Prosecuting Juvenile Piracy Suspects

Duncan Gaswaga, a former judge of the Seychelles Supreme Court who has presided over numerous piracy trials, asked the following question: "What is a judge to do when a bearded piracy suspect facing justice asserts that he is fourteen?" This book addresses this important question by focusing on the treatment of juvenile piracy suspects under international law within national prosecutorial regimes. Beginning with the modern-day Somali piracy model, and exploring the reasons for piracy organizers and financiers to have employed Somali youth as pirates, author Milena Sterio analyzes the relevant international legal framework applicable to the treatment of juvenile criminal suspects, such as international human rights law, international criminal law, including the statutes of several international and ad hoc tribunals, as well as legal issues related to the use of child soldiers, as a parallel to the use of child pirates.

This volume examines recent national piracy prosecutions involving juvenile suspects in Germany, Spain, India, Italy, Malaysia, the Seychelles, and the United States, developing a set of recommendations and best practices for all piracy prosecuting nations dealing with juvenile suspects to refer to in developing their national policy toward the treatment of juvenile piracy suspects.

Milena Sterio is a Professor of Law and Associate Dean for Faculty Enrichment at Cleveland State University's Marshall College of Law, USA. Her research interests are in the field of international law, international criminal law, international human rights, law of the seas, as well as private international law. She is author of *The Right to Self-Determination under International Law* (Routledge, 2012), and co-editor of *Prosecuting Maritime Piracy: Domestic Solutions to International Crime* (Cambridge University Press, 2015). Professor Sterio was the recipient of the Fulbright academic award for spring 2013 and spent a semester researching at Baku State University in Baku, Azerbaijan. Over the past five years, Professor Sterio has established herself as one of the most prominent and influential experts in the field of maritime piracy. She has participated in the work of the United Nations' Contact Group on Piracy off the Coast of Somalia, and is a member of the Piracy Working Group, an academic think tank created within the auspices of the Public International Law and Policy Group. Her academic work has been cited in two piracy prosecutions in the United States' federal courts.

Routledge Research in International Law

For a full list of titles in this series, visit www.routledge.com/Routledge-Research-in-International-Law/book-series/INTNLLAW

Available:

The Rule of Law in the United Nations Security Council Decision-Making Process
Turning the Focus Inwards
Sherif Elgebeily

Sovereignty Conflicts and International Law and Politics
A Distributive Justice Issue
Jorge E. Núñez

Queering International Law
Possibilities, Alliances, Complicities, Risks
Dianne Otto

Prosecuting Juvenile Piracy Suspects
The International Legal Framework
Milena Sterio

Forthcoming titles in this series include:

Technology and the Law on the Use of Force
New Security Challenges in the Twenty First Century
Jackson Maogoto

International Law and the Rights of those Displaced by Armed Conflict
Elena Katselli Proukaki

Regionalism in International Law
Ján Klucka

Nationalization, Natural Resources and International Investment Law
Contractual relationship as a dynamic bargaining process
Junji Nakagawa

China, Cultural Heritage, and International Law
Hui Zhong

Demilitarisation and International Law in Context
The Åland Island
Sia Spiliopoulou Åkermark and Saila Heinikoski

Prosecuting Juvenile Piracy Suspects

The International Legal Framework

Milena Sterio

Routledge
Taylor & Francis Group
LONDON AND NEW YORK

First published 2018
by Routledge
2 Park Square, Milton Park, Abingdon, Oxon OX14 4RN

and by Routledge
605 Third Avenue, New York, NY 10017

First issued in paperback 2021

Routledge is an imprint of the Taylor & Francis Group, an informa business

Publisher's Note
The publisher has gone to great lengths to ensure the quality of this reprint but points out that some imperfections in the original copies may be apparent.

British Library Cataloguing in Publication Data
A catalogue record for this book is available from the British Library

Library of Congress Cataloging in Publication Data
A catalog record for this book has been requested

ISBN 13: 978-1-03-224212-5 (pbk)
ISBN 13: 978-1-138-83933-5 (hbk)

DOI: 10.4324/9781315733470

Typeset in Galliard
by Florence Production Ltd, Stoodleigh, Devon, UK

Contents

Preface

This book addresses the complex legal challenges associated with the prosecution of juvenile piracy suspects. While the book focuses on Somali piracy, its discussion and recommendations are more generally applicable to the prosecution of juvenile piracy suspects, no matter what country and part of the world they may come from. The book first discusses the Somali piracy model and explains the phenomenon of child pirates—impoverished Somali youth who are easily recruited into a piracy endeavor, without understanding its precarious nature and comprehending the legal risks associated therewith. It is this book's overall conclusion that juvenile piracy suspects should face justice, if they are captured, but that they should be treated distinctly from their adult peers, under specialized provisions of various countries' juvenile justice laws. This approach respects the relevant provisions of international human rights law, which dictate that all juvenile suspects must be treated with special care and dignity, while taking into account their young age and ensuring that any penalties that they face provide for re-education and rehabilitation. The overall goal of the book is to provide recommendations and best practices for all piracy-prosecuting nations grappling with the challenge of juvenile piracy suspects, in light of the existing international human rights legal framework.

Additionally, this book provides an innovative account of existing age-determining technologies and tests, which piracy prosecuting nations may be able to utilize in the future in order to assess suspects' age, such as bone and dental X-rays, dental scans, ultra sounds, physical, and cognitive examinations. In order to illustrate some of the challenges related to these age determination procedures and their application to the prosecution of juvenile suspects, this book will examine recent national prosecutions involving juvenile suspects, such as those that have taken place in Germany, Spain, France, Italy, India, Malaysia, the Seychelles, and the United States.

This book concludes that it would be beneficial for all piracy-prosecuting nations to develop legal regimes and policies for the treatment of juvenile piracy suspects. The development of such law and policy would enable nations that prosecute juvenile piracy suspects to conduct more efficient prosecutions, because judges would no longer face uncertainty over what type of treatment should be extended to juvenile suspects. In addition, the development of specific legal regimes and policy regarding the prosecution of juvenile piracy suspects would ensure that all piracy-prosecuting nations would be respecting relevant provisions of human rights law and protecting the rights of all suspects. It is this book's recommendation that piracy-prosecuting nations should engage in extensive age assessments and inquiries, starting with questioning the suspects themselves, and ending with medical and forensic examinations. It is also this book's recommendation that nations should adopt a presumption in favor of juvenile status, and that this presumption should apply any time that age determination tests produce inconclusive results and the suspect's age remains contested. Additionally, this book recommends that states that prosecute juvenile suspects ensure that such suspects are detained separately from their adult peers, and that, during the penalty phase, their young age is taken into consideration and that the sentence imposed provide for rehabilitative and re-educational opportunities. Juvenile pirates are neither "Lost Boys" nor criminals; they should face justice but under conditions that respect their young age and provide opportunities for their reintegration into society.

Although numerous other academics and experts in the field of maritime piracy have written about other important legal issues related thereto, no other literature has been published to date on the specific subject of juvenile piracy suspects. This book thus addresses an important gap in piracy literature by providing an exciting account of modern-day challenges that prosecuting nations face when the accused asserts to be underage.

Acknowledgments

It is a pleasure to acknowledge the advice, input, and assistance that I have received in the writing of this book.

Work on this book has been funded by research grants provided by my home institution, the Cleveland-Marshall College of Law. This book is the result of longstanding support provided to me over the past ten years by this institution. In particular, I have benefited from outstanding research assistance provided by Elisabeth Leonard, who has been unfailingly helpful with all the chapters in this book. I have also received continuous assistance and support from the Cleveland-Marshall College of Law Library. Finally, I have sought the advice and have benefited from insights provided by colleagues at other institutions. Professor and Dean Michael Scharf from Case Western Reserve University School of Law and Professor Michael Newton from Vanderbilt Law School have helped me develop various arguments presented throughout this book. I have also relied on the work of other scholars in the field of maritime piracy—Sandra Hodgkinson, Ved Nanda, Laurie Blank, Jon Bellish, Eugene Kontorovich, Mark Drumbl, and Yvonne Dutton.

This book has also benefited from the comments of participants at various conferences, including the American Society of International Law Annual Meetings, the Law and Society Annual Meetings, the Central States Law Schools' Association Annual Meetings, at which I presented parts of this book.

Above all, I am grateful to my family: my husband, Frederic Girault, and my children, Luca, Lara, and Elena. I dedicate this book to you and thank you for your unconditional support and understanding.

Introduction

Duncan Gaswaga, a former judge of the Seychelles Supreme Court who has presided over numerous piracy trials, asked the following question: "What is a judge to do when a bearded piracy suspect facing justice asserts that he is fourteen?"[1] This book addresses this important question by focusing on the treatment of juvenile piracy suspects under international law within national prosecutorial regimes. This book uses the terms "child" or "children" and "juvenile" interchangeably; moreover, this book adopts the Convention on the Rights of the Child definition of a "child" to mean any individual who is under the age of eighteen. This approach of defining child or juvenile pirates as those under the age of eighteen is consistent with the norms of international human rights law, and adopted by some of the most notable scholars in this area of law.[2] While some may disagree with this approach and may argue that older children aged sixteen and seventeen should not be entitled to the same rights, privileges, and protections as those afforded to very young children, it is this author's conclusion that all individuals under the age of eighteen lack intellectual, moral, and physical maturity and that they deserve legal protections associated with juvenile status. The latter is particularly true in the Somali context, where youth "bear the brunt of the weak economy," have engaged in maritime piracy, "a livelihood that may be illicit and dangerous but is also potentially lucrative,"[3] and, as the blockbuster

1 Private conversation between the author and Justice Duncan Gaswaga, Fall 2012.

2 The United Nations Convention on the Rights of the Child defines children as persons under the age of eighteen. United Nations Convention on the Rights of the Child, G.A. Res. 44/25, Art. 1, Annex, U.N. Doc. A/RES/44/25 (Nov. 20, 1989) (entered into force Sept. 2, 1990). In addition, child soldiers as a protected class are understood to be individuals under the age of eighteen. *See* Cape Town Principles and Best Practices (Apr. 27–30, 1997) (definitions), available at *www.unicef.org/emerg/files/Cape_Town_Principles(1).pdf*; The Paris Principles: Principles and Guidelines on Children Associated with Armed Forces or Armed Groups (February 2007), Prin. 2.1, available at *www.child-soldiers.org/childsoldiers/Paris_Principles_March_2007.pdf*; for a detailed treatment of child soldiers, *see also* Mark A. Drumbl, *Reimagining Child Soldiers in International Law and Policy* (2012).

3 Jon Bellish, *The Issue of Juvenile Piracy*, *in* PROSECUTING MARITIME PIRACY: DOMESTIC SOLUTIONS TO INTERNATIONAL CRIMES 275 (Scharf *et al.* eds. 2015).

movie "Captain Phillips" accurately portrays, where youth may easily fall prey to recruiting efforts of piracy organizers and financiers, without fully comprehending the risks associated with this criminal endeavor. Thus, this book's recommendations and best practices regarding the treatment of juvenile piracy suspects apply to all such suspects under the age of eighteen.

After nearly 200 years, maritime piracy reemerged off the coast of Somalia as a major economic and humanitarian problem. Over the past few years, Somali pirates have seized hundreds of vessels, taken thousands of crewmembers and passengers hostage, and extracted hundreds of millions of dollars in ransom payments. Although the number of piracy attacks has decreased off the Horn of Africa, piracy has proliferated to other areas of the world such as the Gulf of Guinea on the West African coast as well as Asia. Thus, piracy remains a relevant global issue that will continue to command the attention of governments, international organizations, and scholars interested in this area.

One of the key initiatives in combatting modern-day piracy has been the increase of national prosecutions of suspected pirates across the globe. Hundreds of Somali piracy suspects have faced justice in the national courts of countries such as Germany, France, Spain, Italy, India, Malaysia, and the United States. In addition, piracy suspects have been prosecuted in the national courts of Kenya, the Seychelles, and Mauritius—these nations have concluded transfer agreements with major maritime nations, allowing for captured pirates to be "outsourced" to these three countries for prosecution purposes. As Professor Michael Scharf has observed, "[a]s a result, there have been far more developments in the law relating to piracy in the past 6 years that there were in the preceding 200 years."[4]

One of the main features of the Somali piracy model has been the use of child pirates. Estimates indicate that up to one-third of all pirates operating off the coast of Somalia are less than fifteen years old.[5] Child pirates are easily recruited into piracy endeavors because the Somali economy is particularly weak and children often live under dire conditions. In addition, Somali youth often lack intellectual and moral maturity in order to fully appreciate and comprehend the risks associated with piracy. In some instances, because of the Somali clan structure, youth may be under full control of adults belonging to higher societal clans and may not have any meaningful choices as to whether or not to "sign up" for a piracy operation. Youssef M., a pirate convicted in Germany and aged between sixteen and nineteen at the time of his offenses, described how he became

4 Michael P. Scharf, *Introduction*, *in* PROSECUTING MARITIME PIRACY: DOMESTIC SOLUTIONS TO INTERNATIONAL CRIMES 2 (Scharf *et al.* eds. 2015).

5 Romeo Dallaire, Hugh Williamson, and Shelly Whitman, *Child Pirates Are Everybody's Problem*, THE GLOBE AND MAIL (Feb. 10, 2012) (noting that about a third of the pirates captured recently are reported to be 14 or 15); see also Sonia Messaoudi, *Child Pirates: A Key Issue For Respecting Child's Rights and Halting Piracy*, blogspot (Oct. 23, 2012), available at *http://piracy-law.com*.

involved in piracy. According to Youssef, he worked as a night watchman for a fishing boat, starting at the age of thirteen. He was then approached by a man who offered to pay Youssef more if Youssef would pilot a boat. Subsequently, this man paid Youssef $500 for a larger piracy operation—but Youssef himself was never told that the boat he was piloting would engage in a piracy attack. According to Youssef:

> It was only on board . . . that I realized we were supposed to hijack a cargo ship . . . No one mentioned in my presence that there was a possibility of getting arrested by an international naval coalition. I did not think very hard about whether I should participate . . . [n]evertheless it seemed as if everything had been planned ahead of time and I had no choice.[6]

Youssef's story is indicative of paths of so many other Somali children who have engaged in piracy and illustrate perfectly the quagmire facing piracy-fighting nations: if child pirates are captured on the high seas, should they be treated like victims and released, or should they be subjected to criminal prosecutions, because of the serious nature of the piracy crimes which they have committed? Are child pirates victims or criminals, "Lost Boys" or violent offenders? Because many nations have chosen to treat child pirates as criminals and have prosecuted juvenile piracy suspects, it is important to develop appropriate legal regimes applicable to such juvenile suspects. Piracy-prosecuting nations that handle cases involving juvenile piracy suspects need to be aware of their legal obligations, under human rights law, regarding the treatment of juveniles, and need to be prepared to tackle difficult legal issues associated with this type of prosecutions, including age determinations, pre-trial and post-trial detention issues, and other specific rights that attach to all juvenile suspects, including those accused of piracy. While some of these challenges are more general in nature and may arise in other legal contexts, such as immigration proceedings, others are specific to piracy and will be explored in this book.

This book focuses on the complex challenges associated with the prosecution of juvenile piracy suspects. The book discusses relevant international law, including human rights law and international criminal law applicable to the issue of juvenile suspects generally, and then applies this general framework to the specific prosecution of juvenile piracy suspects. This book also draws a parallel between child soldiers and child pirates, and recommends that although the two legal categories are distinct, enough similarities exist to warrant similar treatment of both groups of individuals. Additionally, this book provides an innovative account of existing age-determining technologies and tests, which piracy prosecuting nations may be able to utilize in the future in order to assess suspects'

6 SPIEGEL ONLINE, *A Precedent or a Farce? Court Faces Daunting Hurdles in Hamburg Pirate Trial*, (Jan. 18, 2011), available at www.spiegel.de/international/world/a-precedent-or-a-farce-court-faces-daunting-hurdles-in-hamburg-pirate-trial-a-740122.html.

age. In order to illustrate some of the challenges related to the prosecution of juvenile suspects that nations have already faced, this book examines recent national prosecutions involving juvenile suspects, such as those that have taken place in Germany, Spain, France, Italy, India, Malaysia, the Seychelles, and the United States.

The overall goal of the book is to provide recommendations and best practices for all piracy-prosecuting nations dealing with the challenge of juvenile piracy suspects, in light of the existing international legal framework. It is this book's conclusion that if piracy-prosecuting nations adopt such recommendations and best practices, this will lead toward more efficient prosecutions, which will respect the rights of all juvenile suspects, in accordance with relevant international human rights law. While this book focuses on the Somali piracy model and discusses the prosecution of Somali juvenile piracy suspects, its recommendations are universally applicable and will be useful to all nations grappling with legal issues associated with the prosecution of juvenile piracy suspects from any part of the world. In addition, this book will be useful in other legal contexts where a person's age poses a significant issue—because those who are under the age of eighteen are often entitled to specific, and often preferential, treatment. Thus, this book will be useful in the immigration context, where asylum applicants often claim juvenile status, as well as in general criminal law proceedings of most nations, where domestic penal laws provide for distinct treatment of juvenile suspects.

In Part I, this book describes the modern-day Somali piracy model, and explores reasons why piracy organizers and financiers have resorted to employing Somali youth to serve as pirates. In Part II, the book discusses the relevant international legal framework applicable to the treatment of juvenile criminal suspects, such as international human rights law (the United Nations Convention on the Rights of the Child, the International Covenant on Civil and Political Rights, etc.), international criminal law, including the statutes of several international and ad hoc tribunals, as well as legal issues related to the use of child soldiers, as a parallel to the use of child pirates. The book applies this legal framework to the issue of juvenile piracy, and argues that international law requires that juvenile piracy suspects be treated distinctly from their adult peers. In Part III, the book discusses available forensic and medical tests and technology, which piracy prosecuting nations can utilize in order to assess any suspect's age. This part also examines recent national piracy prosecutions involving juvenile suspects, such as those in Germany, Spain, France, Italy, India, Malaysia, the Seychelles, and the United States. Last, in Part IV this book develops a set of recommendations and best practices, which all piracy prosecuting nations dealing with juvenile suspects could refer to in developing their national policy toward the treatment of juvenile piracy suspects.

Abdiwali, a juvenile pirate prosecuted in Germany in 2011, has addressed his German lawyer as follows:

> You are a father and brother to me. Your rule of law is a miracle on earth. All the expense, and two lawyers fighting just for me, and I don't have to

> pay any money at all! I have rights—I didn't know that. I am grateful that I have the chance to learn this. It all seems like a fairy tale to me.[7]

Despite significant legal challenges, as well as moral and ethical dilemmas, posed by the prosecution of juvenile piracy suspects, no other scholarly literature has been published to date on this specific subject. This book fills an important gap in piracy literature by providing an exciting account of modern-day challenges, which prosecuting nations face when the accused asserts to be underage. Devising the best legal regimes and policy for the treatment of suspects such as Abdiwali, who are at times a victim and a criminal and who may deserve both rehabilitation and punishment, is a crucial task that will facilitate prosecutions of juvenile piracy suspects throughout the world.

7 Beate Lakotta, *Torture? Execution? German Justice Through the Eyes of a Somali Pirate*, SPIEGEL ONLINE (Apr. 7, 2011), available at www.spiegel.de/international/world/torture-execution-german-justice-through-the-eyes-of-a-somali-pirate-a-755340.html.

Part I

The Problem of Juvenile Pirates in Somalia

Part I of this book will introduce the Somali piracy model and the use of juveniles therein. Chapter 1 will discuss the basics of Somali piracy, including the pirates' modus operandi, their motivation, and their ability to exploit the lawless situation in Somalia. Chapter 2 will then focus on a more specific discussion of issues related to the use of child pirates. This chapter will also discuss piracy prosecutions in Kenya, the Seychelles, and Mauritius, countries that have signed transfer agreements with capturing nations and where some child pirates have faced justice already.

1 The Basics of the Somali Piracy Model

Introduction

This chapter will explore the basic model of Somali piracy. Somali pirates launch attacks using small boats or "skiffs," which can surprise a target vessel sailing through the Indian Ocean. After a successful piracy attack, pirates will haul the captured vessel and its crew to the Somali shore, from where they will begin negotiations for a hefty ransom. Within Somalia, piracy has thrived due to lawlessness throughout the country's territory and a poor economic condition. Since 1991, Somalia has been a failed state, and pirates have operated off its coast with a high degree of impunity. Most law enforcement operations geared to combat piracy are led and organized by powerful maritime nations, as well as by regional and international organizations, but not Somali forces. Within Somalia, pirates have faced very few repercussions. In addition, piracy in Somalia is fueled by a poor economic situation. An average Somali citizen earns as little as $600 per year. Piracy is thus a crime of opportunity for young Somali men: a successful vessel seizure, which had not, until recently, been viewed as particularly risky, can yield each pirate thousands of dollars. Sadly, many such pirates are children.

This chapter will explore the above issues by describing the pirates' *modus operandi*, by highlighting the enormous economic cost of piracy, by emphasizing the need to adequately address the piracy problem from a deterrence perspective, and by focusing on the most important international treaties, laws, and regulations available to maritime-fighting nations. In addition, this chapter will discuss the present political and security conditions in Somalia, and will conclude that because this nation is unable to tackle the problem of maritime piracy, the international community needs to remain involved in combatting this serious threat, which could spread to other parts of the African continent and the rest of the world. This chapter will thus lay the groundwork for exploring more specific piracy-related issues—those that focus on the use of juveniles to perform piratical attacks, which will be addressed starting in Chapter 2.

Modus Operandi: A Crime of Opportunity

Piracy blossomed off the coast of Somalia starting in the late 2000s. In 2008, Somali pirates took nearly six hundred crewmembers hostage; several hundred of these crewmembers, as well as a dozen ships, were held by the pirates for many months, and were released only after their home countries and/or shipping companies paid millions of dollars in ransom.[1] Somali pirates became more aggressive in their operations during this period, attacking larger ships. In 2008, they seized the Faina, which was carrying Russian tanks and ammunition, as well as the supertanker Sirius Star, which was carrying two million barrels of oil.[2] In 2008, the United Nations Security Council, recognizing the seriousness of the threat posed by Somali piracy, passed Resolution 1816, which states that piracy "exacerbate[s] the situation in Somalia[,] which continues to constitute a threat to international peace and security in the region."[3] The International Maritime Bureau ("IMB") reported that in 2011, 439 piracy attacks occurred worldwide, 237 of which took place off the coast of Somalia. In 2010, the IMB reported a similar figure of 445 attacks, and in 2009, a total of 406 piracy attacks took place.[4] Over the past several years, the number of crewmembers taken hostage significantly increased—from 188 in 2006 to 1,181 in 2010. While the overall number of piracy attacks off the coast of Somalia has decreased since 2011, most commentators attribute the decline to the large presence of patrolling vessels in the Indian Ocean and to the frequent use of private armed guards on board merchant vessels.[5] Despite this decline, most commentators agree that piracy incidents could become more frequent once again if patrolling vessels and private armed guards departed these piracy-infested waters. According to IMB Director Pottengal Mukundan:

> Although the number of acts of piracy reported in Somalia has significantly decreased, there can be no room for complacency. The drop in reported attacks is due to proactive naval actions against suspect Pirate Action Groups, the employment of privately contracted armed security personnel and the preventive measures used by the merchant vessels (as per latest Best Management Practices recommendations). The attacks will rise to past levels if the naval presence is reduced or vessels relax their vigilance.[6]

1 James Kraska and Brian Wilson, *Fighting Pirates: The Pen and the Sword*, 25 WORLD POL'Y J. 41 (2009) [hereinafter Kraska and Wilson, *Fighting Pirates*].

2 James Kraska and Brian Wilson, *Piracy Repression, Partnering and the Law*, 40 J. MAR. L. & COM. 43, 43 (2009); *see also* James Kraska and Brian Wilson, *Combatting Piracy in International Waters*, WORLD POL'Y BLOG (Feb. 23, 2012), www.worldpolicy.org/blog/2011/02/23/combatting-piracy-international-waters (noting that pirates have become increasingly skilled at hijacking and that kidnap experts were stunned at the seizure of the Sirius Star, whose side had been regarded as too high for pirates to scale).

3 S.C. Res. 1816, ¶ 13 (June 2, 2008).

4 *Piracy Attacks in East and West Africa Dominate World Report*, ICC COM. CRIME SERVS. (Jan. 19, 2012), www.icc-ccs.org/news/711-piracy-attacks-in-east-and-west-africa-dominate-world-report.

5 *See IMB Advises Continued Vigilance as Maritime Piracy Attacks Decline*, ICC COM. CRIME SERVS. (Apr. 15, 2013), www.icc-ccs.org/news/841-imb-advises-continued-vigilance-as-maritime-piracy-attacks-decline.

6 *Id.*

Thus, piracy is an ongoing global issue that should continue to occupy the attention and resources of many maritime nations in the near future, and one that should command continuous scholarly attention.

The pirates' *modus operandi* is relatively simple. Somali pirates congregate on a "mother ship" and then divide into smaller groups that sail out on tiny skiffs.[7] Using powerful weapons such as AK-47s and hand-propelled grenades, Somali pirates attack civilian ships carrying cargo through the Gulf of Aden, a body of water between Yemen and Somalia. Once the victim's vessel has been overtaken, the pirates typically hijack its cargo and kidnap its crewmembers. The cargo is often resold to willing buyers or held for ransom. The crew is held hostage in Somalia until either the hostages' home country or the shipowners pay, at times, multi-million dollar ransoms.[8] In most instances, crewmembers are released unharmed, but those held hostage have described their captivity as a horrific ordeal; in addition, the pirates have killed several hostages.[9] The pirates themselves routinely go unpunished: once they release the hostages, the pirates simply plan another lucrative capture.

The reasons why Somali pirates have had a high success rate until recently are relatively simple. First, Somali pirates operate mostly in the Gulf of Aden, a major global shipping route, where the number of potential targets is higher than elsewhere. Second, Somali pirates are able to use the region's geography to their advantage. Somalia has the longest coastline in Africa, making it difficult to patrol, and it is populated by coastal towns where pirates easily blend in with other insurgent groups. Because the Gulf of Aden is a relatively narrow body of water, pirates are also able to anchor smaller ships to shore fairly quickly, which allows them to secure the crew and cargo while they wait for ransom. Third, Somalia is a failed state with a weak, unstable central government and no effective police force; thus, pirates are able to operate with impunity from Somali coastal towns. In fact, news accounts suggest that entire towns on the coast of Somalia happily lived off the proceeds of piracy for several years.[10] Fourth, piracy is a lucrative business: reports indicate that a single seizure of a ship can earn each individual

7 *See generally* Eugene Kontorovich, *International Legal Responses to Piracy off the Coast of Somalia*, ASIL INSIGHTS (Feb. 6, 2009), www.asil.org/insights/volume/13/issue/2/international-legal-responses-piracy-coast-somalia (describing the pirates' typical operational style and goals).

8 *Id.*

9 In 2012, pirates, in protest of a delayed ransom payment, killed a Syrian hostage held for two years by Somali pirates; another hostage was wounded. *See* Abdi Guled, *Somali Pirates Kill Hostage Over Delayed Ransom*, THE WORLD POST (Sept. 1, 2012), www.huffingtonpost.com/2012/09/01/somali-pirates-hostage-killed_n_1848937.html; *see also Deaths of Hostages Held by Somali Pirates 'Increasing,'* BBC NEWS (June 22, 2012), www.bbc.com/news/world-africa-18548810 (reporting that according to an International Maritime Bureau report, thirty-five hostages held by Somali pirates in 2011 died; reporting also that "[h]alf of those held were subjected to punching and slapping and 10 percent suffered violent abuse such as being locked in freezers, burned with cigarettes and having their fingernails pulled out with pliers.").

10 Kraska and Wilson, *Fighting Pirates*, *supra* note 1; *see also* Kontorovich, *supra* note 7.

pirate up to $150,000. In Somalia, where yearly earnings average about $600, this amount is staggering to Somali youth, including juveniles under the age of eighteen, who see few other employment options in their war-torn home land.[11] Finally, piracy in Somalia has thrived because of a lack of global cooperation in suppressing pirate attacks. Pirates work at a supranational level: they attack a vessel owned by a company headquartered in one country; the vessel itself flies the flag of a second country and employs crewmembers coming from multiple other countries. Therefore, a piracy attack almost never harms the interests of a single country but instead concerns multiple nations. Moreover, many crewmembers come from the developing world, and major maritime powers such as the United States and the United Kingdom have shown relatively little interest in paying ransoms to rescue non-nationals, even in situations where such hostages' home countries may be unable to pay for their release.[12] The lack of global cooperation with law enforcement regarding Somali piracy, combined with a failure to prosecute detained pirates, has significantly contributed to Somali pirates' high success rates up until a few years ago.

The situation changed starting in 2011, when maritime nations pooled resources and efforts to create a coordinated response to the piracy threat, through joint patrolling operations, joint law enforcement and information sharing, as well as joint prosecutorial efforts to ensure that captured suspects are brought to justice. For example, an international naval fleet consisting of American, French, Russian, Indian, and British warships formed off the coast of East Africa. In addition, Chinese naval ships have been seen in these waters for the first time since the Middle Ages![13] Another reason that Somali piracy seems to be on the decline is because of shipping companies' recent efforts to combat this threat. Shipping companies, despite being the entities most directly affected by pirate attacks, initially did very little to solve the issue. Instead, shipping companies have exacerbated the Somalia piracy problem by paying increasingly high ransoms in exchange for the release of hijacked ships, cargo, and kidnapped crewmembers.[14] Over the past few years, however, shipping companies have addressed the problem of maritime piracy by increasingly employing private armed guards on board merchant vessels sailing through the Gulf of Aden and other piracy-infested waters; this somewhat successful tactic has, however, significantly increased the shipping companies' operating costs and has contributed to the already elevated economic cost of piracy.

11 Kontorovich, *supra* note 7.

12 See Vivienne Walt, Why the Somali Pirates Keep Getting Their Ransoms,TIME (Apr. 20, 2009), www.time.com/time/world/article/0,8599,1892366,00.html.

13 Mateo Taussig-Rubbo, "Pirate Trials, the International Criminal Court, and Mob Justice: Reflections on Postcolonial Sovereignty in Kenya," *Humanity: An International Journal of Human Rights, Humanitarianism and Development*, 2010–1, p. 57.

14 *Id.*

Economic Cost of Piracy

As pirate attacks increased over the last few years in the Gulf of Aden and elsewhere off the Somali coast, so did shipping companies' cargo transportation costs for any ships sailing in these treacherous waters. Estimates indicate that shipping companies may be losing between thirteen and fifteen billion dollars per year due to pirate attacks.[15] To minimize the risk of ships falling prey to Somali pirates, shipping companies have devoted significant attention to their shipping routes. In order to avoid the most dangerous places, routes have sometimes been recalculated and lengthened, thus requiring more fuel and more paid days at sea for crewmembers.[16] Moreover, because of the increased risk of pirate attacks, insurance premiums have soared: whereas shipping companies previously paid as little as $500 per voyage, they now face rates as high as $20,000 for vessels passing through the pirate-infested waters. According to a recent report, insurance premiums for ships traveling through the Gulf have increased by as much as 350 percent, and premiums for kidnap and ransom coverage have reportedly increased by as much as 1,000 percent.[17]

Shipping companies' labor costs have also increased. In light of the dangers of the pirate-infested Gulf of Aden, shippers have needed to increase crewmembers' salaries to entice them to serve on vessels deployed through these waters. Even with higher salaries, some crewmembers may simply be unwilling to expose their own lives to the dangers posed by piracy. Thus, recruiting for shipping companies may become a difficult exercise, requiring additional efforts and expense.[18] In addition, shipping companies have begun to routinely employ private armed guards on board merchant vessels. Many states have also recently authorized the use of private armed guards on board their merchant ships. Today, between 40 and 60 percent of ships sailing through the Gulf of Aden are protected by an armed security guard.[19] Security companies providing these services typically charge around $30,000 to secure a vessel's safe transit through a dangerous, piracy-affected area.[20] Many shipping companies have willingly undertaken this cost, because although employing guards on every ship adds to the company's overall labor costs, this strategy has proven to be one of the most

15 Kraska and Wilson, *Fighting Pirates*, *supra* note 1.

16 Kaivan H. Chinoy, *Anarchy on the High Seas—Is Arming Merchant Vessels the Way Forward?*, AVA MARINE SURVEYORS & CONSULTANTS, http://psm.du.edu/media/documents/industry_initiatives/industry_reports/ava_marine-high-seas-piracy-and-arming-vessels.pdf (last visited Feb. 3, 2016).

17 *Id.*

18 InterManager: Criminalisation and Piracy Damage Seafarer *Recruitment*, BAIRD MAR. (Mar. 22, 2010), www.bairdmaritime.com/index.php?option=com_content&view=article&id=6004:intermanager-criminalisation-and-piracy-damage-seafarerrecruitment&catid=113:ports-and-shipping&Itemid=208.

19 John Clark Levin, *Arming Captain Phillips*, WALL ST. J. (Oct. 16, 2013) www.wsj.com/articles/SB10001424052702304106704579137903414164412.

20 *Id.*

effective tools in combatting piracy. According to Andrew Shapiro, former United States Assistant Secretary of State, "[t]he ultimate security measure a commercial ship can adopt is the use of privately contracted armed security teams."[21] Numbers prove Mr. Shapiro's point: by the end of 2013, not a single ship employing private armed guards had been successfully hijacked by Somali pirates. However, shipping companies must remain vigilant, and must continue to invest significant resources toward combatting the piracy threat. If armed guards cease to be used in the Gulf of Aden, attacks will re-flourish in all likelihood. Moreover, piracy has spread to the West Coast of Africa, and smaller-scale attacks have been reported in Asia, Indonesia, and in the Bay of Bengal.[22] It may be likely that shipping companies will be obliged to arm all of their vessels—a cost that would significantly impact shipping markets and global commerce in general.

Finally, in addition to increasing costs on the front-end of the shipping process, piracy has driven up costs in other ways. In some cases, pirates have demanded multi-million dollar ransoms after successfully hijacking a ship and kidnapping its crewmembers, and the shipping companies have met those demands in almost every instance by paying large sums of cash to the pirates. These pirate-imposed costs have substantially increased shipping companies' expenses and could cause significant long-term economic problems in the shipping industry if piracy in Somalia, and elsewhere, is not addressed. The financial problems that Somali pirates have brought upon shipping companies are particularly relevant in light of the ongoing global financial crisis. According to one recent analysis, "[i]nstability from maritime piracy in the Gulf of Aden is sending ripples throughout the global supply chain, which is already reeling from the collapse of shipping rates brought on by the worldwide economic slowdown."[23] As the economic crisis has peaked, consumption has declined, demand for merchandise and raw materials has dropped, and fewer ships are needed to transport goods. The result has been a decrease in shipping prices and lower profits for shipping companies. Moreover, shipping companies' abilities to borrow money and work closely with large lenders may have been negatively affected by the banking crisis.[24] A significant decline in existing cash flow coupled with the need to expend large sums of cash to pay pirate ransoms may wreak havoc on shipping companies' finances and may threaten their long-term financial stability. In addition, the financial strain of increasing global fuel costs is exacerbated by the need to purchase additional fuel to avoid pirate-infested shipping routes. Finally, if shipping companies are forced to incur additional expenses to equip their ships with security officers, weapons, pirate-tracking devices, and other technological mechanisms to combat pirates, their financial future and well-being in today's volatile economy may become uncertain.[25]

21 *Id.*
22 *Id.*
23 Kraska and Wilson, *Fighting Pirates*, *supra* note 1.
24 *Id.*
25 Kraska and Wilson, *Fighting Pirates*, *supra* note 1.

In addition to combatting piracy because of its impact on economics of the shipping business, it is crucial to address the piracy threat from a deterrence perspective, to ensure that Somali youth and juveniles do not continue to devote their lives to criminal enterprise. The section below will discuss issues related to deterring piratical activity.

Piracy and Deterrence

Piracy is a serious criminal activity. Pirates are criminal offenders subject to universal jurisdiction;[26] from a deterrence standpoint, not fighting them sends the wrong message to pirates, particularly juvenile pirates, and other criminal and terrorist organizations. This is especially true if pirates are routinely released after capture, or if only a few of those captured are prosecuted. This issue is particularly relevant in the context of juvenile piracy suspects—most capturing states have routinely released juvenile suspects, because of perceived logistical and legal complexities involved in handling the detention and eventual prosecution of juvenile suspects. While deterrence is essential in the fight against piracy, it is difficult to judge how efficacious prosecutions would be to deter the spread of Somali piracy. Young men and boys living in poverty on the Somali coast may not be deterred at all by the possibility of facing legal consequences when considering whether to become a pirate. For poor Somali youth and children, the prospect of earning thousands of dollars may outweigh the unlikely possibility of being caught and prosecuted. While deterrence alone may not solve the Somali pirate problem, it remains an important part of the solution.

Deterrence of Somali pirates through criminal prosecutions remains important for several reasons. From a local Somali standpoint, if prospective pirates believe the chances of capture and prosecution significantly outweigh the probability of profit, then there is a possibility that more recruits would be dissuaded from engaging in this criminal activity.[27] The recently-proliferated model of employing armed guards on board merchant vessels sailing through the Gulf of Aden and elsewhere in the Indian Ocean underscores the notion that Somali youth view piracy as a crime of opportunity: statistics show that almost no vessels employing armed guards have been successfully pirated, although some such vessels have been attacked.[28] Statistics also show that the piracy model has been seriously undermined by the use of private armed guards on board merchant vessels,

26 *See* United Nations Convention on the Law of the Sea art. 101, Oct. 7, 1982, 1833 U.N.T.S. 41–42 [hereinafter UNCLOS].

27 *See* Michael Bahar, *Attaining Optimal Deterrence at Sea: A Legal and Strategic Theory for Naval Anti-Piracy Operations*, 40 VAND J. TRANSNAT'L L. 1, 41 (2007) (arguing that the perceived probability of capture will likely have a deterrent effect on the Somali pirates).

28 *Repelling Pirate Attacks: The Measures To Protect A Ship*, THE TELEGRAPH (Feb. 10, 2014), www.telegraph.co.uk/sponsored/culture/captain-phillips-film/10367534/security-against-pirate-attacks.html (reporting that Somali piracy has plummeted since 2008 and 2009, because of the use of private armed guards on board shipping vessels).

because the presence of such armed guards seriously raises the risks inherent in each piracy attack.[29] Somali pirates fear being harmed or killed by armed guards, and their risk of capture, as well as the possibility of eventual criminal prosecution, have drastically increased through the presence of armed guards on merchant vessels. Thus, Somali pirates and Somali youth may be rethinking whether piracy truly pays off.

It would be foolish to assume that piracy has been eradicated, or that the international community can back off and no longer invest resources in capturing and prosecuting suspected pirates. If international criminals such as Somali pirates are not routinely prosecuted and punished, other potential criminals, such as weapons-smugglers and narcotics-traffickers, may think that hard-to-prosecute crimes routinely go unpunished and that they may flout international law with impunity. This may lead to an overall increase in international crime. Thus, pirates should be fought, captured, and routinely prosecuted because the whole world has an interest in deterring international crimes, especially those that involve juvenile offenders, who could potentially be rehabilitated and redirected toward other meaningful life opportunities.

Existing International Laws on Maritime Piracy

Piracy is a crime under international law; several important international treaties define piracy and provide piracy-fighting nations with relevant legal tools in prosecuting piracy offenders. In addition, the international community, and in particular the United Nations Security Council, has been involved in addressing maritime piracy by drafting resolutions and other documents that allow nations engaged in combatting piracy to access Somali waters in order to pursue offenders and fend off attacks.

Article 15 of the 1958 Convention on the High Seas ("Convention on the High Seas") and Article 101 of the United Nations Convention on the Law of the Sea ("UNCLOS") both contain the most universally accepted definition of piracy:

> (1) Any illegal act of violence, detention, or any act of depredation, committed for private ends by the crew or the passengers of a private ship or a private aircraft, and directed: (a) On the high seas, against another ship or aircraft, or against persons or property on board such ship or aircraft; (b) Against a ship, aircraft, persons or property in a place outside the jurisdiction of any State.[30]

While some scholars have criticized the restrictive nature of the piracy definition in the Convention on the High Seas and UNCLOS, arguing that the two treaties

29 *See* Levin, *supra* note 19.

30 UNCLOS, *supra* note 26, art. 101; United Nations Convention on the High Seas art. 15, Apr. 29, 1958, 450 U.N.T.S. 11, 90 [hereinafter Convention on the High Seas].

actually narrowed the scope of piracy from its roots in customary law, most agree that the above definition reflects international custom as it stands today.[31] Nonetheless, the Convention on the High Seas and the UNCLOS definition of piracy is restrictive for several reasons. First, the definition requires that the violent act be committed for private aims.[32] Although some scholars believe that the private aims requirement is intended to eliminate conduct committed on behalf of states or by state actors from the definition of piracy, other scholars argue that this requirement disqualifies acts committed for political and ideological reasons from being considered piracy.[33] These scholars suggest that an act of maritime terrorism committed to advance the political goals of a group, like al-Qaida or the Palestine Liberation Organization ("PLO"), may not qualify as piracy under the Convention on the High Seas/UNCLOS definition.[34]

Second, the above piracy definition requires that the violent act be committed on the high seas.[35] The reasons for this limitation are logical: under traditional international law, anything that happens within the territorial sovereignty of a given state is a matter for that state alone to address and rectify.[36] Because the crime of piracy is closely linked to the idea of universal jurisdiction, if the scope of piracy extends into a state's territorial waters, the universality of the crime collides with the territorial sovereignty of that state. Therefore, the high seas requirement for piracy is rational from an international law standpoint. The high seas requirement nonetheless disqualifies many acts of maritime violence from the definition of piracy. For example, if Somali pirates strike within the twelve nautical-mile territorial sea of their home country, this act would not constitute piracy under the Convention on the High Seas/UNCLOS definition. Consequently, the Convention on the High Seas/UNCLOS jurisdictional regimes, which provide any nation interested in capturing pirates with the possibility of extending universal jurisdiction over such captured pirates, are not useful in the Somali context.[37]

31 Jon D. Peppetti, *Building the Global Maritime Security Network: A Multinational Legal Structure to Combat Transnational Threats*, 55 NAVAL L. REV. 73, 92 (2008).

32 UNCLOS, *supra* note 26, art. 101(a); Convention on the High Seas, *supra* note 30, art. 15.

33 *See, e.g.*, Bahar, *supra* note 27, at 27 ("Unless . . . terrorists were commissioned by a state, they are private actors."); *see also id.* at 27–37 (discussing in detail why acts committed by terrorists can qualify as piracy). *But see* Peppetti, *supra* note 31, at 92 (arguing that the private ends restriction has contributed to the most commonly adopted view that acts of violence committed for religious, ethnic, or political reasons, such as acts of maritime terrorism, cannot be treated as piracy).

34 Lawrence Azubuike, *International Law Regime Against Piracy*, 15 ANN. SURV. INT'L & COMP. L. 43, 52 (2009) (noting that the commonly held view is that acts of violence committed on religious, ethnic, or political grounds cannot be treated as piracy).

35 Under UNCLOS, the area comprised of twelve miles into the sea from the coastline of the littoral state constitutes the littoral state's territorial waters; any areas beyond the territorial waters are considered part of the high seas. UNCLOS, *supra* note 26, art. 3; *see also* Azubuike, *supra* note 34, at 50 (articulating the twelve nautical mile requirements of UNCLOS and noting that up to 200 nautical miles may be claimed by the mainland country as an economic zone).

36 *See* Bahar, *supra* note 27, at 18.

37 Peppetti, *supra* note 31, at 92–93.

Another limiting factor is that the Convention on the High Seas/UNCLOS piracy definition requires the presence of two vessels for an act to qualify as piracy —an aggressor vessel must attack a victim vessel.[38] Therefore, if hijackers board the victim vessel at its last port of entry and then overpower the ship's crew on the high seas, this act would not constitute piracy under the Convention on the High Seas/UNCLOS definition, because only one vessel is involved. While some scholars have argued that two vessels may not be required under the Convention on the High Seas/UNCLOS definition,[39] the majority view and the plain reading of these conventions indicate that their drafters envision the presence of two vessels in their definition of piracy.[40] Overall, the Convention on the High Seas and UNCLOS codify the law of piracy narrowly, perhaps regrettably eliminating a multitude of acts of maritime aggression from the definition of piracy.

In addition to limiting the definition of piracy, the Convention on the High Seas/UNCLOS impose restrictions on states' ability to capture and prosecute pirates.[41] The conventions provide that any state has jurisdiction to capture pirates on the high seas, as follows:

> On the high seas, or in any other place outside the jurisdiction of any State, every State may seize a pirate ship or aircraft, or a ship taken by piracy and under the control of pirates, and arrest the persons and seize the property on board.[42]

The concept of universal jurisdiction over pirates is limited to the high seas, as these conventions do not authorize nations to pursue pirates in a state's territorial waters. These conventions further state that the capturing nation may then prosecute pirates in its domestic courts.[43] Article 19 of the Convention on the High Seas and Article 105 of UNCLOS provide: "The courts of the State which carried out the seizure may decide upon the penalties to be imposed, and may also determine the action to be taken with regard to the ships, aircraft or property, subject to the rights of third parties acting in good faith."[44] Under these

38 UNCLOS, *supra* note 26, art. 101(a)(i); Convention on the High Seas, *supra* note 30, art. 15.

39 *See* Bahar, *supra* note 27, at 38–39 (arguing that UNCLOS drafters merely intended to exclude from the definition of piracy "criminal acts by one passenger or crewmember against another" and also arguing that case law on piracy does not support a two-ship requirement).

40 *See*, e.g., Azubuike, *supra* note 34, at 53 (explaining that the two-ship requirement is reasonable because it "emanates from the notion that a ship [being attacked] is always under the jurisdiction of the flag State," so that "any act or offense committed on board [that] ship is subject to the domestic laws of the flag State"); *see also* UNCLOS, *supra* note 26, art. 101 (providing that piracy consists of violent acts committed "by the crew or the passengers of a private ship or a private aircraft" directed "against another ship or aircraft") (emphasis added).

41 UNCLOS, *supra* note 26, art. 105; Convention on the High Seas, *supra* note 30, art. 19.

42 *Id.*

43 *Id.*

44 *Id.*

conventions, however, the capturing nation may not transfer seized pirates to a third country for prosecution.[45] The idea of universal jurisdiction, therefore, gives limited options to piracy-fighting states, as their authority to pursue pirates ceases to exist outside the high seas, and the opportunity to prosecute pirates arises only in cases where the capturing state is also willing to prosecute.[46] If an act of maritime violence does not fall within the scope of the Convention on the High Seas/UNCLOS, the perpetrators cannot be apprehended or prosecuted under these conventions' jurisdictional basis. Consequently, countries willing to capture, detain, and prosecute violent maritime offenders may be forced to look to other laws in order to justify their anti-piracy operations.

Whereas the Convention on the High Seas/UNCLOS provisions sometimes leaves gaps with regard to the capture and prosecution of pirates, the Convention for the Suppression of Unlawful Acts Against the Safety of Maritime Navigation ("SUA Convention" or SUA) attempts to aid states in their fight against maritime violence by broadening the jurisdictional basis for the capture and prosecution of maritime aggressors.[47] The SUA Convention is considered an anti-terrorist treaty, and rather than defining piracy, it lists a series of maritime criminal offenses that are prohibited under the convention. The list includes the following acts that, if committed, would likely endanger the safe navigation of the vessel: seizing or taking control of a ship by force or the threat of force, performing an act of violence against a person on board a ship, destroying or damaging a ship or its cargo, placing devices or substances on a ship that are likely to destroy that ship, knowingly communicating false information to a ship, and injuring or killing any person in connection with any of the above acts.[48]

The SUA Convention does away with the restrictive elements of the Convention on the High Seas/UNCLOS definition of piracy. First, the SUA Convention does not have the private aims requirement of the Convention on the High Seas/UNCLOS treaties; thus, maritime terrorist acts driven by politics and ideology, and not simply private aims, fall within the SUA Convention framework.[49] Second, the SUA Convention authorizes states to pursue maritime aggressors not only on the high seas, but anytime the victim vessel is in some

45 This conclusion follows from a close reading of the Convention on the High Seas and UNCLOS, and many scholars have embraced it. *See*, e.g., Kontorovich, *supra* note 7 (relating the history of article 105 of UNCLOS, which does not allow a transfer of captured pirates to third parties for prosecution, and comparing that provision to the SUA Convention).

46 Note, however, that some scholars have argued that the Convention on the High Seas and UNCLOS do not prohibit a non-capturing state from prosecuting seized pirates. *See*, e.g., Azubuike, *supra* note 34, at 54–55 (arguing that the jurisdiction of the capturing state is not exclusive but merely permissive because customary law provided for universal jurisdiction over pirates and UNCLOS codified customary law).

47 Convention for the Suppression of Unlawful Acts Against the Safety of Maritime Navigation art. 3, Mar. 10, 1988, 1678 U.N.T.S. 221 [hereinafter SUA Convention].

48 *Id.* at art 3(1)(a)-(g).

49 *Id.*

form of international transit.[50] Third, the SUA Convention no longer requires the presence of two vessels; if hijackers board the ship when it is docked and overwhelm its crew and passengers at a later point in time, this act would fall within the SUA Convention definitional framework.[51] Moreover, the SUA Convention affords states more liberty in their attempts to prosecute aggressors.[52] States under the SUA Convention framework may capture aggressors anywhere, and capturing states may transfer pirates to a third state for prosecution purposes.[53]

While the SUA Convention attempts to eliminate the restrictive elements of the Convention on the High Seas/UNCLOS definition of piracy, the former has not been as widely ratified and is not generally considered a part of customary international law.[54] Regrettably, a number of the countries most affected by piracy, such as Indonesia, Malaysia, and Somalia, have not ratified the SUA Convention.[55] Thus, the SUA Convention may theoretically represent an attractive option for piracy-fighting countries, but its practical reach may prove limited because of its lack of universal acceptance and ratification.[56]

Starting in 2008, the international community began to seriously address the Somali piracy threat. Toward this goal, the United Nations Security Council has adopted several resolutions that have addressed concerns about hijackings in Somali waters.[57] These resolutions have authorized nations that patrol the Gulf of Aden to enter Somali territorial waters to fight or pursue pirates, and have

50 *Id.* at art. 4.

51 *Id.* at art. 3.

52 *See* SUA Convention, *supra* note 42, art. 3 & 4.

53 The SUA Convention authorizes, and under certain circumstances requires, member states to establish jurisdiction over the perpetrators, either by extraditing them to another member state or prosecuting the perpetrators themselves. The following states are required to take measures necessary to establish jurisdiction over the perpetrators: the state of which the perpetrator is a national, the state in whose territorial waters the act was committed, and the flag state of the victim vessel. The following states are permitted to exercise jurisdiction over the offenses: the state of which the victim is a national, the state where the perpetrator has a habitual residence, or the state where the offense was committed if the motive was to compel a state to perform or to abstain from an act. Erik Barrios, *Casting A Wider Net: Addressing the Maritime Piracy Problem in Southeast Asia*, 28 B.C. INT'L & COMPO L. REV. 149, 154–55 (2005).

54 *See* Azubuike, *supra* note 33, at 56.

55 *See id.* (expressing doubts as to the practical effectiveness of the SUA Convention, as it only applies to countries that have adopted the convention).

56 The SUA Convention has not been widely ratified by states for a variety of reasons. States may feel that the SUA Convention modifies the approach to piracy from the traditional view of piracy as sea-robbery toward piracy as a form of maritime violence and possibly maritime terrorism. States may feel reluctant to change their traditional conception of piracy, especially if they have not been targets of maritime terrorism. *See* Malvina Halberstam, Benjamin N. Cardozo School of Law, Comments at the American Society of International Law Annual Meeting (Mar. 26, 2009) [hereinafter ASIL Meeting] (describing the impediments to ratifying the broader SUA Convention).

57 S.C. Res. 1851, (Dec. 16, 2008); S.C. Res. 1846, (Dec. 2, 2008); S.C. Res. 1844, (Nov. 20, 2008); S.C. Res. 1838, (Oct. 7, 2008); S.C. Res. 1816, (June 2, 2008).

called on all states to cooperate in efforts to capture and prosecute offenders. The first resolution adopted, Resolution 1816, authorized nations patrolling the Gulf of Aden to enter Somali territorial waters "for the purpose of repressing acts of piracy and armed robbery at sea," and, while in Somali waters, to "[u]se . . . in a manner consistent with action permitted on the high seas with respect to piracy under relevant international law, all necessary means to repress acts of piracy and armed robbery."[58] Resolution 1816 effectively "make[s] the rules of international law concerning piracy on the high seas applicable also to territorial waters, inter alia permitting pursuit from the high seas into these waters."[59] Moreover, Resolution 1816 gives patrolling nations the authority to use force within Somali territorial waters.[60]

Another resolution passed by the United Nations Security Council in December 2008, Resolution 1851, gives patrolling nations the authority to "undertake all necessary measures that are appropriate in Somalia, for the purpose of suppressing acts of piracy and armed robbery at sea."[61] The Council's use of the expression "in Somalia" apparently authorizes action not only within Somali territorial waters but also on mainland Somalia.[62] The expansive language of Resolution 1851 arguably expands the scope of "hot pursuit" of pirates by allowing the chase to continue from Somali waters to Somali land.[63] However, this expansion challenges the traditional international humanitarian law principle that civilians may not be targeted with force on land, except in cases of self-defense. Somali pirates are also Somali civilians, albeit dangerous ones. It is unclear how or if Resolution 1851's expanded authorization will be employed in reality.[64]

Together, these resolutions are designed to facilitate the task of safeguarding the Gulf of Aden by extending patrolling nations' jurisdictional and legal enforcement reach into Somalia. The resolutions, however, are limited in their scope because: (1) they only apply to Somalia; (2) they are not meant to establish any new rules of customary piracy law; (3) they require consent of the Somali government for any undertaken action; (4) they require the patrolling nations to respect international humanitarian law; and (5) they pertain only to the current patrolling nations in the Gulf of Aden.

58 S.C. Res. 1816, *supra* note, ¶¶ 7(a)-(b).

59 Tullio Treves, Piracy, Law of the Sea, and Use of Force: Developments off the Coast of Somalia, 20 EUR. J. INT'L L. 399, 400, 404 (2009).

60 *See* S.C. Res. 1816, *supra* note 57, ¶ 7(b) (referring to the "all necessary means" language).

61 S.C. Res. 1851, *supra* note 57, ¶ 6.

62 See generally Steven R. Obert, Using Force on Land to Suppress Piracy at Sea: The Legal Landscape of A Largely Untapped Strategy, 25 DUKE J. COMP. & INT'L L. 197, 207 (2014).

63 S.C. Res. 1851, *supra* note 56, ¶¶ 2, 6; *see also* Kontorovich, *supra* note 4 (arguing that the language in Resolution 1851 broadens the use of force against pirates because a state can pursue the pirate once on dry land).

64 Kontorovich, *supra* note 7 (explaining that the powers granted by the anti-pirate resolutions have gone "largely if not entirely unutilized, with military action against pirates taking place in international waters and confined to small, reportedly defensive incidents").

Subsequent United Nations Security Council Resolutions affirm the Resolutions mentioned above and build on the latter's existing framework, by focusing on establishing a comprehensive judicial framework regarding piracy suspects, to ensure that many different states have the willingness and capacity to prosecute such suspects. Resolution 1897, adopted in 2009, requests states with relevant jurisdiction over piracy offenses under international law and national legislation cooperate in determining jurisdiction and in the investigation and prosecution of piracy suspects captured off the coast of Somalia, as well as to ensure that all pirates handed over to judicial authorities are subject to a judicial process.[65] Resolution 1918, adopted in 2010, calls on states to criminalize piracy as part of their domestic law.[66] In addition, this Resolution asks the Secretary-General to present to the United Nations Security Council within three months on possible options to further the aim of prosecuting and imprisoning piracy suspects off the coast of Somalia, including, in particular, options for creating special domestic chambers possibly with international components, a regional tribunal, or an international tribunal and corresponding imprisonment arrangements.[67] Resolution 1950, adopted in 2010, stresses the need to prosecute the individuals involved in planning and financing piracy, and expresses particular concern about the involvement of juveniles in piracy operations.[68] Resolution 1976, adopted in 2011, further emphasizes the need to go after international criminal networks involved in piracy operations, and calls on states to consider the establishment of specialized Somali courts to try suspected pirates both in Somalia and in the region, including an extraterritorial Somali specialized anti-piracy court.[69] Resolution 2015, adopted in 2011, further emphasizes the necessity to establish specialized anti-piracy courts in Somalia and other states.[70] This Resolution underlines the importance for such courts to have jurisdiction over not only suspects captured at sea, but also anyone who incites or intentionally facilitates piracy operations, including key figures of criminal networks involved in piracy who illicitly plan, organize, facilitate, or finance and profit from such attacks.[71] Overall, the above-mentioned Security Council Resolutions demonstrate the international community's continuous concern over the rise of maritime piracy off the coast of Somalia and, despite their limited reach, contribute toward the global fight against piracy by enhancing law enforcement and prosecutorial tools available to all states involved in this fight.

65 S.C. Res. 1897, ¶3, ¶6–10 (Nov. 30, 2009).
66 S.C. Res. 1918, ¶2 (Apr. 27, 2010).
67 S.C. Res. 1918, *supra* note 66, ¶4.
68 S.C. Res. 1950, ¶13 (Nov. 23, 2010).
69 S.C. Res. 1976, ¶17, ¶26 (Apr. 11, 2011).
70 S.C. Res. 2015, ¶4 (Oct. 24, 2011).
71 S.C. Res. 2015, *supra* note 71, ¶17.

Somalia: Unable and Unwilling to Combat Maritime Piracy

Although piracy is a dangerous crime everywhere in the world, its occurrence in Somalia has been particularly troubling because of this country's inability to address this problem. This factor alone necessitates the international community's continual involvement with this issue.

Somalia is a failed state. Since the early 1990s, Somalia has not had a stable government, and its fragile government is currently battling warlords and militant Islamic groups for control of the country.[72] The country does not have a functional economy, and its official law enforcement operations are slim, with gangs of paramilitary groups and rebel forces controlling the streets of Mogadishu and other towns. Until recently, piracy has thrived in this cowboy culture of inefficient government, and everyday life is ruled by violence. A functional Somali government is so absent that some Somali coastal towns have established pirate-centric societies where piracy not only enjoyed local support, but local governments relied on it.[73] Many of these piracy-driven micro economies have dried up because of the recent decrease in successful piracy attacks, caused by both the international community's integrated efforts to combat piracy and the increasing use of armed guards on board merchant vessels. However, if efforts to thwart the threat of piracy in Somalia are not continued, piracy will re-surge in Somalia, not only undermining efforts to stabilize the country, but also seriously threatening regional and international peace and stability.

In addition, piracy can spread elsewhere from Somalia. Other African states, whether Somali neighbors or located farther away, could fall prey to powerful pirate operations, especially if such operations become firmly rooted in Somalia and ruled by powerful warlords enjoying Somalia government support. In recent years, piracy has blossomed off the West Coast of Africa, in the Gulf of Guinea, where pirate networks operate a similar ransom-driven model.[74] Other regional

72 Kontorovich, *supra* note 7 (noting that Somalia has not had a stable government since 1991 and lacks the capacity to keep its territorial waters secure); *see also* Jane G. Dalton *et al.*, Introductory Note to United Nations Security Council: Piracy and Armed Robbery at Sea—Resolutions 1816, 1846 & 1851, 48 INT'L LEGAL MATTERS 129, (2009) (attributing the rise in piracy in Somalia to "violent political and economic instability, . . . the lack of a viable infrastructure to counter lawlessness, and the continued proliferation of ever-more-sophisticated small arms and light weapons").

73 *See* Mohamed Ahmed, *Pirate Stock Exchange Helps Fund Hijackings*, FIN. POST (Canada), Dec. 1, 2009, www.financialpost.com/newssectors/story.html?id=2289558 (describing how the pirates have set up "maritime companies" in some coastal villages) (quoting a local Somali government official who stated that "[p]iracy-related business is the main profitable economic activity in our area and as locals we depend on their output"). The official described how local districts are given a percentage of the pirates' ransom, which they then use to improve infrastructure, such as hospitals and schools.

74 Adeniyi Adejimi Osinowo, *Combating Piracy in the Gulf of Guinea*, AFRICA SECURITY BRIEF, No. 30, February 2015, available at *http://africacenter.org/wp-content/uploads/2015/02/ASB-30-Feb-2015-Combating-Piracy-in-GoG.pdf* (noting that in 2012, the Gulf of Guinea surpassed the Gulf of Aden as the area with the highest number of reported piracy attacks in the world).

pirate networks could be created, posing a significant threat to global commerce and human safety.[75] Moreover, piracy can endanger commercial and tourist routes, undermining the regional economy and exposing neighboring states to many potential problems.[76] These potential problems include economic non-viability, political and civil unrest caused by poverty, and border instability provoked by the need to expend vast resources on the fight against piracy. In addition, Somali piracy can threaten global peace and security if pirates start collaborating with other maritime trafficking groups, such as those who smuggle narcotics or weapons of mass destruction, either for a financial or political cause. Thus, the development of Somali piracy could contribute to the spread of maritime violence, endangering sea routes everywhere and supporting dangerous factions across the globe. These global implications, highlighted below, show why a continued global response is needed to curb and eventually eliminate this menace.

Conclusion

The Somali piracy model, employing youth and juveniles to violently attack merchant vessels sailing through the Gulf of Aden, has thrived for several years. Those who have reaped the highest benefit from this criminal enterprise are not the young pirates themselves, but instead, piracy organizers and financiers, who have invested in piracy attacks and have profited from this "business" opportunity. It appears that global efforts by the international community, which have included joint patrolling and law enforcement operations, as well as increased legal cooperation to bring suspected pirates to justice, coupled with the shipping industry's willingness to invest in the training and deployment of armed guards on board merchant vessels, have contributed to a decrease in piracy attacks off the Somali coast. However, it is highly probable that piracy would re-flourish in Somalia if such efforts were discontinued, and it is thus critical that the international community remain involved in anti-piracy operations. In addition, because piratical operations have been performed by Somali youth and children, it is even more crucial for the international community to continue to address the piracy crisis in Somalia, to ensure that this country's children are oriented toward meaningful opportunities as opposed to a life of piracy. The next chapter will discuss the use of juveniles to perform piratical acts, and will focus on legal and prosecutorial efforts to combat piracy, including the prosecution of juvenile suspects.

75 Kraska and Wilson, *supra* note 1, at 43 (arguing that piracy could contribute to regional instability in East Africa).

76 *Id.* ("Beyond the immediate threat to crews, property, and ships, maritime piracy endangers sea lines of communication, interferes with freedom of navigation and the free flow of commerce, and undermines regional stability").

2 Using Juveniles to Perform Piratical Acts

Introduction

Piracy attacks are financed and organized by "businessmen" who often reside abroad, in places such as Dubai or London. In order to execute an attack, piracy organizers will often recruit young men and boys, prone to participating in a criminal enterprise for lack of better job or schooling options. Sadly, pirates as young as twelve have been detained and prosecuted in places such as New York, Germany, Spain, India, Italy, Malaysia, and the Seychelles.[1] In many instances, juvenile pirates play the same role as adult pirates on a pirate vessel: they may engage in violent acts such as shooting, manhandling captured victims, helping to operate the vessel, or providing other types of assistance on board. In many piracy prosecutions, all suspected pirates detained onboard a single pirate vessel will be prosecuted together, under a joint criminal enterprise-type legal theory, which allows prosecutors to charge all suspects involved in a single piracy incident with the same crime.[2] Prosecutors thus do not have to distinguish between the different roles played by different piracy actors on board a skiff; instead, they can charge everybody with the crime of piracy. For juvenile pirates, this essentially means that they will be charged with the crime of piracy, even though their role in the attack may have been minor. Convicting all those involved in a violent

1 *See*, e.g., Lauren Hahn, *Comment, Juvenile Justice and Piracy: Prosecutions of Juvenile Pirates in the United States*, GEO. MASON L. REV. 241, 241–42 (2012).

2 For example, in the Seychelles, where many pirates have been prosecuted pursuant to transfer agreements between apprehending nations and the government of the Seychelles, all pirates who are caught onboard a single pirate vessel are typically prosecuted together under a joint criminal enterprise theory of "common intention." For a discussion of piracy prosecutions in the Seychelles, *see* Milena Sterio, *Piracy off the Coast of Somalia: The Argument for Pirate Prosecutions in the National Courts of Kenya, The Seychelles, and Mauritius*, 4 AMSTERDAM L.F. 104, 106 (2012). Similarly, all pirates caught together on a pirate vessel are being prosecuted together in Mauritius, another nation that has signed transfer agreements with capturing nations. *See*, e.g., Sulakshna Beekarry, *Legal, Political and Strategic Initiatives of Mauritius, with Special Focus on Collaboration Between Developed and Developing Countries*, *in* MARITIME SECURITY AND PIRACY: GLOBAL ISSUES, CHALLENGES AND SOLUTIONS 1, 1–6 (Bimal N. Patel and Hitesh Thakkar eds., 2012).

crime, such as piracy, of the most serious crime (piracy) is advantageous, as it provides prosecutors with powerful legal tools in the global fight against piracy; however, such an approach poses problems in terms of handling juvenile suspects appropriately. Most, but not all, countries' domestic criminal systems distinguish between adult and juvenile criminal suspects, and most countries treat juveniles differently. This chapter will conclude that juvenile piracy suspects should be separated from their adult partners-in-crime and should be prosecuted and detained distinctly.

The Recruitment of Juveniles to Conduct Piracy Attacks

Piracy in Somalia has thrived in a "cowboy" climate of violence and poverty. Pirates operate out of coastal Somali towns, where they are able to dock their own skiffs freely, and where they haul back their hijacked property and hostages. Coastal towns in Somalia have benefitted economically from the proceeds of piracy and thus have had no incentive to participate in anti-piracy operations.[3] The Somali government has no effective control of the various coastal regions where pirates operate, and is unable to respond with any effective law enforcement or military operation against pirates.[4] Reports indicate that piracy is supported by powerful Somali warlords, who exercise control over their respective regions of influence, and who routinely finance pirate attacks and reap the benefits thereof in case of a successful hijacking and ransom payment.[5] As one scholar noted recently,

> Piracy has evolved into a far-reaching enterprise, with support sometimes provided by the Somali diaspora and a 'business model' in which pirates receive payment based on different kinds of 'shares.' . . . As a matter of everyday practice, deals with Somali pirates are often carried out in a business-like manner.[6]

The situation has changed somewhat, in light of the recent decrease in the number of successful attacks, and by most accounts, piracy-supported micro economies of Somali coastal towns have essentially dried up.[7] However, the piracy business

3 *See* Mohamed Ahmed, *Pirate Stock Exchange Helps Fund Hijackings*, FIN. POST (Dec. 1, 2009), available at www.financialpost.com/news-sectors/story.html?id=2289558 (describing that pirates have set up "maritime companies" in coastal villages).

4 *See* James Kraska and Brian Wilson, *Fighting Pirates: The Pen and the Sword*, 25 WORLD POL'Y J. 41, 46 (2008); *see also* Eugene Kontorovich, *International Legal Responses to Piracy off the Coast of Somalia*, ASIL INSIGHTS (Feb. 6, 2009), available at www.asil.org/insights090206.cfm.

5 *See* Ahmed, *supra* note 3.

6 Mateo Taussig-Rubbo, Pirate Trials, the International Criminal Court, and Mob Justice: Reflections on Postcolonial Sovereignty in Kenya, 1 HUMAN. 51, 56 (2011).

7 Harry Haddon, *Recession Hits Somalian Pirates: Kingpin Quits As Hijackings Dry Up*, 2OCEANSVIBE.COM (Jan. 11, 2013), available at www.2oceansvibe.com/2013/01/11/recession-hits-somalian-pirates-kingpin-quits-as-hijackings-dry-up/ (describing that one of the most powerful

model could become successful again if the international community were to cease investing efforts into piracy prevention.

Piracy-related business operations often involve juvenile pirates, who are easily recruited off the streets of Somali coastal towns and persuaded to participate in a future piratical attack. One of the opening scenes in the blockbuster film, "Captain Phillips," depicts a sleepy Somali coastal town visited by piracy recruiters; upon hearing that recruiters are present, dozens of young men and boys swarm a central area of town in order to sign up for a piracy "job."[8] This scene, albeit part of a Hollywood fictional film, most likely accurately portrays the recruitment process and the dire economic reality that Somali youth face on a daily basis.

Piracy experts believe that a piracy team on any given skiff is composed of an older boss (typically, a thirty to fifty-year-old man), several foot soldiers (typically, from eighteen to thirty years of age), and at least one youth under the age of eighteen. Often called "walalo" [little brother] by the rest of the crew, boys typically serve in a supportive capacity, but can be called upon to act as gunmen on boarding parties or hostage guards if push comes to shove.[9] Most juvenile pirates are orphans and/or delinquents, and are commonly recruited around Puntland.[10] Estimates indicate that about a third of all pirates are juveniles.[11]

Much like other child soldiers, juvenile pirates are recruited to serve specific tactical and operational functions. Children as young as nine or ten are typically prized by commanders and piracy organizers for being agile, submissive, trustworthy, daring, and largely impervious to legal prosecution.

> [T]he socio-economic factors (e.g. poverty, armed violence, lack of educational or employment opportunities, orphanhood, displacement and exposure to disease) that make children vulnerable for use by armed groups exist in each of the major areas where piracy is currently reported. In addition, in many of the regions where piracy exists, children are being used by terrorist groups, criminal gangs and within state and non-state armed groups (e.g. in Somalia, Nigeria and Haiti). Therefore, the use of children and youth by pirate groups could be viewed as a natural extension of these armed groups.[12]

Somali piracy kingpins decided to quit the piracy business, most likely because of the decrease in successful piratical attacks).

8 CAPTAIN PHILLIPS (Sony Pictures 2013).

9 Today in Seychelles, *Detaining and Protecting Child Pirates*, FACEBOOK (Mar. 18, 2014), available at www.facebook.com/todayinsey/posts/635900863114394.

10 *Id.*

11 Child Pirates: Raising awareness about a serious issue, RADIO CANADA INT'L (Mar. 20, 2013), available at www.rcinet.ca/english/daily/interviews-2012/14–23_2013–03–20-child-pirates-raising-awareness-about-a-serious-issue/.

12 Carl Conradi, *Mitigating Children Involvement in Maritime Piracy*, 10 CANADIAN NAV. REV. 16, 16 (2014), available at www.navalreview.ca/wp-content/uploads/public/vol10num2/vol10num2art3.pdf.

Youssef M., a Somali youth aged between sixteen and nineteen at the time of his arrest, was tried in the national courts of Hamburg, Germany.[13] He described how he became involved in piracy. His story is representative of those of countless other child pirates.[14] When he was around the age of thirteen, Youssef began working as a night watchman for a fishing boat; he was paid less than one U.S. dollar per night.[15] In 2010, a man approached Youssef and offered him an increased pay of two to three U.S. dollars a day to pilot a boat. Later, the same man offered Youssef 500 U.S. dollars for a larger operation—a piracy attack against a German cargo ship, the MV Taipan.[16] Youssef, however, claimed that he was duped into taking part in this operation:

> It was only on board . . . that I realized we were supposed to hijack a cargo ship . . . . No one mentioned in my presence that there was a possibility of getting arrested by an international naval coalition. I did not think very hard about whether I should participate . . . [n]evertheless it seemed as if everything had been planned ahead of time and I had no choice. However, I was never threatened by anyone.[17]

It is possible that Youssef's story is not entirely trustworthy and that Youssef did know what he was signing up for; it is also entirely possible, however, that Youssef spoke the truth before the Hamburg court. Youssef and most of his under-age peers are easily recruited into piracy endeavors precisely because they do not understand the dangers associated with piracy, nor the consequences that they may face if caught and prosecuted. Child pirates, like child soldiers, are precious to their bosses because they may be willing to accomplish tasks that adults do not want to undertake. Moreover, as one of the sections below will explore, child pirates when caught are more often released, because very few prosecuting nations want to bother with setting up a separate trial for a juvenile offender.[18] Piracy organizers may be aware of the fact that child pirates are often caught-and-released and may be even more inclined to employ them for some piracy jobs. The sections below will address the different prosecutorial options that piracy-fighting nations have upon catching a suspect, as well as the difficult legal issues associated with prosecuting juvenile piracy suspects.

13 *A Precedent or a Farce? Court Faces Daunting Hurdles in Hamburg Pirate Trial*, SPIEGAL ONLINE (Jan. 18, 2011), available at www.spiegel.de/international/world/a-precedent-or-a-farce-court-faces-daunting-hurdles-in-hamburg-pirate-trial-a-740122.html [hereinafter *A Precedent of a Farce?*].

14 Danielle Fritz, *Child Pirates From Somalia: A Call for the International Community to Support the Further Development of Juvenile Justice Systems in Puntland and Somaliland*, 44 CASE WES. RES. J. INT'L L. 891 (2012).

15 *A Precedent or a Farce*, *supra* note 13.

16 *Id.*

17 *Id.*

18 See *infra*.

International Law on Piracy: Limited Prosecutorial Options

Under UNCLOS, any nation has the right to capture pirates on the high seas.[19] The capturing nation also has the right, under this convention, to prosecute pirates.[20] However, UNCLOS does not specifically condone the right for capturing nations to transfer pirates to third states for prosecution purposes. Many scholars have written on this issue: some have concluded that UNCLOS precludes pirate transfers to third states for prosecution, while some have argued that nothing in UNCLOS specifically prohibits such transfers, and that such transfers ought to be permitted in order to broaden the scope of anti-piracy measures.[21] This point is particularly important because while many nations have been willing to capture pirates, most are not willing to prosecute them in their domestic courts.[22] Piracy prosecutions are generally viewed as politically and logistically challenging and costly, and most nations have been unwilling to spend time and money on such burdensome investigative and prosecutorial efforts.[23] Some pirates have been tried in domestic courts of the capturing nation, but most of those prosecutions occurred after pirates directly threatened the national interests of the prosecuting state by attempting to attack one of its vessels or to kidnap one of its nationals.[24] Instances of Somali pirates' prosecutions based on true universal jurisdiction are extremely rare.[25]

In fact, piracy in its modern application in Somalia seems like a truly universal crime involving many different states. Merchant ships often fly flags of convenience, incorporating in countries such as Panama, Liberia or the Bahamas, which offer lenient requirements with respect to labor and safety regulations on board, and thus lower incorporation and operating costs.[26] Wealthy individuals often own such merchant ships or corporations originating from wealthy developed

19 United Nations Convention on the Law of the Sea art. 105, Oct. 7, 1982, 1833 U.N.T.S. 41–42 [hereinafter UNCLOS].

20 *Id.*

21 For the view that UNCLOS prohibits the transfer of pirates by the capturing state to third states for prosecution purposes, *see also* Kontorovich, *supra* note 4. This view also follows from a strict, narrow interpretation of UNCLOS article 105. For the opposite view, that UNCLOS does not specifically preclude the transfer of pirates to third states, see for example Lawrence Azubuike, *International Law Regime Against Piracy*, 15 Ann. Survey Int'l & Comp. L. 43, 52 (arguing that the jurisdiction of the capturing state is merely permissive because under customary law, jurisdiction over pirates was universal and UNCLOS codified customary law); *see also* J. Ashley Roach, *Countering Piracy Off Somalia: International Law and International Institutions*, 104 Am. J. Int'l L., 397, 404 (2010) (arguing that UNCLOS does not specifically prohibit the transfer of pirates to third states for prosecution).

22 *See id.* at 415.

23 Kontorovich, *supra* note 4.

24 For a detailed examination of jurisdictional basis exercised over Somali pirates by different countries, *see* Eugene Kontorovich and Steven Art, *An Empirical Examination of Universal Jurisdiction for Piracy*, 104 Am. J. Int'l L. 436, 436 (2010).

25 *See id.* at 436.

26 Taussig-Rubo, *supra* note 6, at 57.

states. Moreover, ship captains and crewmembers may come from a variety of different states, often migrating toward less developed, poorer states. The pirates themselves are from Somalia, and they may be caught by a naval ship from yet another, typically powerful maritime nation. With such a mixture of nationalities and states involved, the state that captures the pirates may only exercise universal jurisdiction, and must act as an agent on behalf of the global community in the latter's fight against Somali piracy.[27] Alas, capturing states have been reluctant to exercise universal jurisdiction over Somali pirates in these instances. After all, why should a country like the United Kingdom, if it captures Somali pirates, pay for the exercise of universal jurisdiction on behalf of a Liberian vessel owned by a Dutch corporation and employing a Philippine crew? "Universal jurisdiction in this context might appear more like a burden, a kind of self-sacrifice for a global public good."[28] When the captured suspect is a juvenile, the prospects of finding a prosecuting nation that would willingly exercise universal jurisdiction, on behalf of all mankind, are even more dire—prosecutions of juvenile suspects require special procedures and separate detention facilities, in light of relevant international human rights law instruments. Thus, many capturing nations may be forced to release juvenile suspects, because of the general lack of attractiveness of universal jurisdiction piracy prosecutions coupled with the legal complexity caused by the juvenile status of the alleged offender.

Capturing states face a difficult issue indeed: what to do with captured pirates, and in particular, with captured juvenile suspects, in instances where the capturing state is unwilling to prosecute them in its own courts? In addition, even if the capturing nation can find a third state, which is willing to prosecute pirates, international law may prohibit such a transfer to a third state. States that are signatory to major human rights treaties, like the European Convention on Human Rights and the International Covenant for Civil and Political Rights, have a so-called *non-réfoulement* obligation not to transfer anyone to a place where he or she may be mistreated.[29] In light of these legal difficulties, some NATO countries have routinely released captured pirates, including juvenile suspects, resulting in a "catch-and-release" attitude that has only exacerbated the piracy problem in Somalia. The catch-and-release policy has been applied frequently to juvenile pirates, because neither the capturing nor the prosecuting nations want to deal with issues related to the distinct treatment of juvenile suspects. Some nations, like Russia, have even resorted to drastic measures: after a Russian ship captured Somali pirates, the latter were released on a tiny boat in the middle of the Indian Ocean, with no food, water, or navigation devices.[30] The fate of these pirates remains unknown, but even Russian authorities have acknowledged that

27 *Id.*

28 *Id.*

29 Kontorovich, *supra* note 4.

30 *Freed Somali pirates 'probably died'—Russian source*, BBC News (May 11, 2010), available at http://news.bbc.co.uk/2/hi/8675978.stm.

these Somalis probably died.[31] This attitude is far from desirable in international law, but nonetheless illustrates the frustration that some piracy-fighting nations have experienced when dealing with captured pirates.

Possible solutions to this issue include either a broader interpretation of UNCLOS and customary law, arguing that international law does not specifically prohibit capturing states from transferring piracy suspects, including juveniles, to third states for prosecution, or reliance on other conventions, such as SUA and other anti-terrorism treaties, which do not limit capturing states to prosecution in their own courts. Most piracy-fighting nations have preferred to transfer pirates to third states for prosecution purposes, and have creatively circumvented the restraints of international law by relying on broader definitions of piracy described above. In addition, major maritime nations have begun to increasingly rely on stable regional partners, like Kenya, the Seychelles, and Mauritius, which have offered the use of their national courts for the purposes of prosecuting captured Somali pirates. This transfer model, and its implications for the prosecution of juvenile suspects, will be explored in the section below.

Prosecuting Piracy Suspects in National Courts

> Some countries provide a navy, others can help with prosecution.[32]

The preferred approach of many piracy-fighting nations has been to use regional partners, such as Kenya, the Seychelles, and Mauritius, and to transfer captured pirates to the national courts of these states. All three nations have been affected by piracy because of their geographic location and because of the potential harm to these nations' tourism revenues brought about by the threat of pirate attacks. Major maritime powers have requested these nations' assistance in prosecuting Somali pirates because of these nations' position in East Africa and the Indian Ocean; these nations have been willing thus far to extend their domestic courts to Somali piracy prosecutions. It is clear, however, that none of these nations have been particularly keen on prosecuting juvenile suspects, because of different international law requirements that apply to the treatment of such suspects.

Kenya

As early as 2006, Kenya began prosecuting Somali pirates in a specialized piracy court in Mombasa. Pursuant to various secret and public Memoranda of Understanding (MOU), which Kenya signed with the United States, the United

31 *Id.*

32 C. Houreld, *Warships Fill Up with Pirates after Kenya Bails*, ASSOCIATED PRESS, April 15, 2010, available at http://abcnews.go.com/International/wirestory?id=10384342&page;eqI.

Kingdom, as well as with the European Union, Kenyan courts have been asserting jurisdiction over Somali pirates captured by naval ships of other countries. Some of these MOUs are secret and allow executive branch officials to act with no direct oversight by anyone. It is thus unclear how and why such MOUs bestow jurisdiction on Kenyan courts, in light of international law's possible prohibition on pirate transfers, discussed above.[33] Either Kenyan courts are exercising universal jurisdiction on behalf of the capturing state, or international law should be read more broadly to authorize non-capturing states to prosecute pirates as well. Regardless of this jurisdictional issue, Kenyan judges at first appeared willing to take on Somali piracy prosecutions. In a 2006 appellate decision by the High Court of Kenya, which affirmed jurisdiction over the initial group of Somalis delivered to Kenya by the United States in 2006, the High Court determined that even if Kenya had not ratified UNCLOS, and had not provided for an offense of piracy in its domestic criminal law, the lower trial court was "bound to apply international norms and instruments since Kenya is a member of the civilized world and not expected to act in contradiction to expectations of member states of the United Nations."[34]

Similarly, the Kenyan government initially approved the use of Kenyan courts for Somali piracy prosecutions, despite the fact that most of the transferred pirates never directly harmed Kenya. In exchange for such governmental and prosecutorial cooperation, Kenya demanded and enjoyed substantial financial support by wealthy donor states.[35] In its first few years, the transfer program operated somewhat smoothly, resulting in the prosecution and conviction of numerous pirates. However, it is unclear how many of these piracy suspects prosecuted in Kenyan courts may have been juveniles. In addition, it appears that Kenyan authorities prosecuted most of the piracy suspects in groups, and it is unclear whether any attempt was made to separate juvenile offenders from the adult offenders or to distinguish between their respective sentences.[36] Other issues raised regarding Kenyan piracy prosecutions involving juvenile suspects included: the lack of appropriately trained defense counsel, the prosecution of juvenile piracy suspects in adult courts, the lack of appropriate detention facilities to house juvenile suspects, and the difficulty associated with contacting the juvenile suspects' respective families in Somalia.[37]

33 Taussig-Rubbo, *supra* note 6, at 59.

34 Hassan M. Ahmed v. Republic, (2009) K.L.R. (H.C.K.) (Kenya) (Azangalala, J.). It should be noted that at least one scholar has questioned whether Kenya's lowest level trial courts, magistrate's courts, are actually empowered to exercise universal jurisdiction. J. T. Gathii, *Jurisdiction to Prosecute Non-National Pirates Captured by Third States Under Kenyan and International Law*, 31 Loy. L.A. Int'l & Comp. L. Rev. 363 (2009).

35 Taussig-Rubbo, *supra* note 4, at 60 (discussing issues related to donations by wealthy states to Kenya for piracy prosecutions).

36 Danielle Fritz, *supra* note 14, at 899 (noting that "[l]awyers handled the cases of entire groups of pirates but no one specifically represented minors").

37 *Id.* at 899–901.

In addition to this issue, various problems have surfaced over the past few years. Donor states became concerned with the general treatment of pirates, including juvenile suspects, in Kenyan courts and prisons.[38] Corruption issues plagued the program, with allegations that money donated to support piracy trials was going elsewhere. Kenyan officials became concerned that Kenya was being exploited as a dumping ground by wealthy maritime nations that were uncomfortable with simply killing pirates yet unwilling to employ their own courts to prosecute them. Thus, the rapport between Kenya and the major maritime nations, which sought to donate money to Kenya in exchange for Kenya's acceptance to prosecute Somali pirates, quickly turned sour.

> Donor states thus transfer pirates to Kenya yet seem unable to let them go, concerned about Kenyan standards and equipment. And the Kenyans, understandably, are unwilling to let the foreign donors depart without offering some aid. That these awkward transactions are ambivalently situated as benevolent gifts, reciprocal exchanges, or unseemly transfers nicely articulates the complexity and variability of the bonds between Kenya and the donors.[39]

Additionally, in 2009 Kenya became the subject of an International Criminal Court (ICC) investigation, focused on post-election violence of 2007 and allegations that groups operating in Kenya committed crimes against humanity.[40] It is thus possible that Kenya, in a quid pro quo, decided to rebel against the international community, because of the latter's determination that Kenya should be subjected to ICC scrutiny, by halting piracy trials in Mombasa. In April 2010, Kenyan Attorney General Wako announced the end of the piracy program. The Kenyan Attorney General proclaimed that foreign nations were "rubbishing our [Kenyan] judicial system." He also lamented that foreign nations would "dump" pirates on Kenya and then "forget about what happened."[41] It is uncertain whether the ICC investigation into Kenyan violence prompted the Kenyan government's sudden reversal of position with respect to piracy prosecutions, but according to one rumor, the Kenyan Attorney General himself was on the ICC list of possible suspects.[42] It thus seems plausible that the Kenyan

38 *Id.* at 898 ("Criticisms of the Kenyan courts, in particular, have include inadequate resources and laws to conduct effective piracy trials, a foundering criminal justice system, and an overall judicial system that fails to meet the minimum standards necessary to protect piracy suspects").

39 Taussig-Rubbo, *supra* note 4, at 60.

40 On November 26, 2009, the ICC Prosecutor requested authorization from the court to open an investigation into violence that occurred in 2007 in Kenya, in the aftermath of presidential elections, because of allegations that such violence constituted crimes against humanity. *See*, e.g., *How the ICC Became Involved in Kenya*, The Int'l Crim. Cts. Kenya Monitor, available at www.icckenya.org/background/ (last visited Feb. 7, 2016).

41 Fred Mukinda and Alphonce Shiundu, *Kenya Laments Pirates' Burden*, Daily Nation, (Mar. 20, 2012), available at www.nation.co.ke/News/-/1056/889976/-/vrw9dl/-/index.html.

42 Taussig-Rubbo, *supra* note 4, at 61.

authorities were concerned with the ICC investigation and therefore decided to retaliate against the international community by halting piracy prosecutions. Ultimately, in June 2010, Kenya, in another stark change of heart, announced that it was back in the pirate transfer model.[43] An additional promise of a financial contribution by donor states may have prompted the Kenyan reversal of position—indeed, the EU pledged more funding and paid for the building of a new courtroom in Mombasa.[44]

Somewhat unexpectedly, piracy prosecutions in Kenya were halted, when the Kenya High Court at Mombasa ruled that Kenya's magistrate level courts, which had been the ones where all pirate prosecutions had been taking place, did not have jurisdiction over piracy offenses unless the offenses took place in Kenyan territorial waters.[45] The High Court focused on Section 5 of Kenyan penal law, which provides that "[t]he jurisdiction of the Courts of Kenya for the purpose of this Code extends to every place within Kenya, including territorial waters."[46] According to the High Court, this provision, because it is the one defining all jurisdictional ability of Kenyan courts, trumps another piracy provision, Section 69(1), which provides that "[a]ny person who in territorial waters or upon the high seas, commits any act of piracy jure gentium is guilty of the offence of Piracy."[47] This ruling by the Kenya High Court effectively precluded any additional piracy prosecutions in Kenyan magistrate level courts, because none of the Somali piracy incidents had taken place in the Kenyan territorial sea. The Kenyan Attorney General appealed this ruling, and a special five-judge panel of appellate judges was formed in Nairobi to hear this, as well as two other appeals, and to sort through these difficult jurisdictional issues.[48] The appellate panel reversed the trial court, effectively re-instituting piracy prosecutions in Kenya once again.[49]

While it is possible, based on the success of initial piracy prosecutions in Mombasa, that Kenya has the potential to prosecute non-national pirates in fair and neutral trials, it is also important to highlight that Kenyan proceedings have been marred by allegations of human rights violations, and by some judges' unwillingness to assert jurisdiction over Somali piracy suspects.[50] These issues are of particular importance in the context of juvenile suspects and the type of judicial

43 *Id.*

44 *Id.*

45 M. M. Hashi *et al.*, (2009) K.L.R. (H.C.K.) (Kenya), available at http://piracylaw.files.wordpress.com/2011/01/in-re-mohamud-mohamed-hashi-et-al1.pdf; *see also* Roger L. Philips, *Kenya: No Jurisdiction to Try Piracy?*, COMMUNIS HOSTIS OMNIUM (Jan. 27, 2011), available at http://piracylaw.com/2011/01/27/kenya-no-jurisdiction-to-try-piracy/.

46 M. M. Hashi *et al.*, (2009) L.R.K. (H.C.K.) (Kenya).

47 *Id.*

48 Maureen Mudi, *Kenya: Special Court to Hear Mombasa Piracy Case*, NAIROBI STAR, (Sept. 30, 2011), available at http://allafrica.com/stories/201109301201.html.

49 Attorney Gen. v. M. M. Dashi *et al.*, (2010) K.L.R. (Ct. App. Nairobi) (Kenya), available at http://kenyalaw.org/CaseSearch/view_preview1.php?link=38656751089581753125617.

50 *See* Taussig-Rubbo, *supra* note 4, at 65.

proceeding that such suspects are exposed to in the national courts of Kenya. If adult suspects' rights are potentially being violated in Kenyan prisons, it is highly likely that juveniles may be treated even more harshly and may be experiencing higher levels of violence. Moreover, the above-mentioned delays in piracy prosecutions have resulted in lengthy pre-trial detention periods for all suspects, including juveniles. This is problematic because international human rights law instruments mandate that juveniles should only be detained pre-trial as a measure of last resort and for the minimum amount of time necessary.[51] Additionally, if Kenyan authorities have shown reluctance to prosecute adult suspects, it is very likely that they will turn away juvenile suspects, for a host of pragmatic reasons. These reasons include the logistical complexity associated with the detention of juvenile suspects pre-trial, during the trial itself, and post-trial, as well as legal challenges involved in the actual prosecution of juvenile suspects. As will be discussed in Chapter 3 below, various international human rights treaties and other international law instruments impose a duty on all states to treat juveniles who have entered the criminal process with special care. It is unclear that piracy-prosecuting nations, such as Kenya, are willing to spend significant resources in order to develop adequate procedures that would apply to juvenile piracy suspects. Thus, while major maritime nations should continue to explore the potential of successful piracy prosecutions in Kenya, involving adult and juvenile suspects, other allies, such as the Seychelles and Mauritius, should continue to be engaged and approached.

The Seychelles

The Seychelles is an island nation in the Indian Ocean, consisting of 115 islands scattered over an area of 450,000 square miles. Several pirate attacks have occurred sufficiently close to the Seychelles to alarm this nation's government and to prompt it to participate in the fight against Somali piracy.[52] In fact, the Seychelles' economy derives most of its revenue from tourism, and the prospect of Somali piracy spreading toward the Seychelles could deter tourists from visiting this beautiful nation. For this reason, the Seychelles' government has a direct interest in both preventing pirate attacks from taking place, and in ensuring that all detained pirates are effectively prosecuted.[53] Thus, the Seychelles' government, pursuant to the Kenyan model, has entered into several MOUs with major

51 Fritz, *supra* note 14, at 900.

52 *Pirate Attacks on Sailing Yachts-Piracy Warnings*, YACHT PALS (Oct. 2, 2009), available at http://yachtpals.com/pirates-yachts4092 (reporting on several pirate attacks off the Seychelles' coast in 2009).

53 Jennie Ryan, *Seychelles President Urges Greater Anti-Piracy Measures*, JURIST (Dec. 5, 2011), available at http://jurist.org/paperchase/2011/12/seychelles-president-urges-greater-anti-piracy-measures.php (noting that the Seychelles yacht tourism has been harmed by pirate attacks, and that the price of shipping from the Seychelles has drastically increased).

maritime nations. Under the terms of these MOUs, capturing nations deliver pirates to the Seychelles for prosecution in the Seychellois courts. In each instance, the Seychelles government has discretion to accept or reject the transfer.[54] In order to facilitate piracy prosecutions in the Seychelles, this nation's parliament revised the offense of piracy under the Seychellois penal law in 2010.[55] Before the revision, the offense of piracy did not exist as an independently defined crime under the Seychelles' law and was instead defined as follows under the Seychellois penal law: "[a]ny person who is guilty of piracy or any crime connected with or akin to piracy shall be liable to be tried and punished according to the law of England for the time being in force."[56] The Seychellois courts interpreted the phrase "time being in force" as referring to the common law prevailing in England as of June 29, 1976 (herein after referred to as the relevant time) when the Seychelles attained independence from Great Britain. In order to facilitate piracy prosecutions, the Seychelles' Parliament added a new piracy definition to its penal law. Under the revised Section 65(4) of the Seychelles Penal code, piracy is defined as follows:

> (a) Any illegal act of violence or detention, or any act of depredation, committed for private ends by the crew or the passengers of a private ship or aircraft and directed:
>   (i) the high seas, against another ship or aircraft, or against persons or property on board such a ship or aircraft;
>   (ii) against a ship or an aircraft or a person or property in a place, outside the jurisdiction of any State;
>
> (b) Any act of voluntary participation in the operation of a ship or an aircraft with knowledge of facts making it pirate ship or a pirate aircraft; or
>
> (c) Any act described in paragraph (a) or (b) which, except for the fact that it was committed within a maritime zone of Seychelles, would have been an act of piracy under either of those paragraphs.[57]

Moreover, section 65(5) further provides that:

> A ship or aircraft shall be considered a pirate ship or pirate aircraft if:
>
> (a) It had been used to commit any of the acts referred to in subsection (4) and remains under the control of the persons who committed those acts; or

54 Milena Sterio, *Piracy off the Coast of Somalia: The Argument for Pirate Prosecutions in the National Courts of Kenya, The Seychelles, and Mauritius*, 4 AMSTERDAM L. F. 104, 115 (2012).

55 *Seychelles MPs Adopt Anti-Piracy Law*, HAABA (Mar. 16, 2010), available at www.haaba.com/node/395898/topic/it.

56 The Republic v. Abdi Ali, Sentencing, Crim. Side No. 14, ¶ 2 (Nov. 3, 2010) (Sey.) (citing Penal Code 2010, § 65 (Sey.)) (on file with author).

57 The Republic v. Mohamed Aweys Sayid, Crim. Side No. 19, ¶¶ 11–12, (Dec. 15, 2010) (Sey.) (citing Penal Code, 2010 § 65(4) (Sey.)) (on file with author).

(b) It is intended by the person in dominant control of it to be used for the purpose of committing any of the acts referred to in subsection (4).[58]

The new piracy provision in the Seychelles law is modelled closely on the UNCLOS definition of piracy, and thus corresponds to customary international law. However, the new law is broader in its reach than UNCLOS in several respects. First, the revised Section 65 criminalizes the offense of conspiracy to commit piracy, enabling Seychellois prosecutors to go after piracy conspirators and enablers in addition to prosecuting the executioners.[59] Second, Section 65(4) effectively dispenses with the "high seas" requirement of the UNCLOS definition of piracy, by stipulating that acts committed in the Seychelles' maritime zone will amount to piracy, provided that other requirements of the piracy definition are satisfied.[60] Finally, it should be noted that Section 23 of the Seychelles Penal Code enables prosecutors to charge several defendants with the same offense, as long as all of such defendants had a "common intention" to commit the crime in question.[61] Thus, the Seychelles' prosecutors have been charging groups of Somali pirates, who had all participated in the same piracy incident, with the same offenses under the "common intention" theory of criminal liability.[62] This greatly facilitates piracy prosecutions in the Seychelles' courts. However, the revised Seychellois law does not mention juvenile piracy suspects, and the prosecution of groups of pirates under the "common intention" theory of liability has resulted in criminal proceedings involving adults and juveniles lumped together and typically convicted of the same offense, regardless of their respective ages. In most cases, the Supreme Court of the Seychelles makes no mention of the age of the accused, and in some cases, the Court, while recognizing the young age of the defendants, has failed to adequately consider the implications of such young age recognition.[63]

Several piracy prosecutions involving both adults and juveniles have taken place in the Seychelles' courts. The international community has assisted the Seychelles in Somali piracy prosecutions in various ways. Like Kenya, the Seychelles have benefited from financial aid by donor states as well as by assistance from the United Nations Office on Drugs and Crime (UNODC). Thus, a new prison wing was built to accommodate pirate detainees, and new, larger courtrooms are currently being built.[64] The Seychelles prosecutors and judges have also benefited from translation and interpretation assistance by skilled United Nations employees.[65]

58 *Id.* at ¶¶ 12–13 (citing Seychelles Penal Code, Section 65(5)) (on file with author).

59 Penal Code (Amendment) Bill, 2010, § 65 (Sey.) (amending Penal Code 1955, CAP. 73 (Sey.)).

60 *Id.* at § 65(4).

61 *Id.* at § 23.

62 *See*, e.g., Mohamed Aweys Sayid, Crim. Side No. 19.

63 *See* Fritz, *supra* note 14, at 902–903.

64 Sterio, *supra* note 54, at 117 (citing Jennie Ryan, *Seychelles President Urges Greater Anti-Piracy Measures*, JURIST (Dec. 5, 2011) http://jurist.org/paperchase/2011/12/seychelles-president-urges-greater-anti-piracy-measures.php.

65 *Id.*

Finally, some donor states, like the United Kingdom, have assisted the Seychelles in piracy prosecutions by sending skilled British-trained prosecutors to work in the Seychelles' Attorney General's office; these British prosecutors devote most of their time to piracy prosecutions, but they also help in prosecuting other, non-piracy cases thereby relieving the burdensome workload of the Attorney General's small legal staff.[66] None of these efforts have been directed toward tackling the issue of juvenile piracy. In Seychelles, like in Kenya, juveniles are often detained together with their adult counterparts, and it is unclear whether juvenile suspects are provided with more adequately trained defense counsel who are apt in working with juveniles and addressing their particular needs. While it appears that the Seychellois prosecutorial model may satisfy standards of international justice more so than the Kenyan model, it is uncertain whether the needs of juvenile piracy suspects have been appropriately addressed in the Seychelles' courts. More specific cases involving juvenile piracy suspects prosecuting in the Seychellois courts will be discussed below, in Chapter 8.

The Seychelles transfer program has somewhat successfully supplemented the Kenyan model. The Seychelles government appears willing and eager to use the Seychellois court for the purpose of prosecuting Somali pirates, even in instances where the Seychelles' interests have not been directly threatened by the act of piracy, on a true universal jurisdiction model. However, because of capacity issues associated with the small island nation of the Seychelles, major maritime nations have been searching for other stable regional partners, like Mauritius.

Mauritius

Mauritius is another Indian Ocean island nation, located to the southeast of Somalia.[67] Mauritius has not been directly harmed by any piracy incidents, and the Somali pirates have not travelled as far south in their piratical endeavors. However, Mauritius has also been identified by the international community as another possible regional partner in the global fight against piracy.

In July 2011, Mauritius concluded an MOU with the European Union, pursuant to the Kenyan and Seychellois models. Under the terms of the MOU, pirates detained by European forces will be transferred to Mauritius for prosecution in this country's national courts.[68] In order to facilitate such piracy prosecutions, Mauritius has revised its criminal law to model the piracy offense on UNCLOS more closely.[69] Under the new Mauritian law, the piracy offense is identical to the one found in UNCLOS, thus requiring the presence of two vessels

66 *Id.*

67 *See*, e.g., DISCOVER MAURITIUS, available at www.mauritius.net (last visited Feb. 10, 2016).

68 *Pirates to be Prosecuted in Mauritius*, DEFIMEDIA (Jan. 13, 2012), available at www.defimedia.info/newssunday/nos-news/item/4435-pirates-to-be-prosecuted-in-mauritius.html?tmpl=component&print=1.

69 *Id.*

(aggressor and victim), and a violent act committed for private aims on the high seas. In addition to the offense of piracy, the new Mauritian law also provides for the offense of a "maritime attack," which is defined as follows:

> (a) an illegal act of violence or detention, or any act of depredation for private ends by the crew or the passengers of a private ship or a private aircraft, and directed –
>
> (i) against persons or property on board a ship or aircraft, as the case may be; or
>
> (ii) against a ship or aircraft, as the case may be; or
>
> (b) any act of inciting or of intentionally facilitating an act described in paragraph (a) within the territorial sea or the internal, historic and archipelagic waters of Mauritius.[70]

The new Mauritian law conceives of piracy in broader terms than UNCLOS, because it adds the offense of "maritime attack" to criminalize acts that fall short of the traditional definition of piracy because they may be committed in the Mauritian territorial waters.[71] Finally, the new law also criminalizes acts such as the hijacking and destroying of ships, and the act of endangering safe navigation of ships.[72] In this respect, the Mauritian law resembles the SUA approach—it criminalizes a series of different maritime offenses including violence against ships or persons onboard ships. The drafters of this law seemed to have blended UNCLOS and SUA, to come up with a law that encompasses the traditional definition of piracy found in UNCLOS, and that also adopts a broader approach in its anti-piracy reach by criminalizing other maritime offenses falling short of piracy. Finally, the new law specifically contemplates the transfer of detained pirates to Mauritius by the authorities of the capturing state for prosecution in Mauritian courts.[73] By all accounts, the revision in the Mauritian Penal Code was dictated by European Union authorities, which promised financial and logistical assistance to the Mauritius transfer model on the condition that Mauritius pass and implement a new penal code provision on piracy.[74] Like Kenya and the Seychelles, Mauritius has chosen not to address the issue of juvenile piracy suspects directly. Mauritian law does not specifically provide for disparate treatment of juvenile piracy suspects, and in all likelihood, juvenile suspects will be detained and prosecuted alongside adult suspects in the Mauritian criminal justice system. The lack of specific legal provisions protecting the status of juvenile piracy

70 Piracy and Maritime Violence Act 2011, (No. XXVIII), art. 3 (Dec. 13, 2011) (on file with author).

71 *Id.*

72 *Id.* at art. 4, 5.

73 *Id.* at art. 8.

74 *Pirates to be Prosecuted in Mauritius*, *supra* note 68 (reporting that the disbursement of EU funds was subject to Mauritius passing the above-mentioned Piracy and Maritime Violence Bill; reporting also that the bill was enacted on December 13, 2011).

suspects may be viewed as a significant oversight by the international community, involved in the global fight against piracy.

Upon the successful passage of the above-discussed revised piracy law, Mauritius, like Kenya and the Seychelles, has benefitted from financial assistance by the European Union, implemented through the UNODC.[75] It has been reported that these donations will be used for judicial and prosecutorial capacity building in Mauritius, as well as for infrastructure such as the building or upgrading of prisons, courthouses and police headquarters.[76] It is unclear, however, whether the international donations will be used to build juvenile detention facilities, which would allow Mauritian authorities to separate juvenile piracy suspects from adult ones. Finally, like the Seychelles, Mauritius has concluded post-prosecution transfer agreements with the federal government of Somalia, as well as with Puntland and Somaliland, two of the more stable regions in Somalia.[77] The revised Mauritian penal law, described above, specifically contemplates the possibility of transfer of pirates convicted in Mauritius to third states for detention purposes.[78] Mauritius, like the Seychelles, may face prison capacity issues and may thus wish to explore the possibility of repatriating convicted pirates to their homeland, for prolonged detention purposes. The possibility of transferring convicted juvenile pirates to Somalia poses additional challenges. While this option may be attractive, if Somali detention facilities are updated and rebuilt to include separate juvenile prisons, and if relatives of convicted juvenile pirates can be located in Somalia and implicated in the juvenile's rehabilitation process, the success of post-conviction transfers of convicted juveniles will depend on Somalia's ability to welcome them home in a meaningful way. "The possibility of returning these children to semi-autonomous regions in Somalia may serve the dual function of holding children accountable for their actions while emphasizing rehabilitation and reintegration into their home society as the ultimate goal."[79]

Thus far, one prosecution of Somali pirates has taken place in Mauritius, after the pirates were captured on the high seas by the French authorities and transferred to Mauritius, pursuant to the above-mentioned transfer agreement with the European Union.[80] The Mauritian trial level court initially found the pirates

75 *Id.* (reporting that the European Union donated over 4 million Euros to Mauritius to assist in piracy prosecutions). For a detailed discussion of UNODC efforts in Kenya, the Seychelles and Mauritius, *see* Counter-Piracy Programme: Support to the Trial and Related Treatment of Piracy Suspects, 7 UNODC, Sept.-Oct. 2011, available at www.unodc.org/documents/Piracy/UNODC_Brochure_Issue_7_WV.pdf [hereinafter UNODC, *Counter-Piracy Programme*].

76 Pirates to be prosecuted in Mauritius, *supra* note 68; see also UNODC, Counter-Piracy Programme, supra note 75.

77 *Id.*

78 Piracy and Maritime Violence Bill, *supra* note 70, art. 8.

79 Fritz, *supra* note 14, at 910.

80 Mauritian Piracy Trial, Waltons & Morse LLP, available at www.waltonsandmorse.com/mauritian-piracy-trial/.

not guilty, but the Supreme Court overturned the not guilty verdict and the case was remanded for further proceedings at the trial court.[81] None of the pirates prosecuted in this incident alleged to be juvenile, and it remains to be seen how Mauritian authorities will handle prosecutions where defendants raise a juvenile age claim. It would seem advisable for Mauritius, like for Kenya and the Seychelles, to develop specific policies that would apply to the detention and prosecution of juvenile suspects. A more detailed proposal for the development of such policies is discussed in Chapter 10.

Conclusion: Prosecuting Juvenile Pirates—A Problem With No Adequate Solution?

As the above discussion demonstrates, most piracy attacks are organized and financed by individuals residing outside of Somalia, and implemented using impoverished Somali youth. For the most part, young Somali men are enticed into participating in a piracy attack "by private ends, such as escaping poverty, pursuing lucre, and securing some financial gain amid dire conditions and paucity of opportunities."[82] In addition, Somalia's hierarchical clan structure contributes to the Somali youth's willingness to participate in piratical endeavors, because success in a piracy gang often elevates the status of the youth pirate within Somali society. If caught, juvenile pirates are either released back to Somalia, to the hands of those who exploited them in the first place, or they are prosecuted in places like Kenya, the Seychelles, or Mauritius. Because most countries do not have adequate procedures in place to handle the detention and prosecution of juvenile piracy suspects, such suspects—at times as young as twelve—are often prosecuted alongside adult suspects.[83] Juvenile pirates are thus often charged with the crime of piracy, even though their role in the actual piracy attack may have been minor. Charging juvenile piracy suspects with the same crimes as their adult counterparts and prosecuting them all together poses significant problems in light of applicable international human rights law. As Chapter 3 below will discuss, international human rights law imposes positive obligations on all states to establish separate criminal processes for juvenile offenders, to detain all juvenile suspects separately from the adult suspects, and to only impose punishments that contain a rehabilitative and restorative goal and function.

81 Mike Schuler, *Suspected Pirates Found Not Guilty in Mauritius*, GCAPTAIN (Nov. 6, 2014), available at http://gcaptain.com/2014/11/06/suspected-pirates-found-not-guilty-in-mauritius/#.VqfXX4-cGUk (reporting on the pirates' acquittal by the Mauritius trial court); *see also* The Director of Public Prosecutions v. Abdoulkader Mohamed Ali *et al.*, 2015, No. 8702, 452 SCJ (Mauritius) (reversing the trial court and ordering the remittance of the case to the trial court) (on file with author).

82 Mark A. Drumble, *Child Pirates: Rehabilitation, Reintegration, and Accountability*, p. 12 (on file with author).

83 *See*, e.g., Lauren Hahn, *Juvenile Justice and Piracy: Prosecutions of Juvenile Pirates in the United States*, GEO. MASON L. REV. 241, 241–42 (2012).

In light of such international human rights law obligations, most countries' domestic criminal systems distinguish between adult and juvenile criminal suspects, and most countries treat juveniles differently. However, the international community and piracy-prosecuting nations have paid very little attention to the specific issue of prosecuting juvenile piracy suspects. As discussed above, novel piracy laws passed in piracy-prosecuting nations such as Kenya, the Seychelles, and Mauritius, failed to address the issue of juvenile pirates. Despite the fact that a report by the United Nations Secretary-General suggested that the Security Council "would need to consider whether special provision should be made for [juvenile piracy suspects'] treatment," most Security Council resolutions passed on the subject of Somali piracy do not address the phenomenon of child pirates.[84] The so-called Lang Report, submitted by Jack Lang, Special Adviser to the Secretary-General on Legal Issues Related to Piracy off the Coast of Somalia, which focused on criminal justice mechanisms and suggested the establishment of a specialized piracy court in Puntland, Somalia, and in Tanzania, did not specifically discuss any accommodations that juvenile suspects would be entitled to.[85] Thus, it appears that most piracy-prosecuting nations are unsure how their existing international human rights obligations would apply to juvenile piracy suspects, and are often inclined to simply refuse to handle any juvenile suspects. An additional hurdle in this context is the fact that piracy suspects often allege that they are below the age of eighteen, but are unable to factually prove their juvenile status. A prosecuting nation may be unsure how to treat this type of suspect, and in instances where the suspect's nexus to the prosecuting nation is slim and where the only basis of jurisdiction is universality, most prosecuting authorities decline to proceed. This results in the catch-and-release of juvenile suspects and in their return to the same Somali clans where they were recruited into piracy to begin with. This cycle will continue unless the issue of juvenile pirates is seriously considered by the international community and prosecuting nations.

The next chapter will examine international treaties that impose a general duty on all member states to distinguish between juvenile and adult suspects. This duty applies equally in the piracy context.

84 United Nations Security Council, Report of the Secretary-General, S/2010/394 (July 26, 2010), pp. 21–22, para. 46.

85 Letter dated 24 January 2011 from the Secretary-General to the President of the Security Council, Annex (Report of the Special Adviser to the Secretary-General on Legal Issues Related to Piracy off the Coast of Somalia), page 3.

Part II

International Law on the Treatment of Juvenile Criminal Suspects

Part II of the book will focus on relevant international legal provisions regarding the treatment of juvenile criminal suspects. These provisions are also relevant in the context of Somali piracy, where juvenile suspects are most often prosecuted under the national criminal laws of various nations, and where such prosecuting nations are members of relevant international treaties and bound by customary law. Chapter 3 will focus on international human rights law on the treatment of juvenile criminal suspects, including the Convention on the Rights of the Child and the International Covenant on Civil and Political Rights. Chapter 4 will draw a parallel between the treatment of child soldiers and child pirates and will use relevant international criminal law, on the treatment of the former, as a guideline about the treatment of the latter.

3 International Human Rights Law on the Treatment of Juvenile Suspects

Introduction

Major human rights treaties, international criminal law documents and other instruments recognize that juvenile suspects need to be treated distinctly within any criminal investigation or prosecution. These include the International Covenant on Civil and Political Rights, the Convention on the Rights of the Child, International Labor Organization Convention Concerning the Prohibition and Elimination of the Worst Forms of Child Labor (No. 182), the Geneva Declaration of the Rights of the Child of 1924, the U.N. Standard Minimum Rules of the Administration of Juvenile Justice (Beijing Rules), the United Nations Rules for the Protection of Juveniles Deprived of Their Liberty, and the United Nations Guidelines for the Protection of Juvenile Delinquency (Riyadh Guidelines), as well as the statutes of major international criminal tribunals and war crimes chambers, such as the International Criminal Court, the International Criminal Tribunal for Yugoslavia, the International Criminal Tribunal for Rwanda, the Special Court for Sierra Leone, the Extraordinary Chambers in the Courts of Cambodia, and the United Nations Transitional Administration in East Timor.

This chapter will first discuss whether international human rights law and international criminal law impose on states a duty to establish a reasonable Minimum Age of Criminal Responsibility, before turning to a discussion of relevant international law instruments themselves. This chapter will conclude that international human rights law and international criminal law, while failing to provide for a specific minimum age of criminal responsibility, clearly establish the need for states to differentiate in their treatment of juvenile versus adult criminal suspects, as well as the necessity to erect special protections of minors within any state's criminal system. This conclusion applies to the prosecution of juvenile piracy suspects within countries bound by above-mentioned human rights norms and other international criminal law instruments.

Minimum Age of Criminal Responsibility

Most family law and human rights law experts and many states agree with the idea that each individual needs to reach a minimum age of criminal responsibility

("MACR") before he or she can be held accountable for his or her actions.[1] While the concept of MACR has received near universal acceptance, neither family nor international law have ever established a generally agreed upon precise age at which one would incur criminal responsibility. As of today, 174 states have established a MACR, and establishing a MACR is required by major human rights instruments. Article 40(3)(a) of the Convention on the Rights of the Child (CRC) requires that:

> States Parties shall seek to promote the establishment of laws, procedures, authorities and institutions specifically applicable to children alleged as, accused of, or recognized as having infringed the penal law, and, in particular:
> a) The establishment of a minimum age below which children shall be presumed not to have the capacity to infringe the penal law.[2]

In addition, Article 4.1 of the United Nations Minimum Rules for the Administration of Juvenile Justice (Beijing Rules) states that MACR "shall not be fixed at too low an age level, bearing in mind the factors of emotional, mental and intellectual maturity."[3] Commentary to Article 4 suggests that drafters of the Beijing Rules envisioned the creation of MACRs that are parallel to the age at which a child gains other social rights and responsibilities within his or her own national system:

> The minimum age of criminal responsibility differs widely owing to history and culture. The modern approach would be to consider whether a child can live up to the moral and psychological components of criminal responsibility; that is, whether a child, by virtue of her or his individual discernment and understanding, can be held responsible for essentially anti-social behaviour. If the age of criminal responsibility is fixed too low or if there is no lower age limit at all, the notion of responsibility would become meaningless. In general, there is a close relationship between the notion of responsibility for delinquent or criminal behaviour and other social rights and responsibilities (such as marital status, civil majority, etc.).
>
> Efforts should therefore be made to agree on a reasonable lowest age limit that is applicable internationally.[4]

The above-cited instruments clearly demonstrate that the underlying policy goal of international justice should be to determine the minimum age at which an individual has sufficient moral, intellectual, and emotional maturity in order

1 Jon Bellish, *The Issue of Juvenile Piracy*, *in* PROSECUTING MARITIME PIRACY: DOMESTIC SOLUTIONS TO INTERNATIONAL CRIMES 276 (Michael P. Scharf *et al.*, eds. 2015).

2 Convention on the Rights of the Child, art. 40(3)(a), *opened for signature* Nov. 20, 1989, 1577 U.N.T.S. 44 (entered into force Sept. 2, 1990) [hereinafter CRC].

3 G.A. Res. 40/33, United Nations Standard minimum Rules for the Administration of Juvenile Justice (the "Beijing Rules"), annex ¶ 4.1, (Nov. 29, 1985) [hereinafter Beijing Rules].

4 *Id.* art. 4.1, Commentary.

to bear criminal responsibility; however, the above-cited instruments also demonstrate that states are currently free to determine such a minimum age according to their own national laws and policies. Unsurprisingly, this has resulted in a tremendous disparity of MACRs at the national level. Don Cipriani has compiled MACRs for each of the United Nations member states as of 2009.[5] He found that MACRs range, at the national level, from zero to sixteen years of age. While five states had the highest MACR of sixteen years of age, eighteen nations and four states within the United States had no statutory MACR.[6] A total of twenty-six nations had an MACR established at the age of seven.[7] Some nations had embraced the notion of MACR but did not attach a specific age to it and instead believed that individuals could be held criminally responsible at the age of puberty. In one nation, the Comores, males reach MACR at puberty whereas females reach it upon marriage.[8] Within the United States, MACRs vary from state to state—in North Carolina, children may be held criminally responsible as young as six,[9] but in Oregon children may be held criminally responsible at age eleven.[10]

At the international level MACRs vary from one international body to another. The statutes of the International Criminal Tribunal for Yugoslavia (ICTY)[11] and the International Criminal Tribunal for Rwanda (ICTR)[12] do not mention a particular MACR, although in practice, neither of the tribunals has ever prosecuted a defendant under the age of eighteen.[13] It is thus unclear whether the Statutes

5 Don Cipriani, CHILDREN'S RIGHTS AND THE MINIMUM AGE OF CRIMINAL RESPONSIBILITY: A GLOBAL PERSPECTIVE 98–108 (2009).

6 *Id.* The eighteen nations include Bahrain, Cambodia, Cuba, the Democratic Republic of Congo, France, Luxembourg, Malaysia, the Marshall Islands, Mauritius, Micronesia, Mozambique, Nauru, Nepal, Pakistan, Poland, the Solomon Islands, Somalia, and Sudan. The four states include California, New Jersey, Pennsylvania, and Vermont. *Id.*

7 *Id.* These nations include the Bahamas, Brunei, Egypt, Estonia, Grenada, India, Jordan, Kuwait, Lebanon, Lesotho, Liberia, Libya, Malawi, Mauritania, Myanmar, Namibia, Papua New Guinea, Qatar, the Seychelles, Singapore, South Africa, Swaziland, Thailand, Tonga, Trinidad and Tobago, and the United Arab Emirates. *Id.*

8 *Id.*

9 N.C. GEN. STAT. ANN. § 7B-1501.

10 OR. REV. STAT. ANN. § 419A.004 (West 2012). The minimum age of criminal responsibility is thirteen in Georgia, Illinois, and New Hampshire. *See* GA. CODE ANN. § 15–11–560 (West 2012); 705 ILL. COMP. STAT. ANN. 405/1–8; N.H. REV. STAT. ANN. § 628:1. Many states do not have a MACR, however, for a comprehensive list of state MACR's *see* Joshua Seth, *Age of Criminal Responsibility*, THE EXAMINER (Nov. 22, 2012), available at www.examiner.com/article/age-of-criminal-responsibility.

11 S.C. Res. 827, Statute of the International Criminal Tribunal for the Former Yugoslavia (May 25, 1993), available at www.icty.org/x/file/Legal%20Library/Statute/statute_sept09_en.pdf.

12 S.C. Res. 955, Statute of the International Tribunal for Rwanda (Nov. 8. 1994), available at www.ohchr.org/EN/ProfessionalInterest/Pages/StatuteInternationalCriminalTribunalForRwanda.aspx.

13 In fact, the ICTY has considered the young age of a defendant (twenty-three) as a mitigating factor. *See* Prosecutor v. Furundzija, Case No. IT-95–17/1-T, Trial Chamber, Judgment, 284, 291 (ICTY 1998), reprinted in 38 I.L.M. 317, 373 (1999); *see also id.* at 291, reprinted in 38 I.L.M.at 375 (stating that it is "especially mindful of the age of the accused," and expressing "support for rehabilitative programmes in which the accused may participate while serving his sentence" for defendant who was twenty-three at the time of his crimes).

of these two tribunals purposely omitted a provision establishing an MACR, thereby indicating that the Tribunals were unwilling to prosecute anyone under the age of eighteen, or whether the omission can be interpreted as allowing these Tribunals to prosecute juveniles.[14]

Article 6 of the Rome Statute of the International Criminal Court (ICC) specifically excludes individuals under the age of eighteen from the court's jurisdiction, but the Rome Statute does not specifically mention a MACR ("[t]he Court shall have no jurisdiction over any person under the age of 18 at the time of the alleged commission of a crime.").[15] Some scholars have argued that the pragmatic desire to avoid creating a separate juvenile justice system motivated the drafters of the Rome Statute to restrict jurisdiction to individuals over the age of eighteen, and that Article 6 effectively leaves the decision of whether to prosecute a juvenile accused of international crimes to national courts.[16] In other words, the ICC jurisdictional limitation does not apply to other national and international tribunals and does not prevent them in any way from choosing to prosecute a person under the age of eighteen.

The Statute for the Extraordinary Chambers in the Courts of Cambodia (ECCC) does not establish a clear MACR either; instead, the Statute incorporates Article 14 of the International Covenant on Civil and Political Rights (ICCPR), which states that in case of juveniles, any judicial procedure should take into account their age and the desirability of promoting their rehabilitation.[17] It may be argued that the ECCC statute thus establishes jurisdiction over juvenile offenders and thereby sets MACR at an age lower than eighteen.

The Statute of the Special Court for Sierra Leone establishes an MACR of fifteen, and provides that juveniles between the ages of fifteen and eighteen may be prosecuted by the court but that they should be treated distinctly:

> The Special Court shall have no jurisdiction over any person who was under the age of 15 at the time of the alleged commission of the crime. Should any person who was at the time of the alleged commission of the crime between 15 and 18 years of age come before this court, he or she shall be treated with dignity and a sense of worth, taking into account his or her young age and the desirability of promoting his or her rehabilitation, reintegration into and assumption of a constructive role in society, and in

14 *See* Matthew Happold, *Child Soldiers: Victims or Perpetrators?*, 29 U. La Verne L. Rev. 56, 85 (2008); *see also* Paola Konge, *International Crimes & Child Soldiers*, 16 Sw. J. Int'l L. 41, 48 (2010).

15 ICC Statute, art. 6.

16 Matthew Happold, *The Age of Criminal Responsibility in International Criminal Law*, *in* International Criminal Accountability and the Rights of Children 6 (Karin Arts and Vesselin Popovski eds. 2006).

17 Law on the Establishment of the Extraordinary Chambers in the Courts of Cambodia for the Prosecution of Crimes Committed During the Republic of Kampuchea, art. 33, NS/RKM/1004/006 (Oct. 27, 2004).

> accordance with international human rights, in particular the rights of the child.[18]

Despite the fact that the Special Court had jurisdiction over juveniles between the ages of fifteen and eighteen, the Prosecutor indicated, shortly after the Court was established, that he would not prosecute children, but that he would focus instead on prosecuting those who forced children to commit horrible crimes.[19]

Finally, the United Nations Transitional Administration in East Timor (UNTAET) establishes a clear-cut MACR at the age of twelve, and provides for special treatment for juveniles between the ages of thirteen and sixteen.[20]

> For the purposes of the present regulation, any person under 18 years of age shall be deemed a minor. A minor under 12 years of age shall be deemed incapable for committing a crime and shall not be subjected to criminal proceedings. A minor between 12 and 16 years of age may be prosecuted for criminal offences only in accordance with such rules as may be established in subsequent UNTAET regulations on juvenile justice; provided, however, that minors between 12 and 16 years of age may be prosecuted under the provisions of the present regulation for any offence which under applicable law constitutes murder, rape, or a crime of violence in which serious injury is inflicted upon a victim.[21]

UNTAET thus treats children aged seventeen as adults, while providing for future special juvenile justice regulations for minors between the ages of twelve and sixteen, and while exposing the latter to criminal responsibility only if they are accused of having committed serious crimes.[22]

In the United States Office of Military Commissions case against Omar Khadr, the commission ruled that "neither international law nor international treaties binding upon the United States prohibit the trial of a person for alleged violations of the law of nations committed when he was fifteen years of age."[23] It is unclear whether this view would be espoused by all in the international community. It appears that international law obliges states to establish an MACR, but that international law does not provide much specific guidance about what the MACR

18 Statute of the Special Court for Sierra Leone, art. 7, ¶1 (Aug. 14, 2000).

19 Press Release, Special Court Prosecutor Says He Will Not Prosecute Children, Pub. Affairs Office of the Special Court for Sierra Leone (Nov. 2, 2002).

20 United Nations Transnational Administration for East Timor, On Transitional Rules of Criminal Procedure, Rule 45.1, UN Doc. UNTAET/REG/2000/30 (Sept. 13, 2000).

21 *Id.*

22 *Id.*

23 Ruling on Defense Motion for Dismissal Due to Lack of Jurisdiction Under the MCS in Regard to Juvenile Crimes of a Child Soldier para. 18, Khadr, No. D-022 (Military Comm'n, Apr. 30, 2008).

should be. Some scholars believe that the trend in international law may be toward established MACR in the mid-teens, while others argue that the Rome Statute of the ICC and the CRC clearly establish an emerging consensus that children should be shielded from criminal liability.[24] One could conclude that most international instruments seem to agree that MACR should not be set an age lower than twelve.

In light of the above, one can conclude that "a high level of inconsistency in state practice regarding the specific age at which an individual can be held criminally responsible prevents a universal MACR from being established as a matter of customary law."[25] Some level of consensus appears to exist within the international community about the necessity to set MACR at an age when a juvenile has a reasonable understanding about the nature and severity of the crime that he or she has committed—perhaps around the age of twelve. This in turn leaves piracy-prosecuting nations at liberty to determine their own MACRs and to apply those to juvenile piracy suspects, as long as such MACRs are not too low. As Chapter 10 below will discuss, it is this book's recommendation that piracy-prosecuting nations should not prosecute juvenile piracy suspects below the age of twelve, in light of existing international law on MACRs.

Juvenile Suspects' Rights under Multilateral Treaties

In addition to determining an appropriate MACR, a nation contemplating or engaged in the prosecution of juvenile piracy suspects must also determine which international treaties and other instruments create additional binding norms, which apply specifically to the treatment of juveniles. It should be noted that all norms of international human rights law apply equally to adults and to juveniles. For example, fundamental principles of international criminal law, such as *nullum crimen sine lege*, apply equally to children as they do to adults. Instead of perusing all of international human rights law, the section below will focus specifically on those provisions that are limited to the treatment of juveniles during judicial processes. These provisions establish that juvenile suspects in all judicial proceedings, including piracy prosecutions, must be provided with greater protections that go beyond the minimum standards of treatment afforded to adults.

International Covenant on Civil and Political Rights and the Geneva Conventions

The International Covenant on Civil and Political Rights (ICCPR) is one of the most important multilateral human rights treaties and the cornerstone of the

24 *See* Happold, *supra* note 16, at 11. *But see* Nienke Grossman, *Rehabilitation or Revenge*, 38 GEO. J. INT'L L. 323, 357 (2007).

25 Bellish, *supra* note 1, at 277.

so-called International Bill of Human Rights.[26] The ICCPR currently has 168 state parties, and Somalia became a member of this treaty in 1990.[27] Two different ICCPR articles specifically address the rights of juvenile suspects.

Article 10(2)(b) addresses the rights of juveniles in the context of pre-trial detention, by providing that "[a]ccused juvenile persons shall be separated from adults and brought as speedily as possible for adjudication."[28] Article 10(3) similarly requires that if convicted, juvenile offenders "shall be segregated from adults and be accorded treatment appropriate to their age and legal status."[29] In addition, Article 10(3) requires member states to generally take into account a juvenile's age throughout his or her encounter with the penal system. Article 14(4) builds on the requirements of Article 10(3), by stating that any judicial proceedings applied to juveniles should take into account their age and "the desirability of promoting their rehabilitation."[30] Article 14(1) further specifies that where the interests of the juvenile would be better served if his or her sentence were kept confidential, the authorities of the relevant state should not render his or her sentence public.[31]

In conclusion, the ICCPR requires member states to consider the juvenile suspect's age at all stages of judicial proceedings, starting with pre-trial detention and ending with sentencing. These requirements, when applied to juvenile piracy prosecutions, would impose on piracy-prosecuting states the obligation to separate juvenile piracy suspects from their adult counter-parts, and to subject the former to a particular judicial process that would pay particular attention to their young age and to the desirability of their rehabilitation.

In addition to the ICCPR, an important norm of international humanitarian law dealing with children involved in armed conflict and expressed in the Additional Protocol I to the Geneva Conventions pertains to the treatment of juveniles. Although Somali pirates operate outside the paradigm of any armed conflict, the parallel between the use of child soldiers and child pirates, as will be explored in Chapter 4, is sufficiently strong to justify a reference to international legal norms pertaining to the former. Article 77 of the Additional Protocol I to the Geneva Conventions specifies that "[i]f arrested, detained or interned for reasons related to the armed conflict, children shall be held in quarters separate

26 The ICCPR, along with the International Covenant on Economic, Social, and Cultural Rights and the Universal Declaration of Human Rights form the International Bill of Human Rights. *See Fact Sheet No. 2 (Rev. 1), the International Bill of Human Rights,* U.N. OFF. OF THE HIGH COMMISSIONER OF HUM. RTS. www.ohchr.org/Documents/Publications/FactSheet2Rev.1en.pdf.

27 United Nations Treaty Collection, Status of the International Covenant on Civil and Political Rights, available at https://treaties.un.org/pages/ViewDetails.aspx?src=IND&mtdsg_no=IV-4&chapter=4&lang=en.

28 International Covenant on Civil and Political Rights, art. 10, *opened for signature* Dec. 19, 1966, 999 U.N.T.S. 171 (entered into force on Mar. 23, 1976) [hereinafter ICCPR].

29 *Id.*

30 *Id.* at art. 14.

31 *Id.*

from the quarters of adults."[32] Although Somalia is a not party to this treaty, Additional Protocol I has 174 state parties and is widely seen as representing customary law, which would bind Somalia and any other state involved in piracy prosecutions.[33] According to the International Committee on the Red Cross, Rule 120 of customary international humanitarian law espouses the same idea as Article 77 of the Additional Protocol I, that children should be detained separately from adults: "Children who are deprived of their liberty must be held in quarters separate from those of adults, except where families are accommodated as family units."[34]

Like the ICCPR, Additional Protocol I, as well as customary international humanitarian law, impose a duty on all member states to detain juvenile suspects separately from the adult ones; to the extent that this treaty and accompanying customary law can be used by analogy in the piracy context, they would impose a duty on piracy-prosecuting states to provide for distinct detention facilities segregating juvenile piracy suspects from adults.

Convention on the Rights of the Child and International Labor Organization Convention Concerning the Prohibition and Elimination of the Worst Forms of Child Labor (No. 182)

The Convention on the Rights of the Child (CRC) is the most widely ratified human rights treaty in the world. Currently, the United States is the only country that is not a member of the CRC (Somalia was the last country to accede to this treaty in 2015).[35] The CRC is a specialized human rights treaty that focuses on the rights of children—those defined by this treaty as a "human being below the age of 18 years unless, under the law applicable to the child, majority is attained earlier."[36] Article 3 of the CRC establishes that in all aspects of juvenile treatment, including court proceedings, "the best interests of the child shall be a primary consideration."[37]

32 Protocol Additional to the Geneva Conventions of 12 August 1949, and Relating to the Protection of Victims of International Armed Conflicts (Protocol I), art. 77(4), June 8, 1977, 1125 U.N.T.S. 3 [hereinafter Additional Protocol I].

33 International Committee on the Red Cross, Treaties and State Parties to Such Treaties, Protocol Additional to the Geneva Conventions of 12 August 1949, and relating to the Protection of Victims of International Armed Conflicts (Protocol I), June 8, 1977, available at www.icrc.org/applic/ihl/ihl.nsf/States.xsp?xp_viewStates=XPages_NORMStatesSign&xp_treatySelected=470.

34 *Customary IHL, Rule 120. Accommodation for Children Deprived of Their Liberty*, INT'L COMM. OF THE RED CROSS, www.icrc.org/customary-ihl/eng/docs/v1_rul_rule120 (last visited Feb. 15, 2016).

35 G.A. Res. 44/25, Status of the Convention on the Rights of the Child, Nov. 20, 1989, https://treaties.un.org/Pages/ViewDetails.aspx?src=IND&mtdsg_no=IV-11&chapter=4&lang=en.

36 Convention on the Rights of the Child, art. 1, *opened for signature* Nov. 20, 1989, 1577 U.N.T.S. 44 (entered into force on Sept. 2, 1990).

37 *Id.* art. 3.

This is particularly relevant in the context of criminal proceedings, where other policy considerations of retribution, deterrence, and rehabilitation may carry equal weight within different jurisdictions. According to the CRC, if a child is the subject of a criminal proceeding, rehabilitation should be more important than retribution or deterrence because of the "best interest of the child" approach of this treaty.[38]

Several provisions of the CRC address the rights of juvenile suspects once they have become the subject of a criminal investigation or proceeding. Article 40 requires that member states establish a MACR, as mentioned above, and that:

> A variety of dispositions, such as care, guidance and supervision orders; counseling; probation; foster care; education and vocational training programmes and other alternatives to institutional care shall be available to ensure that children are dealt with in a manner appropriate to their well-being and proportionate both to their circumstances and the offence.[39]

Article 12 establishes that every child has the right to be heard, particularly in judicial and other proceedings, either directly or through a representative.[40] Article 37 details a list of particular protections that a juvenile is entitled to during any judicial proceedings, including immunity from capital punishment or life sentences without the possibility of parole, that detention of a child should only be imposed as a matter of last resort, that juveniles should be incarcerated separately from adults, and that juveniles have the right to contact their parents or guardians.[41] Thus, like the ICCPR, the CRC imposes on its member states a general duty to treat juvenile suspects distinctly from adult ones, by, for example, detaining the former separately from the latter and by requiring states to take a child's age into account during the entirety of judicial proceedings.

In addition to the above provisions, the CRC contains another Article particularly relevant to the context of piracy prosecutions. Article 32 provides that member states shall ensure that children are not exploited economically by engaging in work that "is likely to be hazardous or to interfere with the child's education, or to be harmful to the child's health or physical, mental, spiritual, moral or social development."[42] This Article may be interpreted as imposing an additional obligation on Somalia, or any other states where juveniles may be actively recruited into piracy, to ensure that children do not become participants in such dangerous endeavors, and to impose additional criminal liability on those who entice children into becoming pirates.

38 *Id.* art. 23.
39 *Id.* art. 40.
40 *Id.* art. 12.
41 *Id.* art. 37.
42 *Id.* art. 32.

In addition to Article 32 of the CRC, the International Labor Organization Convention Concerning the Prohibition and Elimination of the Worst Forms of Child Labor (Child Labor Convention), which entered into force in 2000 and which has 180 member states, including Somalia, obliges states to ensure the prohibition and elimination of the worst forms of child labor.[43] Article 3 of the Child Labor Convention defines child labor in four different ways, two of which are relevant in the context of Somali piracy. These two definitions of child labor include: "the use, procuring or offering of a child for illicit activities" and "work which, by its nature or the circumstances in which it is carried out, is likely to harm the health, safety or morals of children."[44] Using children to perform piratical acts satisfies the definitions of child labor in Article 3, because it constitutes the use of a child for an illicit activity, and because piracy amounts to "work," which is by its nature likely to harm the health, safety, and morals of children. The Child Labor Convention obligates member states to both "prevent the engagement of children in the worst forms of child labour" and to "provide the necessary and appropriate direct assistance for the removal of children from the worst forms of child labour."[45] The Child Labor Convention may be even more important than the CRC within the context of Somali piracy and the use of juveniles to perform piratical acts, because Somalia is a member of the former but not of the latter. The Child Labor Convention thus imposes a positive obligation on the Somali government to prevent the enlistment of children into piracy and to provide help with the removal of children from piratical endeavors.

Other International Law Instruments Relevant for Children's Rights

In addition to the above-mentioned human rights treaties, other international law documents reference the need to treat juvenile suspects differently from adult suspects. These instruments include the Geneva Declaration of the Rights of the Child of 1924, the Beijing Rules, the United Nations Rules for the Protection of Juveniles Deprived of Their Liberty, and the United Nations Guidelines for the Protection of Juvenile Delinquency ("Riyadh Guidelines").

The Geneva Declaration on the Rights of the Child was adopted by the League of Nations in 1924. Its main purpose was to establish a duty protection on behalf of all mankind toward children.[46] To this effect, the Declaration

43 *C182—Worst Forms of Child Labour Convention*, INT'L LAB. ORG. (Nov. 19, 2000), available at www.ilo.org/dyn/mormlex/en/f?p=1000;11300:0::NO:11300:P11300_INSTRUMENT_ID:312327.

44 Convention Concerning the Prohibition and Elimination of the Worst Forms of Child Labor (No. 182) arts. 3(b), 3(d) [hereinafter Child Labor Convention].

45 *Id.* at art. 7(2)(a-b).

46 Geneva Declaration on the Rights of the Child, League of Nations (1924) [hereinafter Geneva Declaration].

contains five different provisions, which require that children be given opportunity, nourishment, and relief.[47]

The so-called Beijing Rules were adopted by the United Nations General Assembly in 1985; they include rules and corresponding commentary regarding various aspects of juvenile justice, such as guidance as to the investigation and prosecution of juveniles, guidance with respect to treatment of convicted juveniles, guidance about the investigation of juvenile suspects, etc.[48]

The United Nations Rules for the Protection of Juveniles Deprived of their Liberty was also passed as a General Assembly Resolution in 1990.[49] These rules pertain to the issue of detention of juveniles, such as pre-trial detention, the management of juvenile detention facilities, and the treatment of juveniles by personnel working with juveniles in such detention facilities.[50]

Finally, the Riyadh Guidelines were adopted as a General Assembly Resolution as well, alongside the Beijing Rules.[51] These guidelines relate to the ways in which states treat children and are aimed at encouraging states to adopt social policies, legislation, and other programs related to children in order to ensure that children become productive members of their respective societies. These guidelines emphasize that, "all aspects of society, from the family to the school to the local community to mass media, have a role to play in preventing juvenile delinquency."[52]

In sum, the Declaration, Rules, and Guidelines mentioned above establish a level of consensus within the international community that states owe a duty of protection toward juveniles, that juveniles should be provided with meaningful educational and other societal opportunities, in order to prevent them from engaging in delinquent behavior, and that, if juveniles have entered the criminal process, their cases are treated in a distinct manner that respects their young age. The documents discussed above appear to be consistent with the CRC and other human rights treaties and customary law requiring similar treatment of juvenile suspects and offenders.

Punishment and Sentencing of Juvenile Suspects

As mentioned above, international law imposes a duty on states to seek rehabilitation and reintegration of the child when imposing a criminal sentence on him or her. Both the ICCPR and the CRC embrace the goal of rehabilitation in any

47 *Id.*

48 *Id.*

49 Beijing Rules, *supra* note 3.

50 G.A. Res. 45/113, United Nations Rules for the Protection of Juveniles Deprived of Their Liberty, (Dec. 14, 1990).

51 G.A. Res. 45/112, United Nations Guidelines for the Protection of Juvenile Delinquency (the "Riyadh Guidelines"), (Dec. 14, 1990).

52 Bellish, *supra* note 1, at 283.

criminal proceedings involving a child, and the CRC adopts a specific "best interest of the child" standard in guiding any such criminal proceedings. Standards of juvenile justice, as discussed above, require any prosecuting authority to give primary consideration to a child's well being and to emphasize education and rehabilitation in any sentencing structure. The Riyadh Guidelines, for example, emphasize that states should adopt policies and programs to ensure that children become productive members of their respective societies. The Riyadh Guidelines thus embrace the notion of rehabilitation as an important guiding factor in handling children. The Beijing Rules similarly embrace the goal of rehabilitation regarding juvenile offenders. Rule 17.1 states that a sentence (or "reaction") imposed on a juvenile by a competent state authority "shall always be in proportion not only to the circumstances and the gravity of the offence but also to the circumstances and the needs of the juvenile as well as to the needs of the society" and that "[t]he well-being of the juvenile shall be the guiding factor in the consideration of her or his case."[53] Commentary to Rule 17.1 further clarifies the above language as follows:

> Rule 17.1 (b) implies that strictly punitive approaches are not appropriate. Whereas in adult cases, and possibly also in cases of severe offences by juveniles, just desert and retributive sanctions might be considered to have some merit, in juvenile cases such considerations should always be outweighed by the interest of safeguarding the well-being and the future of the young person.[54]

Michael Custer has explained the goal of rehabilitation in the context of juvenile offenders as follows:

> At the heart of this goals is the understanding that . . . juveniles are more amenable to rehabilitation into productive members of society. Biological and psychological studies have shown that adolescents process information differently than adults, and therefore, have a less sophisticated understanding of the consequences of their action . . . . [T]his lack of full biological maturity also argues for their amenability to rehabilitation. A juvenile offender . . . can be reconditioned and rehabilitated while the brain completes its maturation process, giving the juvenile a higher likelihood for success than an adult who has already reached full maturity.[55]

International courts have already embraced this notion in the context of child soldiers. The Statute of the Special Court for Sierra Leone precluded imprison-

53 Beijing Rules, *supra* note 3, Rule 17.1.

54 *Id.* at Rule 17.1 (Commentary).

55 Michael Custer, *Punishing Child Soldiers: The Special Court for Sierra Leone and the Lessons to be Learned from the United States' Juvenile System*, 19 TEMP. INT'L LAW & COMP. L.J. 449, 470 (2005).

ment of juveniles as punishment, authorized the use of alternative punishments, and required that the Prosecutor ensure that the rehabilitation of child soldiers not be placed at risk through prosecution.[56] Radhika Coomaraswamy, the United Nations Special Representative for Children and Armed Conflict, has argued that no individual under the age of eighteen should undergo prosecution and that courts should focus instead on rehabilitative measures.[57] The Special Court for Sierra Leone accepted this approach de facto, by making a prudential decision not to prosecute juveniles under the age of eighteen. Finally, even those who advocate the position, that prosecution of juvenile suspects does not always prevent rehabilitation, embrace the idea that future courts should always balance the goals of rehabilitation and punitive punishment.[58] In the context of piracy prosecutions, the parallel to the treatment of child soldiers is particularly relevant, as Chapter 4 below will discuss. Juvenile pirates, like child soldiers, may be forced into criminal activity by leaders of their respective societies, and may not willingly engage in any such activity. Juvenile pirates, like child soldiers, may be both victims and offenders and it may be particularly appropriate for jurisdictions prosecuting juvenile piracy suspects to consider scholarship and policy recommendations existing within the context of child soldiers. Many such recommendations include the notion that child soldiers should be directed toward a truth and reconciliation process, rather than prosecuted in traditional courts. This may be an interesting and helpful approach when dealing with juvenile pirates; this approach will be discussed in the Conclusion.

In light of existing international law on the sentencing of juveniles, as well as case law and literature on the treatment of child soldiers, it can be concluded that juvenile pirates may be prosecuted but that any sentence that they receive should emphasize rehabilitation, either within the sentencing nation's society or in Somalia, if the offender is transferred back post-conviction. In addition, before handing down a sentence to a juvenile pirate, the prosecuting court should take into account factors such as the juvenile's ability to make independent decisions within Somalia's clan structure, the degree to which prosecutions of juvenile pirates will constitute a general deterrent for Somali youth, and the severity of life in Somalia as a mitigating factor.

Implications for the Treatment of Juvenile Piracy Suspects

The above-discussed instruments express the international community's concern for the well being of children in general, and emphasize the necessity to treat juveniles distinctly and carefully once they have entered the judicial system. These concerns apply with equal force to the treatment of juvenile piracy suspects

56 *Id.*

57 Anita Snow, *UN Envoy: Rehabilitate Child Pirates*, ARAB NEWS.COM (Nov. 9, 2010), available at http://arabnews.com/world/article184520.ece.

58 *See*, e.g., Custer, *supra* note 55, at 476.

and suggest that piracy-prosecuting nations should always take the suspect's young age into consideration.

In light of the above, it can be concluded that when taken together, norms of international human rights law and international criminal law impose a duty on all piracy-prosecuting states to establish a MACR. While there is no consensus within the international community as to the specific age that criminal responsibility should attach to juveniles, it appears that most states would agree that MACR should not be set lower than twelve years of age. Thus, piracy-prosecuting nations should not impose individual criminal responsibility on suspects younger than twelve. In addition, the above discussion clearly demonstrates that international law instruments impose a duty on all states that subject juveniles to judicial criminal processes to treat juvenile suspects with special care, to detain them separately from the adult incarcerated population, and to only impose punishments that allow for appropriate rehabilitation opportunities. Piracy-prosecuting nations therefore have a specific obligation to treat juvenile suspects in a distinct manner, taking into account their young age and vulnerability, as well as the desirability of their rehabilitation. Finally, the above-discussed international law clearly imposes a duty on states to consider the juvenile pirate's rehabilitation and overall well being when imposing any criminal sentence.

In sum, international human rights law, while failing to provide for a specific MACR, clearly establishes the need for member states to differentiate in their treatment of juvenile versus adult criminal suspects, as well as the necessity to erect special protections of juveniles within any state's criminal system.

Conclusion

Piracy-prosecuting states may prosecute juvenile piracy suspects, as international law does not prohibit the prosecution of juvenile offenders. However, if juvenile piracy suspects are investigated, detained, and put on trial, their cases need to be handled with special care, because of existing international human rights law, international criminal law, and other international law documents, establishing the duty on all states to treat juveniles distinctly from adults and to devote particular care to the possibility of juvenile offenders' rehabilitation and re-education. Piracy-prosecuting states involved in cases of juvenile piracy offenders need to separate juvenile cases and need to treat juvenile defendants with a heightened duty of care. Chapter 9 below will discuss a detailed set of recommendations regarding the best care and treatment of juvenile piracy suspects, in accordance with relevant international law instruments, described above.

4 International Law on the Use of Child Soldiers

An Important Parallel?

Introduction

International law provides norms criminalizing the conduct of those who choose to employ minors in armed conflicts. Although Somali piracy thrives outside an armed conflict, norms pertaining to the treatment of child soldiers in armed conflict are relevant to any discussion of the treatment of child pirates. Child pirates operate in a lawless environment, similar to that of an armed conflict. Additionally, child pirates often exhibit the same characteristics as child soldiers in that both: typically experience hardship and poverty; are often separated from family members; may lack appropriate educational opportunities; and may lack the presence of mind to make informed decisions about their participation in criminal endeavors. While international court decisions on the use of child soldiers will not constitute binding precedent for any court prosecuting juvenile pirates, such decisions can nonetheless provide useful and informative guidance about the imposition of criminal responsibility on those who employ children in order to commit crimes. This chapter will focus on the definition of a child soldier and will draw a parallel between child soldiers and child pirates. This chapter will conclude that using the child soldier paradigm may be helpful in understanding the phenomenon of child pirates and in devising the best strategies to appropriately punish and rehabilitate child pirates. In addition, this chapter will focus on the criminalization of the use of child soldiers. It will also discuss the recent International Criminal Court Lubanga decision, as well as the recent Special Court for Sierra Leone Charles Taylor judgment, as examples of international court decisions criminalizing the use of child soldiers, which may constitute important parallels in a potential prosecution of a piracy organizer employing child pirates.

Definition of a Child Soldier

> And when you no longer have anyone on earth, neither mother nor father nor brother nor sister, and you are little, a little darling in a screwed-up and barbarous country where everyone slits throats, what do you do? Of course

> you become a small soldier, a child soldier, to eat and to cut throats in turn. Nothing else remains.[1]

Two international law instruments provide the current operational definition of a child soldier: the Cape Town Principles of 1997 and the Paris Principles of 2007.[2] The former focused on the issue of child soldiers in Africa, whereas the latter, developed at a Conference in Paris co-hosted by the French government and by the United Nations Children's Fund (UNICEF) was of a more global scope and included representatives from fifty-eight countries. While the Cape Town Principles use the term "child soldier," the Paris Principles use a broader term of "children associated with armed forces or armed groups," which is defined as follows:

> Any person below 18 years of age who is or who has been recruited or used by an armed force or armed group in any capacity, including but not limited to children, boys, and girls used as fighters, cooks, porters, messengers, spires or for sexual purposes. It does not only refer to a child who is taking or has taken a direct part in hostilities.[3]

The term "armed group" specifically refers to non-state entities, distinct from traditional state-led armed forces, to include rebel movements, insurgencies, and dissident factions. Further, these two instruments take on a broad approach toward defining child soldiers, and include not only those younger than eighteen who carry weapons, engage in combat, or take direct part in the hostilities, but also children who may be used for auxiliary activities, such as cooking, spying, portering, etc., and those forced into sexual servitude. "The impetus among

1 Ahmadou Kourouma, Allah N'est Pas Oblige 100 (2000) ("Et quand on n'a plus personne sur terre, ni père ni mère ni frère ni soeur, et qu'on est petit, un petit mignon dans un pays foutu et barbare ou tout le monde s'égorge, que fait-on? Bien sur on deviant un enfant-soldat, un small-soldier, un child-soldier pour manger et pour egorger aussi à son tour; il n'y a que ça qui reste.").

2 Cape Town Principles and Best Practices, April 27–30, 1997 (definitions) www.unicef.org/emerg/files/Cape_Town_Principles(1).pdf [hereinafter Cape Town Principles]. According to the Cape Town Principles, a child soldier is "any person under 18 years of age who is part of any kind of regular or irregular armed force or armed group in any capacity, including but not limited to cooks, porters, messengers and anyone accompanying such groups, other than family members." The Cape Town Principles specifically include in the definition of child soldiers girls recruited for sexual purposes and forced marriage. Moreover, the definition "does not . . . only refer to a child who is carrying or has carried arms." *Id.*; *see also* The Paris Principles: Principles and Guidelines on Children Associated with Armed Forces or Armed Groups (February 2007), Princ. 2.1, www.child-soldiers.org/childsoldiers/Paris_Principles_March_2007.pdf [hereinafter Paris Principles].

3 Paris Principles, *supra* note 2, at prin. 2.1. As of today 105 states have endorsed the Paris Commitments, which the Paris Principles accompany. The definition includes girls recruited for sexual purposes and for forced marriage. It does not, therefore, only refer to a child who is carrying or has carried arms. *Id.*

policymakers is to discourage distinctions from being drawn between children who serve as combatants and children who do not or who do so only incidentally."[4]

Currently, it is estimated that military recruitment of children and their use in hostilities, in various capacities, takes place in at least twenty countries world wide.[5] The most notable conflicts where child soldiers have been heavily used tend to be situated on the African continent—in the Democratic Republic of Congo, Uganda, Rwanda, Sudan and Sierra Leone.[6] The use of child soldiers is not a purely African problem—child soldiers have also been used in other countries, such as in Afghanistan, Cambodia, Colombia, Indonesia, Nepal, Papua New Guinea, Philippines, Sri Lanka, and Timor-Leste.[7] However, the African conflicts mentioned above have been adjudicated internationally and have caused tribunals in those jurisdictions to render particularly relevant decisions punishing the employment of child soldiers. Thus, this chapter will focus on the use of child soldiers in several African conflicts and will examine the case of law of relevant tribunals sitting in such countries.

While some children take on combat roles, most do not and instead carry out auxiliary roles or accompany typically male adult forces as sex slaves or compelled conjugal partners.[8] Thus, while some children carry out atrocities, such as war crimes, crimes against humanity and genocide, most do not do so directly. This may explain the overall trend in international criminal jurisprudence of not prosecuting child soldiers, and of discouraging national jurisdictions from doing so. As mentioned in Chapter 3, the Statute of the International Criminal Court specifically eliminates persons under the age of eighteen from the Court's jurisdiction, and while the Statute of the Special Court for Sierra Leone de jure allowed for the prosecution of those fifteen years of age or older, the Court's Prosecutor early on announced a policy of not prosecuting juveniles under eighteen.[9] In addition, as noted in

4 Mark A. Drumbl, *Reimagining Child Soldiers in International Law and Policy* 3–4 (2011) [hereinafter Drumbl, *Reimagining*].

5 *See* About the Issues, CHILD SOLDIERS INT'L, available at www.child-soldiers.org/faq.php (last visited Mar. 10, 2016) ("Child soldier use by non-state armed groups is widespread: dozens of groups are known to unlawfully recruit and use boys and girls. However, the record of some governments is also poor. Since 2010, child soldier use by twenty states has been reported either directly in government armed forces or indirectly in armed groups, which they support or are allied to. In addition, around 40 states still have a minimum voluntary recruitment age below 18 years."); *see also* Coalition to Stop the Use of Child Soldiers, CHILD SOLDIERS GLOBAL REPORT 2012 20 (2012).

6 Eben Kaplan, *Child Soldiers Around the World*, COUNCIL ON FOREIGN REL. (Dec. 2, 2015), available at www.cfr.org/human-rights/child-soldiers-around-world/p9331#p6.

7 Drumbl, *supra* note 4, at 15.

8 *Child Recruitment and Use*, OFF. SPECIAL REPRESENTATIVE OF SECRETARY-GEN. CHILD. & ARMED FORCES, available at https://childrenandarmedconflict.un.org/effects-of-conflict/six-grave-violations/child-soldiers/ (last visited Mar. 10, 2016).

9 ICC Statute, art. 26 ("The Court shall have no jurisdiction over any person who was under the age of 18 at the time of the alleged commission of a crime"); Press Release, *Special Court Prosecutor Says He Will Not Prosecute Children*, Pub. Affairs Office of the Special Court for Sierra Leone (Nov. 2, 2002).

Chapter 3, the Yugoslavia and the Rwanda tribunals, while silent on this issue in their respective statutes, never prosecuted any offenders under the age of eighteen.[10] However, some scholars have cautioned against this approach. Mark Drumbl has noted that most child soldiers are not young children; instead, most are adolescents often aged fifteen, sixteen, and seventeen.[11] At times, adolescents, and even younger children are capable of committing acts of violence. In addition, Drumbl has noted that most child soldiers are neither abducted nor forcibly recruited, but instead join an armed force or group willingly.[12] Drumbl thus cautions against viewing all child soldiers as passive victims and instead advocates toward treating child soldiers as a generally protected class, but differentiating among individual class members to, at times, impose criminal responsibility on those who should bear it.[13]

> Fear that child soldiers may become subject of punitive criminal trials has induced a crudely fulsome protectionism that has come to insulate child soldiers from accountability processes generally, regardless of the goals or potentials of those processes. This protectionism needlessly cocoons child soldiers from the tough questions that societies must reckon with in order to come to terms with mass violence. The solution, then, is not for international criminal law to recognize the criminal culpability of children but, instead, for transnational discourse to develop a more fine-grained approach to post-conflict accountability.[14]

It should be emphasized that *stricto sensu*, child pirates are not child soldiers, unless they operate with the paradigm of an international or non-international armed conflict and are members of a group that constitutes an armed force or an armed group. As mentioned above, in the context of the Cape Town and Paris Principles' definitions of child soldiers, armed forces are official state militaries whereas armed groups are organized non-state entities, such as rebel and dissident militias and factions, distinct from official state militaries.[15] In light of this, it can be concluded that most child pirates are not child soldiers because

10 The Statutes of the International Criminal Tribunal for the former Yugoslavia (ICTY) and the International Criminal Tribunal for Rwanda (ICTR) do not explicitly exclude persons under eighteen from their respective jurisdictions, but to date, only adults have been prosecuted by those tribunals. International Legal Standards for the Protection of Children, UNICEF (Sept. 2002), www.unicef.org/emerg/files/ICJC.pdf.

11 Mark A. Drumbl, *Child Pirates: Rehabilitation, Reintegration and Accountability*, 46 Case W. J. Int'l L. 235, 267 (2013) [hereinafter Drumbl, *Child Pirates*].

12 *Id.* at 266.

13 *Id.* at 242–46.

14 *Victims of International Crimes: An Interdisciplinary Discourse* 141 (Thorston Bonacker & Christoph Safferling, eds. 2013).

15 Cape Town Principles, *supra* note 2 ("'Child soldier' . . . is any person under 18 years of age who is part of any kind of *regular or irregular armed force or armed group* in any capacity . . . .") (emphasis added); Paris Principles, *supra* note 2.

although they may operate within a non-international armed conflict (it can be argued, in light of the unrest and violence in Somalia, that this situation rises to the level of a non-international armed conflict), they are not members of an armed group (although piracy gangs function in a group-like manner, most would agree that their level of organization and overall functioning falls below the threshold of an armed force).

First, it can be argued that the current lawless situation in Somalia rises to the level of non-international armed conflict. Non-international armed conflict, under Common Article 3 of the 1949 Geneva Conventions, has been understood to contain two criteria: first, the hostilities must reach a minimum level of intensity, and second, non-governmental groups involved in the conflict must be considered as "parties to the conflict," meaning that they possess organized armed forces and have to be under a certain command structure and have the capacity to sustain military operations.[16] Under Additional Protocol II to the Geneva Conventions, non-international armed conflict is conflict "which take[s] place in the territory of a High Contracting Party between its armed forces and dissident armed forces or other organized armed groups which, under responsible command, exercise such control over a part of its territory as to enable them to carry out sustained and concerted military operations and to implement this Protocol."[17] The International Criminal Tribunal for Yugoslavia has held that non-international armed conflict exists "whenever there is [. . .] protracted armed violence between governmental authorities and organised armed groups or between such groups within a State."[18] It can thus be argued that "[t]he extent and sustained nature of armed violence, and the level of organization of the non-state armed groups fighting, particularly the al-Shabaab, mean that the situation has reached the threshold of an armed conflict. As Somalia is fighting against non-state armed groups, the armed conflict is qualified as being of a non-international character."[19]

However, even if the current situation in Somalia rises to the level of non-international armed conflict, piracy groups would have to constitute armed groups that participate in such conflict, in order for the armed conflict paradigm to apply to piracy itself. This is not the case because piracy groups do not exhibit the same level of organization as an armed group and thus do not constitute an armed group. The non-international armed conflict in Somalia, if one accepts this characterization of the current situation in this country, involves Somali

16 International Committee of the Red Cross, How is the Term "Armed Conflict" Defined in International Humanitarian Law?, Opinion Paper, March 2008, available at www.icrc.org/eng/assets/files/other/opinion-paper-armed-conflict.pdf.

17 Protocol Additional to the Geneva Conventions of 12 August 1949, and Relating to the Protection of Victims of Non-International Armed Conflicts (Protocol II), art 1, para. 1, June 8, 1977, 1125 U.N.T.S. 3 [hereinafter Additional Protocol II].

18 ICTY, The Prosecutor v. Dusko Tadic, Decision on the Defence Motion for Interlocutory Appeal on Jurisdiction, IT-94-1-A, October 2, 1995, para.70.

19 Rule of Law in Armed Conflicts Project, Somalia, available at www.geneva-academy.ch/RULAC/applicable_international_law.php?id_state=204.

government forces, al-Shabaab, and at times members of security forces from Puntland and Somaliland.[20] Piracy groups have not been participants in this conflict, and it appears that local governments of Puntland and Somaliland have at times supported piracy operations and benefited therefrom financially. In addition, piracy groups are not armed forces or armed groups, because they do not possess the necessary degree of organization. Thus, the armed conflict paradigm cannot apply to piracy itself, and child pirates cannot be legally equated to child soldiers.

Nonetheless, important parallels exist between the phenomena of child soldiers and child pirates, and scholarship and policy proposals on the former are particularly useful when devising proposals to deal with the latter. Significant similarities between child soldiers and child pirates include: the fact that most child pirates, like child soldiers, are adolescents aged between fifteen and seventeen;[21] that most child pirates, like child soldiers, are not kidnapped but rather join piracy endeavors voluntarily;[22] the fact that most child pirates, like child soldiers, accomplish auxiliary tasks such as cooking, messengering, cleaning, etc., but that some do engage in acts of actual violence; and that, because of their young age, child pirates, like child soldiers, may experience particular hardships during their engagement in the violent activity. In addition, some evidence suggests that the same socio-economic factors that make children vulnerable for use by armed groups exist within the piracy context. These factors include poverty, violence, lack of educational or employment opportunities, orphans, displacement, and poor medical conditions.[23] In fact, in many areas where piracy has flourished, such as Somalia, Nigeria, and Haiti, children were already being used by terrorist groups, criminal gangs and by state and non-state armed groups, precisely because of the abundance of above-mentioned socio-economic factors.[24] Finally, like child soldiers, child pirates may be seen as desirable by organizers, in part due to their lack of accountability under legal proceedings, under most national systems. In sum, the situation of child pirates is similar to that of child soldiers because "[t]hey are readily available, financially

20 *Id.*

21 Drumbl, *Child Pirates*, *supra* note 11, at 266.

22 *See* Carl Conradi, *The Invisible Phenomenon of Child Piracy*, Canadian Naval Rev. (Feb. 6, 2013), available at www.navalreview.ca/2013/02/ the-invisible-phenomenon-of-child-piracy/ ("While many children are forcibly recruited into piratical activity, others may join 'voluntarily'. Such voluntary enlistment, however, must be understood in terms of the limited choices and circumstances that are available in the child's country. For example, children may view piracy as a means of bettering themselves if they are extremely poor, displaced from their home communities, separated from their families, denied access to educational or employment opportunities, or exposed to armed conflict").

23 Drumbl, *Reimagining*, *supra* note 4, at 13.

24 S. Whitman *et al.*, *Children and Youth in Marine Piracy—Causes, Consequences and the Way Forward*, Dalhousie Marine Piracy Project, Dec. 2012 at 3, available at www.childsoldiers.org/wp-content/uploads/2014/02/Children-and-Youth-in-Marine-Piracy-RDCSI.pdf.

desperate, under or uneducated with little expectation of employment, and continuously exposed to the violence and degradation found in failed and failing states"[25] and because a child pirate faces the same situation as a child soldier "in terms of danger to life, exploitation by adults, and other abuses."[26]

Differences between child soldiers and child pirates of course exist, but may not be strong enough to justify dismissing reliance on scholarship and policy proposals regarding the treatment of child soldiers. As Drumbl has persuasively argued, "comprehensively understanding child piracy—and effectively deterring it—requires coming to terms with the nuanced and diverse experiences of the children, juveniles, and youth who enter piracy gangs, who are a la fois victims and victimizers."[27] The same approach has been advocated by Drumbl, and others, in the context of child soldiers; for reasons explained above, I believe that the parallel between the treatment of child soldiers and child pirates is sufficiently strong to warrant an examination of more abundant materials on child soldiers when devising the best approach toward handling child pirates.

While very few scholars have written thus far on the parallel between child soldiers and child pirates, others, in addition to Mark Drumbl, have highlighted the necessity to adopt a nuanced approach when dealing with child soldiers. Like Drumbl, Diane Marie Amann has also advocated for the adoption of a more nuanced position when dealing with the phenomenon of child soldiers—within the context of the Special Court for Sierra Leone, she has supported then-United Nations Secretary-General Kofi Annan and has, like Annan, argued in favor of establishing a juvenile chamber, within the Special Court, which would have had jurisdiction over juvenile offenders as young as fifteen.[28] This proposal was particularly relevant in the context of the Sierra Leonian conflict, where an estimated 5,000 children fought in the civil war, and where rebels routinely kidnapped children and compelled them to become soldiers. Taking into account this feature of the Sierra Leonian civil war, then-United Nations Secretary General Kofi Annan proposed a draft statute for the Special Court for Sierra Leone, which included the possibility of authorizing charges against juveniles aged between fifteen and eighteen.[29] Annan however encouraged the referral of at least some juvenile cases to a planned Truth and Reconciliation Commission for Sierra Leone, and emphasized that throughout any proceedings juveniles would be "treated

25 *Id.* at 7.

26 *Id.* at 8.

27 Drumbl, *Child Pirates*, *supra* note, at 11.

28 Diane Marie Amann, *Calling Children to Account: The Proposal for a Juvenile Chamber in the Special Court for Sierra Leone*, 29 PEPP. L. REV. 167 (2002).

29 Report of the Secretary-General on the Establishment of a Special Court for Sierra Leone, U.N. SCOR, 52d Sess., U.N. Doc. S/2000/915 (2000) [hereinafter Special Court Report]. Attached to the report are the proposed Agreement between the United Nations and the Government of Sierra Leone on the Establishment of a Special Court for Sierra Leone and the draft Statute of the Special Court for Sierra Leone.

with dignity and a sense of worth, taking into account his or her young age and the desirability of promoting his or her rehabilitation, reintegration into and assumption of a constructive role in society."[30]

For those juvenile offenders whose cases would be sent to the Commission, their cases would be heard in camera, by judges experienced in the administration of juvenile justice, with appropriate legal counsel as well as social assistance and participation by the juvenile's legal guardian, and with special disposition of the case by rehabilitative means, such as community service, foster case, counseling, education, training, disarmament, and reintegration programs.[31] This proposed approach was fully consistent with Annan's view that the decision whether to prosecute child soldiers in the newly established Special Court represented a "moral dilemma," but that the proposed solution of allowing for some prosecutions of most responsible juveniles in the Court while disposing of other juvenile cases through a specialized commission struck "the appropriate balance between all conflicting interests and provide[d] the necessary guarantees of juvenile justice."[32]

The Annan proposal was somewhat diluted and modified by the United Nations Security Council, resulting in the Special Court Statute, which specifically provides that the Court would have no jurisdiction over offenders under the age of fifteen.[33] The Court could theoretically prosecute those aged between fifteen and eighteen, but that in case of such prosecutions of juvenile offenders,

> [H]e or she shall be treated with dignity and a sense of worth, taking into account his or her young age and the desirability of promoting his or her rehabilitation, reintegration into and assumption of a constructive role in society, and in accordance with international human rights standards, in particular the rights of the child.[34]

In addition, the Statute provides that the Court should dispose of cases involving juveniles differently, by ordering "care guidance and supervision orders, community service orders, counseling, foster care, correctional, educational and vocational training programmes, approved schools and, as appropriate, any programmes of disarmament, demobilization and reintegration or programmes

30 Statute of the Special Court for Sierra Leone, Aug. 14, 2000, art. 7(2), U.N.—S.L., available at www.rscsl.org/Documents/scsl-statute.pdf [hereinafter Special Court Statute].

31 *See id.*; *see also id.*, art. 17 (articulating rights of the accused to "a fair and public" trial with defendant present, "subject to measures . . . for the protection of victims and witnesses"; to the presumption of innocence; to information of the nature and cause of charges; to adequate time and facilities for preparation of a defense; to counsel of choice or assignment of counsel if indigent; to examination of adverse witnesses and attendance of favorable witnesses; to an interpreter if needed; and to be free from giving a compelled confession or adverse testimony).

32 Special Court Report, *supra* note 24, ¶ 38.

33 *See* Amann, *supra* note 28, at 177.

34 Statute of the Special Court Statute, *supra* note 30, art. 7(1).

of child protection agencies."[35] Thus, the Statute that was ultimately adopted did not embrace the idea of creating a separate juvenile chamber, but instead adopted a broader formula allowing for the prosecution of older juveniles, with special care.[36] However, Annan's proposal, supported by influential scholar, Diane Marie Amann, is worth highlighting because it adopts a nuanced position in addressing the issue of child soldiers, similar to that advocated by Drumbl. Amann focused on the particular context of living in Sierra Leone, a society ravaged by war, "in which childhood cannot exist, in which responsibility must be assumed at an early age."[37] According to Amann, if children living in this context commit heinous crimes, it may be understandable that the people of Sierra Leone may want to hold them accountable, regardless of their age.[38] Amann supported Annan's proposal for the establishment of a juvenile chamber within the Special Court, because this approach would have allowed for the imposition of some form of accountability against child soldiers while providing them with necessary rehabilitation and reintegration tools. According to Amann, "Special Court prosecutions of juveniles suspected of the most awful crimes may aid both rehabilitation and accountability, and thus serve as one more tool for reconciliation."[39]

Like child soldiers, child pirates are neither heinous criminals nor helpless victims. Many are drawn toward piracy because of precarious socio-economic conditions that they are experiencing in places like Somalia, but many also engage in violent acts voluntarily. Like child soldiers, most child pirates should face some form of accountability, but should also be provided with special rehabilitative opportunities while serving any criminal convictions and post-conviction, when every effort should be undertaken to reintegrate them into society.

Use of Child Soldiers—An International Crime

A corollary to the treatment of child pirates and child soldiers themselves is the recruitment and use of child pirates and child soldiers. Consensus exists within the international community that enlisting child soldiers is a war crime, and that those who do so should be treated harshly. The same conclusion applies to the recruitment and use of child pirates, and it is this book's ultimate recommendation that those who knowingly and willingly employ child pirates should receive the harshest penalties. The section below will discuss the existing international law on the enlistment of child soldiers, and will, by drawing a logical parallel, conclude that the same body of law should apply by analogy in the piracy context.

35 *Id.* art 7(2).
36 *Id.*
37 Amann, *supra* note 28, at 179.
38 *Id.* at 174.
39 *Id.* at 185.

The use of child soldiers in armed conflict is prohibited by several international treaties and firmly espoused by international customary law. Article 77(2) of Additional Protocol I to the Geneva Conventions stipulates that children under the age of fifteen should not participate in hostilities; this prohibition applies, along with the remainder of Additional Protocol I, within the context of international armed conflict.[40] Article 4(3)(c) of Additional Protocol II to the Geneva Conventions adopts the same prohibition in the context of non-international armed conflict.[41] The participation of children in hostilities is prohibited in many military manuals, including those that are applicable in non-international armed conflicts. It is also prohibited under the legislation of numerous States. And under the Statute of the International Criminal Court, using children under the age of fifteen to "participate actively in hostilities" constitutes a war crime in both international and non-international armed conflicts.[42] The phrase "using children to participate actively in hostilities" contained in the Statute of the International Criminal Court was specifically included by the Statute drafters to:

> [C]over both direct participation in combat and also active participation in military activities linked to combat such as scouting, spying, sabotage and the use of children as decoys, couriers or at military checkpoints. It would not cover activities clearly unrelated to the hostilities such as food deliveries to an airbase or the use of domestic staff in an officer's married accommodation. However, use of children in a direct support function such as acting as bearers to take supplies to the front line, or activities at the front line itself, would be included within the terminology.[43]

The Statute of the Special Court for Sierra Leone provides similarly that "[c]onscripting or enlisting children under the age of 15 years into armed forces or groups or using them to participate actively in hostilities" is a serious violation of international humanitarian law over which the Court will have jurisdiction.[44] This prohibition is repeated in Article 38 of the Convention on the Rights of the Child.[45] Finally, the Optional Protocol to the Convention on the Rights

40 Protocol Additional to the Geneva Conventions of 12 August 1949, and Relating to the Protection of Victims of International Armed Conflicts (Protocol I), art. 77(2) June 8, 1977, 1125 U.N.T.S. 3 [hereinafter Additional Protocol I].

41 Additional Protocol II, *supra* note 17, art 4(3).

42 Rome Statute of the International Criminal Court art 8(2)(b)(xxvi), (e)(vii), U.N. Doc. A/ CONF.183/9* (1998), www.un.org/law/icc/statute/contents.htm [hereinafter ICC Statute].

43 Draft Statute of the International Criminal Court, Report of the Preparatory Committee on the Establishment of an International Criminal Court, Addendum, Part One, UN Doc. A/CONF. 183/2/Add.1, 14 April 1998, p. 21 (cited in Vol. II, Ch. 39, § 513).

44 Special Court Statute, *supra* note 30, art. 4.

45 Convention on the Rights of the Child art. 38, opened for signature Nov. 20, 1989, 1577 U.N.T.S. 44 (entered into force Sept. 2, 1990) [hereinafter Child Rights Convention].

of the Child on the Involvement of Children in Armed Conflict establishes the age of recruitment and participation of children in armed conflict at eighteen.[46] Under the African Charter on the Rights and Welfare of the Child, the age-limit for participation in hostilities is eighteen.[47]

In addition to the above-mentioned international treaties, which prohibit the use of child soldiers, the actual practices of using children to take part in hostilities have been condemned by several states and international organizations—with respect to conflicts in the Democratic Republic of the Congo, Liberia and Sudan, inter alia.[48] The international community has condemned the use of child soldiers more generally as well. In a resolution adopted in 1999 on children in armed conflicts, the Security Council strongly condemned the "use of children in armed conflict in violation of international law."[49] In a resolution adopted in 1996 on the plight of African children in situations of armed conflict, the OAU Council of Ministers reaffirmed that "the use of children in armed conflicts constitutes a violation of their rights and should be considered as war crimes."[50] The International Conferences of the Red Cross and Red Crescent in 1986 and 1995 adopted resolutions stressing the prohibition of the participation of children in hostilities.[51] The Plan of Action for the years 2000–2003, adopted by the 27th International Conference of the Red Cross and Red Crescent in 1999, requires that all parties to an armed conflict ensure that "all measures, including penal measures, are taken to stop the participation of children . . . in armed hostilities."[52]

Recent case law by international criminal tribunals further confirms that the international community is unified in its condemnation of the crime of enlisting and using child soldiers. It may be argued, in light of such case law, that the norm prohibiting the enlistment and use of child soldiers is morphing into a norm of customary law. The sections below will discuss two recent judgments, where the defendants were convicted on charges of recruiting and using child soldiers—the Lubanga Case from the International Criminal Court, and the Charles Taylor Case from the Special Court for Sierra Leone.

46 Optional Protocol to the Convention on the Rights of the Child on the Involvement of Children in Armed Conflict art. 1, May 25, 2000, 2173 U.N.T.S. 222 (entered into force Feb. 12, 2002).

47 African Charter on the Rights and Welfare of the Child, art. 2 OAU Doc. CAB/LEG/24.9/49 (entered into force Nov. 29, 1999).

48 *See*, e.g., the statements of Italy (id., § 559) and United States (id., § 569); UN Security Council, Res. 1071 (id., § 572) and Res. 1083 (id., § 572); UN Security Council, Statement by the President (id., § 575); UN General Assembly, Res. 51/112 (id., § 576).

49 S.C. Res. 1261, ¶2 (Aug. 25, 1999).

50 Org. of African Unity [OAU], Council of Ministers, Res. 1659 (LXIV) (1993).

51 25th International Conference of the Red Cross, Res. IX; 26th International Conference of the Red Cross and Red Crescent, Res. II.

52 27th International Conference of the Red Cross and Red Crescent, Res. I (adopted by consensus).

International Criminal Court: The *Lubanga* Case

In the recent Lubanga case, the International Criminal Court (ICC) convicted the defendant, a former warlord from eastern Democratic Republic of Congo, on the charges of recruiting and using child soldiers under the age of fifteen in the Ituri conflict from 2002 to 2003 and sentenced him to fourteen years of imprisonment.[53] In this case, the Special Representative to the Secretary-General for Children and Armed Conflict submitted to the Court an amicus curiae brief arguing in favor of a broader understanding of the phenomenon of using child soldiers. In particular, the Secretary General argued that the distinction between voluntary enlistment and forced recruitment is a distinction without meaning in the context of armed conflict.[54] This is because even the most voluntary acts can be a desperate attempt to survive by children with a limited number of options in the context of war, and that using children to participate actively should be interpreted broadly since children are required to play multiple support roles including spies, messengers, porters, scouts, and cooks that place them in danger.[55] This argument is consistent with the position of prominent scholars on the issue of child soldiers, such as Drumble, as discussed above. The ICC adopted this view in its Lubanga judgment. The Court held that the distinction between voluntary and forced recruitment is artificial and recognized the broader interpretation of the definition of child soldiers to include girls and boys who serve in support roles.[56] "In this sense, the judgment set important international jurisprudence on the crime of recruiting child soldiers and set a precedent for future cases and prosecutions in national courts."[57]

Special Court for Sierra Leone: Charles Taylor

Similarly, the Special Court for Sierra Leone found that enlisting child soldiers under the age of fifteen was a crime under international customary law and has prosecuted several defendants on charges of enlisting and using child soldiers as serious violations of international humanitarian law. In a 2004 case, the Special Court's Appeals Chamber issued a first significant ruling on this issue, holding

53 Prosecutor v. Lubanga Dyilo, Case No. ICC-01/04–01/06, Judgment, ¶ 1 (Mar. 14, 2012). The Trial Court conviction has been confirmed on appeal. Prosecutor v. Lubanga Dyilo, Case No. ICC-01/04–01/06, Confirmation, (Dec. 1, 2014).

54 Amicus Curiae United Nations Special Representative of the Secretary-General on Children and Armed Conflict Submitted in application of Rule 103 of the Rules of Procedure and Evidence at Apex. A pg. 5, Prosecutor v. Thomas Lubanga Dyilo, Case No. ICC-01/04–01/06, Judgment, (Mar. 14, 2012).

55 *Role of the International Criminal Court*, OFF. SPECIAL REPRESENTATIVE SECRETARY-GEN. CHILD. & ARMED CONFLICT, available at https://childrenandarmedconflict.un.org/our-work/role-of-the-icc/ (last visited Mar. 10, 2016) [hereinafter Role of the ICC].

56 Lubanga, Case No. ICC-01/04–01/06 at ¶17.

57 Role of the ICC, *supra* note 55.

that the prohibition on the recruitment or use of children under the age of fifteen had crystallized as customary international law prior to 1996.[58] Subsequently, in 2007, the Special Court found three defendants, Alex Tamba Brima, Brima Bazzy Kamara, and Santigie Borbor Kanu, guilty of war crimes, crimes against humanity, and other serious violations of international humanitarian law, including the recruitment and use of child soldiers, which is punishable under Article 4 of the Special Court Statute.[59] This conviction was the first of its kind regarding the crime of recruiting and using child soldiers, and, according to Human Rights Watch, it constituted "a ground-breaking step toward ending impunity for commanders who exploit hundreds of thousands of children as soldiers in conflicts worldwide."[60]

In 2006, the Special Court for Sierra Leone prosecuted Charles Taylor, the former president of Liberia, on eleven different charges, including the violation of international humanitarian law of enlisting and using child soldiers, punishable under Article 4 of the Special Court Statute.[61] The Court convicted Taylor on this charge and sentenced him to fifty years in prison; the trial court's verdict was upheld on appeal.[62] Taylor's conviction of this crime contributed to and furthered the evolving consensus that the enlistment and use of child soldiers is one of the most serious international crimes. Further, the Charles Taylor case provides a detailed definition of the international crime of enlisting child soldiers.

According to the Special Court for Sierra Leone Trial Chamber, the crime of enlisting child soldiers consists of the following elements:

> [T]he perpetrator conscripted or enlisted one or more persons into an armed force or group or used one or more persons to actively participate in hostilities; such person or persons were under the age of 15 years; the perpetrator knew or should have known that such person or persons were under the age of 15 years.[63]

In addition, according to the Trial Chamber, the actus reus of this crime can be satisfied by either conscripting or enlisting child soldiers under the age of fifteen. "'Conscription' encompasses any acts of coercion, such as abductions and forced

58 Prosecutor v. Norman, Case No. SCSL-2004–15-AR72(E), Decision on Preliminary Motion Based on Lack of Jurisdiction (Child Recruitment), (May 31, 2004), available at www.rscsl.org/Documents/Decisions/CDF/Appeal/131/SCSL-04–14-AR72(E)-131.pdf.

59 Special Court Statute, *supra* note 29, art. 4.

60 *Sierra Leone: Landmark Convictions for Use of Child Soldiers*, HUM. RTS. WATCH (June 20, 2007), available at www.hrw.org/news/2007/06/20/sierra-leone-landmark-convictions-use-child-soldiers.

61 Prosecutor v. Taylor, Case No. SCSL-03–01-T, Judgment, ¶ 12 (May 18, 2012), available at www.scsldocs.org/documents/view/6662–19559.

62 *Charles Taylor War Crimes Conviction Upheld*, BBC NEWS (Sept. 26, 2013), available at www.bbc.com/news/world-africa-24279323.

63 *Taylor*, Case No. SCSL-03–01-T, at ¶ 39.

recruitment of children by an armed group with the purpose of using them to participate actively in hostilities."[64] "Enlistment" is different from "conscription," according to the Trial Chamber, because it "entails accepting and enrolling individuals when they volunteer to join an armed force or group" but does not necessarily involve an "element of express compulsion."[65] Finally, "using" child soldiers to participate actively in the hostilities

> [E]ncompasses putting their lives directly at risk in combat, but may also include participation in activities linked to combat such as carrying loads for the fighting faction, finding and/or acquiring food, ammunition, or equipment, acting as decoys, carrying messages, making trails or finding routes, manning checkpoints or acting as human shields.[66]

In the Charles Taylor case, the Trial Chamber concluded that the prosecution had proved beyond a reasonable doubt that all the elements of the crime of conscripting, enlisting, or using child soldiers were satisfied, and that this crime constitutes a serious violation of international humanitarian law, punishable under Article 4 of the Special Court Statute.[67] The judgment was confirmed on appeal, and Charles Taylor was ultimately sentenced to fifty years of imprisonment.

According to Richard Clark, Director of Child Soldiers International, the Special Court for Sierra Leone Appellate Chamber's confirmation of the Charles Taylor conviction "sends a clear message that political leaders can be held accountable for the recruitment of child soldiers. This judgment confirms that providing arms and supporting armed groups that recruit and use children in hostilities is a war crime."[68] The United Nations Special Representative for Children and Armed Conflict, Leila Zerrougui, expressed a similar sentiment about the Appellate Chamber's ruling, by stating that "[t]his verdict is a milestone for the accountability of those who use child soldiers, and another warning to warlords and military commanders that child recruitment will not go unpunished."[69]

Similar to the parallel explored above, between child soldiers and child pirates, it can be argued that a strong connection exists between the international law prohibition on the enlistment and use of child soldiers and the developing norms on the use of child pirates. Developing such norms, which would impose individual criminal responsibility on piracy organizers who enlist and use child pirates,

64 *Id.* at ¶ 441.
65 *Id.* at ¶ 442.
66 *Id.* at ¶ 444.
67 *Id.* at ¶ 1606.
68 *Special Court for Sierra Leone—Appeals Chamber Confirms Conviction of Charles Taylor*, CHILD SOLDIERS INT'L. (Sept. 26, 2013), available at www.child-soldiers.org/news_reader.php?id=704.
69 *Charles Taylor's Conviction Upheld: A Message That Recruiters Of Child Soldiers Will Be Held Accountable*, U.N. SPECIAL REPRESENTATIVE CHILD. & ARMED CONFLICT (Sept. 26, 2013), available at https://childrenandarmedconflict.un.org/press-release/charles-taylors-conviction-upheld/.

similar to the way in which responsibility is imposed on those who enlist and use child soldiers, is helpful and necessary in order to effectively prosecute gang leaders. In other words, in addition to prosecuting gang leaders who organize piracy attacks for the acts or ordering and organizing the attacks, such leaders could also be charged with crimes related to recruiting, enrolling, enlisting, conscripting, and using child pirates, if such crimes formed part of the prosecuting authority's criminal law, or were developed as novel norms of international law. In fact, international law on piracy, as discussed in Chapters 1 and 2, currently prohibits various modes of participating in a piracy endeavor, but does not contain a separate prohibition on the recruitment and use of child pirates. Some jurisdictions already criminalize the use of minors for criminal purposes,[70] and arguably piracy organizers who use child pirates could be prosecuted in such jurisdictions under such general laws. However, in other jurisdictions piracy organizers face impunity because domestic laws do not allow for charges brought upon the accusation of using child pirates.[71]

This gap in domestic and international law could be fulfilled by developing a treaty-based or customary norm of international law, prohibiting the use of child pirates, in the same way that the use of child soldiers is prohibited, because of significant similarities between child soldiering and child piracy, and by encouraging the development of domestic criminal laws, to specifically prohibit and punish the enlistment and use of child pirates. In addition to developing specific laws on the use of child pirates, jurisdictions prosecuting piracy organizers could take into consideration the use of child pirates as an aggravating factor. Such prosecuting jurisdictions could specifically examine the nature of the child pirate's recruitment (whether it was voluntary or not), as well as the age of the recruit, by choosing to punish more harshly those who forcefully employ particularly young pirates. In sum, the enlistment and use of child pirates is a serious offense, similar to the use and enlistment of child soldiers, and the international community should focus on drawing a legal parallel between the two phenomena by developing international and domestic laws that would penalize the use of child pirates, and that would result in harsher sentences for those who do.

70 Coalition to Stop the Use of Child Soldiers, Child Soldiers—Global Report 2008 (2008), available at http://reliefweb.int/sites/reliefweb.int/files/resources/67012B7F8EB991888525744F0069863A-Child%20Soldiers%20Global%20Report%202008.pdf ("Australia, Belgium and Germany are among a small number of countries that have introduced criminal penalties for individuals who conscript, enlist or use children under the age of 15 at home and abroad. In Norway, Sweden and the USA, such legislation was pending. In the case of Norway it was proposed that conscripting or enlisting children under the age of 18 could be prosecuted as a war crime—a standard higher than the age limit of 15 contained in the Rome Statute").

71 For a detailed discussion of national prosecutions involving child piracy suspects, *see infra* Chapters 6, 7, and 8. For a discussion about the prosecution of piracy organizers, *see* Kenneth Scott, *Prosecuting Pirates: Lessons Learned and Continuing Challenges*, OCEANS BEYOND PIRACY, available at http://oceansbeyondpiracy.org/sites/default/files/attachments/ProsecutingPiratesReportDigital_2.pdf.

Conclusion

Existing international law and state practice support the conclusion that child soldiers participating in hostilities are a particularly vulnerable group, and that child soldiers should be treated with particular care, in order to rehabilitate them and promote their reintegration into society. As discussed above, international law does not prohibit the prosecution of child soldiers, if they commit heinous crimes, but international law imposes a firm obligation on any prosecuting authority to handle juvenile cases separately from those involving adults, and to impose punishments that promote rehabilitation and re-education. In addition, international law and state practice demonstrate that it is a violation of treaty and customary law to enlist and use child soldiers, allowing thereby for the prosecution of those who do. The recent cases of Lubanga and Charles Taylor exemplify the international community's willingness to impose harsh penalties on leaders who willingly use child soldiers to participate in hostilities. As has been argued throughout this chapter, important similarities exist between the phenomenon of child soldiers and child pirates. Thus, legal parallels should be drawn between international law's treatment of child soldiers and those who recruit and employ child soldiers, and existing laws and practices regarding the treatment of child pirates and those who recruit and employ child pirates. It is this chapter's recommendation that international norms should be developed on these issues, to provide for special treatment of child pirates, and for harsher treatment of those who use child pirates. In addition, domestic criminal laws should be developed, in particular in countries actively engaged in piracy prosecutions, to allow for separate justice mechanisms that would apply to juvenile pirates, and to impose harsh penalties on individuals who employ juvenile pirates. While child soldiers and child pirates are not the same, scholars have argued in favor of the adopting the same approach when dealing with the potential prosecution and punishment of child soldiers and child pirates.[72] According to Drumbl, the best approach would be to adopt "modalities of restorative and reintegrative justice that avoid the careless superficiality of immediate release and the retributive heavy-handedness of criminal trials."[73] In addition, the same approach of criminalizing the enlistment and use of child pirates, similar to the use of child soldiers, would contribute significantly to successful prosecutions of those who bear the highest responsibility for numerous piracy attacks—the organizers and financiers.

72 See generally, Danielle Fritz, *Child Pirates from Somalia: A Call for the International Community to Support the Further Development of Juvenile Justice Systems in Puntland and Somaliland*, 44 Case W. Res. J. Int'l L. 891 (2012); Emily Holland, Hijacked Childhoods, *Under the Radar: How the International Community Can Help the Youth Associated with Somali Piracy-and Why It Must*, 17 UCLA J. Int'l L. & Foreign Aff. 175, 211 (2013). Shelly L. Whitman, *Children and Marine Piracy*, 46 Case W. Res. J. Int'l L. 217, 233 (2013).

73 Drumbl, *Reimagining*, *supra* note 4, at 6.

Part III

Age Determinations

A Difficult Challenge

Part III will focus on the issue of age determinations regarding juvenile piracy suspects. If a piracy suspect alleges that he is a juvenile, prosecuting authorities typically conduct medical and forensic age determination procedures to assess the suspect's age. Chapter 5 will discuss existing medical and forensic age determination procedures, including bone and dental X-rays, ultra sounds, medical and cognitive examinations, and magnetic resonance imaging. Chapters 6, 7, and 8 will focus on different countries' national prosecutions of piracy suspects, where the suspects' issue was contested and where prosecuting authorities resorted to different types of age determination procedures. Chapter 6 will discuss national prosecutions in European nations, such as Germany, France, Italy, and Spain. Chapter 7 will discuss national prosecutions in non-European nations, including India, Malaysia, and the Seychelles. Chapter 8 will discuss national prosecutions in the United States, in the federal district courts in New York and in Virginia. Chapters 6, 7, and 8 will thus highlight some of the difficulties associated with age determinations in the context of criminal proceedings.

5 Determining a Suspect's Age

When a Bearded Man States That He is Fourteen

Introduction

Judge Duncan Gaswaga, formerly of the Seychelles Supreme Court, who had presided over several Somali piracy prosecutions, shared the following frustration with the author: if a bearded Somali piracy suspect claims that he is fourteen years old, what should the judge do? Is a judge under a legal obligation to order medical and forensic tests to ascertain the defendant's actual age? Or can a judge simply reject this type of claim if it appears unreasonable that the suspect is actually of the age that he is claiming? This chapter will explore the difficult issue of age determination, by highlighting different legal contexts in which age determinations are necessary, by describing available medical, dental, and other forensic procedures, and by highlighting approaches that have already been adopted by jurisdictions across the world. This chapter will explain why appropriately determining the age of Somali piracy suspects is crucial if one is willing to ensure the protection of juvenile suspects' rights. This chapter will be succeeded by Chapters 6, 7, and 8, which will discuss specific age determinations in Somali piracy prosecutions within European and non-European nations, as well as in the United States.

When and Why are Age Determinations Necessary?

Age determination procedures become necessary in the legal context if the defendant's age—typically whether the defendant is eighteen or not—is relevant for his or her legal status. For most piracy prosecutions conducted in national courts of various nations, determining the suspect's age is crucial, because under most national systems juveniles are entitled to distinct protections and are typically not exposed to the harshest criminal penalties.

Under most national criminal laws, defendants younger than eighteen are prosecuted in specialized juvenile tribunals, and the applicable law consists of juvenile justice provisions, which most often adopt a "best interest of the child" standard and which most often embrace a rehabilitative approach. This approach toward juveniles is dictated by international human rights law, as discussed above in Chapter 3, which requires that juveniles be treated distinctly from adults, and that their young age be taken into account during every phase of the criminal process. Thus, it is very likely that a defendant whose age turns out to be under eighteen will receive more preferential treatment than his or her adult counterpart. It should be noted that several countries' national laws allow for juvenile defendants to face criminal prosecution as adults, typically if they are accused of having committed a particularly heinous crime. In such cases, the defendant's age may not inhibit an adult-like criminal prosecution altogether, but may afford the juvenile defendant with specific rights not available to adults. In addition, the juvenile defendant's young age may still play a part in the sentencing phase, typically weighing in favor of a more lenient punishment.

For example, in the United States, the age of a suspect is relevant for the purpose of assessing whether the suspect's rights were properly respected in the context of Miranda rules. The United States Supreme Court has held that the age of a child subjected to police questioning is relevant to the custody analysis of *Miranda v. Arizona*, 384 U.S. 436 (1966). "It is beyond dispute that children will often feel bound to submit to police questioning when an adult in the same circumstances would feel free to leave. Seeing no reason for police officers or courts to blind themselves to that commonsense reality, we hold that a child's age properly informs the Miranda custody analysis."[1] The United States Supreme Court has also held that mandatory life sentences without parole for those under the age of eighteen at the time of their crimes violates the United States Constitution's Eighth Amendment prohibition on cruel and unusual punishments, and that a "judge or jury must have the opportunity to consider mitigating circumstances before imposing the harshest possible penalty for juveniles."[2] Similarly, the United States Supreme Court has held that the imposition of capital punishment on juvenile defendants is unconstitutional, because juvenile defendants as a class are less culpable than adults, in light of their young age.[3] Thus, United States' courts have recognized that a defendant's young age is important throughout a criminal process, and that particularly harsh sentences may not be applicable to juvenile defendants. Age determinations in this context may be crucial, to ensure that juvenile defendants' rights are adequately protected.

In France, any time that criminal penalties are imposed on juveniles, reintegration and re-education are prioritized over punitive sanctions. Juvenile criminal cases are prosecuted in a specialized jurisdiction, the Juvenile Court. Moreover,

1 JDB v. North Carolina, 2011 WL 2369508 (2010).

2 Miller v. Alabama, 567 U.S. _ (2012); Jackson v. Hobbs, No. 10–9647 (2012) (Miller and Jackson cases held that the imposition of life sentences without parole on juvenile defendants having committed homicidal offenses is unconstitutional; an earlier case, Graham v. Florida, 560 U.S. 48 (2010), had already reached this conclusion for juvenile defendants convicted of non-homicidal offenses).

3 Roper v. Simmons, 543 U.S. 551 (2005); *see also* Juvenile Law Center, Juvenile and Criminal Justice, Miller v. Alabama; Jackson v. Hobbs, available at www.jlc.org/legal-docket/miller-v-alabama-jackson-v-hobbs.

many procedural safeguards exist to ensure that when a child is involved in the proceedings, additional suffering to the child is minimized. For example, if children are suspects in criminal proceedings, they have a right to have their parents and lawyers constantly involved in the proceedings. Moreover, any criminal penalty imposed on the child should prioritize re-education and ensure that the best interest of the child is always taken into consideration during sentencing.

> Finally, the wide range of different measures and sanctions, both educational and punitive, provide a complete and child-adapted criminal justice toolbox. France has established a robust and child-friendly criminal system relying on the specialisation of different legal and non-legal actors. This specialisation at the judicial level allows for both reactivity and proactivity toward children as victims and suspects.[4]

In England, Wales and Northern Ireland, the age of minimum criminal responsibility begins at ten, and a Youth Justice system is in place for children between the ages of ten and eighteen. The majority of children are tried in a Youth Court, although some children may be tried in adult courts for certain serious offenses or if they have been charged with an adult. In general, the juvenile justice system in England, Wales, and Northern Ireland aims at discouraging or preventing the commission of criminal offenses by children, by addressing offending behavior, managing the overall welfare of child offenders to reduce recidivism, as well as introducing a range of out-of-court options. If children are detained, the system works to ensure that their detention is safe and secure, and that the causes of their behavior are adequately addressed.[5]

In Germany, the criminal system for juvenile suspects takes into account the child's age, physical and mental well being, as well as their educational needs. Under German criminal law, a child above fourteen years of age can be held criminally responsible, only if the child is sufficiently mature and morally and mentally developed at the time of the offense, to ensure that this child understands the unlawfulness of the offense and is able to act in line with that understanding. The judge can impose supervisory measures (*Erziehungsmassregeln*), disciplinary measures (*Zuchtmittel*), and a youth penalty (*Jugendstrafe*). Any criminal penalties imposed on a juvenile defendant are aimed at the reintegration of the child and at avoiding recidivism. "In order to achieve this goal, the legal approach to youth

4 Nathy Rass-Masson, *Study on Children's Involvement in Judicial Proceedings, Contextual Overview for the Criminal Justice Phase: France*, available at http://bookshop.europa.eu/en/study-on-children-s-involvement-in-judicial-proceedings-pbDS0313668/?CatalogCategoryID=WTQKABsteF0AAAEjKpEY4e5L.

5 Nathy Rass-Masson, *Study on Children's Involvement in Judicial Proceedings, Contextual Overview for the Criminal Justice Phase: England, Wales and Northern Ireland*, available at http://bookshop.europa.eu/en/study-on-children-s-involvement-in-judicial-proceedings-pbDS0313686/?CatalogCategoryID=WTQKABsteF0AAAEjKpEY4e5L.

crime follows primarily an educational concept. Informal sanctions, such as diversion or suspension are imposed as a rule, especially for first-time offenders."[6]

In Canada, the Youth Criminal Justice Act governs the treatment of youth (ages twelve to eighteen) engaged in criminal activity.[7] The Act provides guidelines regarding definitions of illegal acts, legal procedures to be observed in dealing with the youthful offender, and the range of conditions of available dispositions for youth convicted of a criminal action. The three main guiding principles in this act include the prevention of the crime by addressing root causes of a juvenile offender's behavior, rehabilitation of the juvenile offender and his or her reintegration into society, and the imposition of meaningful sanctions on the juvenile offender, in order to ensure long-term protection of the public. The act also includes sentencing guidelines for judges, which have a strong rehabilitative emphasis. The major sentencing principles contained in this act include the following: all available alternatives to detention must be considered; the sentence should be the least restrictive sentence; the sentence must be most likely to rehabilitate the juvenile offender and reintegrate him or her into society, as well as promote a sense of responsibility in the juvenile offender.[8] The act provides for the possibility of imposing harsher sentences on juvenile offenders between the ages of fourteen and eighteen, who commit violent crimes. However, under the act, parole eligibility dates for convicted juveniles are earlier, and overall the system assumes that the incarcerated juvenile will receive rehabilitative services while in custody. In addition to traditional criminal sentences, the act provides for extrajudicial measures designed to divert youth from the criminal justice system, for extrajudicial sanctions, which are alternatives to traditional court processes, and for probation coupled with rehabilitative services. If juveniles are detained, they are held at appropriate institutional settings designed for youth.[9] In sum, the Canadian criminal justice system treats juveniles differently from adults, and adopts a more lenient, rehabilitative approach toward the former.

Based on the above examination of different national laws regarding the treatment of juvenile suspects, it may be argued that the defendant's age and the determination of whether he or she is a juvenile or not is highly relevant under most national criminal laws. While the sample of countries above is far from exhaustive, the juvenile justice approaches above are representative of general "western" trends for the treatment of juvenile suspects. If a defendant is found

6 Nathy Rass-Masson, *Study on Children's Involvement in Judicial Proceedings, Contextual Overview for the Criminal Justice Phase: Germany*, available at http://bookshop.europa.eu/en/study-on-children-s-involvement-in-judicial-proceedings-pbDS0313669/?CatalogCategoryID=WTQKABste F0AAAEjKpEY4e5L.

7 Robert D. Hoge, *Introduction to the Canadian Juvenile Justice System*, RESOURCE MATERIAL SERIES No.78, at 59, available at www.unafei.or.jp/english/pdf/RS_No78/No78_11VE_Hoge3.pdf.

8 *Id.* at 60.

9 *Id.* at 60–61.

to be a juvenile, he or she is typically prosecuted in a separate system of juvenile justice, where rehabilitative and re-educational approaches are favored over traditional penalties. In cases where a juvenile defendant is prosecuted as an adult, in regular criminal courts, his or her young age is typically taken into account during the sentencing phase, where the harshest penalties may not be available. It is thus understandable why determining the age of Somali piracy suspects is crucial under most national criminal systems, and why juvenile suspects' rights may not be adequately protected if age determinations are conducted in unreliable manners.

It should be noted that age determinations are an important issue in contexts other than piracy. In some specific legal contexts, the defendant's juvenile status may entitle him or her to specific legal protections, which are not available to adults. For example, in the immigration context, children may be more likely to obtain asylum status in wealthy, typically western nations, because of protections extended to children under international human rights laws focusing on children. Children whose asylum claims have been accepted by a western nation are then typically granted access to social and education programs. Because these programs are costly and because most western nations are unwilling to accept unlimited numbers of asylum seekers, government authorities of such nations at times resort to age determination procedures, to limit asylum access for those under the age of eighteen only. In fact, asylum seekers often do not carry birth certificates and passports, and ascertaining someone's age is impossible because of the lack of documentary evidence. Government authorities have, in such cases, resorted to the use of age-determining medical and dental procedures. These procedures unfortunately yield inconclusive results and may result in significant legal errors.

For example, Australian immigration authorities have faced important hurdles in their use of age determination procedures. In 2010, three Indonesian child immigrants were jailed as adults after wrist X-ray tests showed that they were not juveniles. In 2011, they provided birth certificates establishing their juvenile age and status and were then released by Australian authorities.[10] This "illegal" detention of children caused public outrage—because the Australian authorities apparently relied solely on bone and wrist X-rays to ascertain that the asylum seekers were adults, and ignored other documentary and testimonial evidence produced on behalf of these asylum seekers, which tended to show that they were children. This case prompted the Australian Human Rights Commission to hold an inquiry into the age determination practice. This is particularly relevant in Australia, where dozens of other immigrants have been waiting in detention

10 Lindsay Murdoch, *Australia Imprisons Indonesian Boys*, THE NATIONAL AGE (June 14, 2011), available at *www.theage.com.au/national/australia-imprisons-indonesian-boys-20110613–1g0il.html*; Lindsay Murdoch, *Indonesian Children Released From Adult Prison*, THE SYDNEY MORNING HERALD (June 18, 2011), available at www.smh.com.au/national/indonesian-children-released-from-adult-prison-20110617–1g7yq.html.

while their age claims are verified by authorities.[11] The Australian Human Rights Commission in 2012 completed an inquiry into the treatment of individuals suspected of people smuggling offenses who say that they are children. The majority of individuals whose cases were considered by this inquiry were Indonesian nationals who had worked as crew on boats bringing asylum seekers to Australia, and who were subsequently investigated for people smuggling offenses.[12] The inquiry looked into all cases where age had been in dispute since September 2008. The inquiry report, "An age of uncertainty," detailed

> how the Australian Government's failure to seriously question age assessment practices and procedures resulted in some children spending long periods of time detained in adult correctional facilities. In particular, it documents how the acts and practices of the Australian Federal Police, the Office of the Commonwealth Director of Public Prosecutions and the Attorney-General's Department have resulted in breaches of the rights of these individuals. The report encourages the Australian Government to take steps to ensure that in the future, the human rights of all those who come in contact with Australia's criminal justice system are respected.[13]

Australia, however, is not alone in its use of medical procedures to determine an immigration candidate's age. "A 2010 study of 22 European countries found that 16 conduct bone scans and 10 use dental X-rays. The US has used both tests for almost two decades."[14] In the United Kingdom, immigration authorities have grappled with the idea of using bone X-rays to determine age for those seeking permanent entry into this country. In the United States, immigration authorities use both bone X-rays as well as dental scans to conduct age determination procedures.[15] The United States immigration authorities conduct such medical age determination procedures, but also consider other evidence regarding an applicant's juvenile status, including statements made by the alien, or by another individual with personal knowledge of the alien's age, information or records from federal, state, local, or foreign government agencies, documentation

11 Australian press has reported that seventy allegedly juvenile Indonesian asylum seekers were being held in detention by Australian authorities, and that bone X-rays were used as proof of adult status against sixty of them. *See* Murdoch, *Indonesian Children, supra* note 10.

12 Australian Human Rights Commission, Age Assessment in People Smuggling Cases—Inquiry into the Treatment of Individuals Suspected of People Smuggling Offences Who Say That They Are Children, available at www.humanrights.gov.au/our-work/asylum-seekers-and-refugees/projects/age-assessment-people-smuggling-cases-inquiry.

13 *Id.*

14 NEW SCIENTIST, *With No Paper Trail, Can Science Determine Age?* (May 9, 2012), available at www.newscientist.com/article/mg21428644–300-with-no-paper-trail-can-science-determine-age/.

15 Department of Homeland Security Office of Inspector General, *Age Determination Practices for Unaccompanied Alien Children in ICE Custody*, November 2009, available at www.oig.dhs.gov/assets/Mgmt/OIG_10–12_Nov09.pdf.

that can credibly establish date of birth, and assessments of the alien's physical appearance and behavior.[16] The United States' authorities, however, do not collect or track data regarding their use of age determination procedures in the immigration context; it is thus impossible to conclude whether such age determination procedures have been successful or whether they have negatively impacted the rights of potentially juvenile asylum seekers.

Outside of the immigration context, age determination techniques may be relevant in sports. "Sports governing bodies have an interest in ensuring athletes compete in appropriate age bands."[17] Thus, sporting events' participants' age may be relevant and may need to be determined using medical and forensic procedures, in the absence of documentary evidence. However, both the International Olympic Committee and the international football federation, FIFA, have agreed not to use X-rays to resolve age issues.[18]

Thus, age determination issues have arisen in contexts other than piracy, typically in situations where a person's age may entitle him or her to specific protections, such as in immigration/asylum law and sports. The section below will discuss the most commonly available age determining techniques that have been used in contexts such as immigration and sports. Most courts handling the prosecution of juvenile piracy suspects will resort to using some of the same age determination techniques, and most piracy courts will encounter some of the same challenges associated with the use of these techniques in the non-piracy contexts described above.

Most Commonly Available Age Determining Techniques: Bone/Wrist and Dental X-rays

The two most commonly used age determination techniques involve bone X-rays and dental scans. This section will briefly describe these two techniques and will assess their overall effectiveness and utility in conducting age determinations.

If a bone X-ray is used to conduct an age determination, most typically medical professionals will scan wrist bones. "In wrist scans, age is estimated by looking at 20 or so bones initially separated by cartilage, but which progressively move closer to one another until they fuse in the mature wrist."[19] This technique is not without challenges, however. The most commonly used medical reference for this test is a 1959 atlas compiled for doctors to assess healthy bone development, not the patient's age. This atlas includes hundreds of X-ray images of wrists of white middle-class American children, as well as an image of the fully mature wrist of a nineteen-year-old.[20] According to some experts, however, wrists can

16 *Id.* at 11.
17 NEW SCIENTIST, *supra* note 14.
18 *Id.*
19 NEW SCIENTIST, *supra* note 14.
20 *Id.*

be fully mature in children as young as fifteen. Another rival atlas, compiled a few years later, concludes that a mean chronological age for wrist maturity is 17.6 years, with a variance of 1.3 years. This observation leads to the conclusion that most "children" have "adult" wrists before the age of eighteen. In fact, Professor Cole from the University College of London, a prestigious expert in the field of medical age determinations, has concluded that there is a 61 percent statistical probability that a young male will have a mature wrist on his 18th birthday. "In other words a mature wrist x-ray is not informative of whether a young male is over the age of 18 years as more than half of all young men will have achieved skeletal maturity before that age."[21]

Thus, focusing on the development of a person's wrist bone may lead the examiner to conclude that the person is eighteen or older, because his or her wrist bones are fully developed. This in turn means that many children may be designated as adults based on bone scans—this is precisely what happened in the Australian immigration case mentioned above. In addition, the atlas' points of comparison are bones of North American children from mostly wealthy, upper middle class families. This comparison may be meaningless when determining the age of Asian or African individuals whose growth rates, including their wrist bones, may be completely different from their North American counterparts. The atlas authors themselves have noted that one should be reluctant to expect the same level of skeletal growth and development among different world populations, because of factors such as racial differences, illness and food deprivation.[22] Moreover, the atlas' purpose was to assess whether a person's bones are developing in a healthy manner, not to predict the person's age.

> Wrist x-ray analysis is most commonly used by medical practitioners to assess the skeletal development of a child whose chronological age is known. An assessment of this kind is undertaken for the purpose of evaluating other aspects of the child's growth and development. Ordinarily, the medical practitioner wants to know how the child's development compares with that of other children of the same sex and age . . . It is important to bear in mind that the authors of the GP Atlas were not seeking to create a method of establishing the chronological age of young people. Rather, their concern was to establish a means of assessing the skeletal development of children whose chronological age is known. [23]

Another problem with using wrist X-rays to determine a person's age is the subjective nature of this medical test's interpretation. Different radiologists interpreting bone scans may come to different conclusions regarding the person's age. Thus, while the use of bone/wrist X-rays is one of most commonly used

21 Australian Human Rights Commission, *supra* note 12, at 49.

22 *Id.* at 53.

23 Australian Human Rights Commission, *supra* note 12, at 44.

age-determining procedures, this technique has been criticized by many in the scientific community and may produce somewhat unreliable results.

The second commonly used medical technique to determine a person's age consists of dental scans—X-rays that analyze the development of the third permanent molar (wisdom tooth). This particular dental X-ray is typically conducted externally to the mouth (as opposed to placing X-ray films inside the mouth), to determine whether the person has a wisdom tooth that has reached a certain stage of maturity. Specific dental databases have been expressly developed for the purposes of assessing chronological age of the patient. The most widely used of these databases is the Demirjian dental age assessment scale, which was developed in 1973 based on a French-Canadian study sample. "In the context of determining adulthood, a forensic odontologist needs to assess whether the OPG indicates that the wisdom teeth have reached 'Stage H' on the Demirjian scale."[24] The scientific community disagrees about the accuracy of age predictions based on this type of dental scan, but it does appear that dental scans produce slightly more reliable results than bone/wrist X-rays do. Professor Cole, quoted above in the context of bone X-rays, has concluded that the mean age of attainment of one or more Stage H third molars is 19.6 years, with a standard deviation of 1.3 years. Based on these figures, Professor Cole has calculated that there is a 24 percent chance of a person having a Stage H wisdom tooth before the age of eighteen. However, despite the higher statistical accuracy of dental X-rays compared to bone scans, Professor Cole is equally skeptical of using dental analysis to ascertain age. "Thus dental age suffers from the same lack of precision as bone age for forensic age assessment. Ages older than 16 cannot convincingly be excluded using either method."[25]

In addition, similar problems regarding this technology exist as those associated with the use of bone scans. Individuals across the globe reach dental maturity at vastly different stages in life, ranging from the mid-teens through a person's early twenties. Moreover, the Demirjian scale mentioned above and used for determining wisdom teeth maturity, is based on a study sample of French-Canadian children. This raises the question of whether assessing the teeth of children coming from different parts of the world "against that age assessment scale might be subject to inherent error based on differing ethnicity, socio-economic status and nutrition."[26]

It is unclear that using both bone and dental X-rays on the same individual to assess his or her age will decrease the margin of error and lead toward more accurate results. Subjecting the same individuals to two different X-rays may expose the person to unnecessary radiation, which in turn raises important ethical issues. It would be fair to conclude that medical experts do not agree that the use of bone and dental scans to determine a person's age is the most preferred

24 *Id.* at 58.

25 Australian Human Rights Commission, *supra* note 12, at 58.

26 *Id.* at 60.

method. Instead, some experts, including Professor Cole, as well as Al Aynsley-Green, an emeritus professor of child health at the University College of London, have argued that "the best hope is in detailed assessments of physical and psychological development by specially trained paediatricians, skilled in combining different aspects of growth to make an informed estimate of age."[27] The section below will discuss other age-determining procedures, including the use of a more holistic, non-exclusively medical approach.

Other Age-Determining Procedures Available

Other age-determining processes exist that involve using biomedical markers, including physical examination, clavicle (collar bone) x-ray, magnetic resonance imaging, and ultrasound of the wrist or elbow. The section below will briefly describe these procedures and will conclude that they suffer from some of the same flaws as bone and dental X-rays and that they should be used cautiously.

Physical examinations require a medical practitioner to assess height, weight, skin and visible signs of sexual maturity. These assessments are then compared to reference data, in order to allow for an approximate chronological age to be calculated.[28] While this method is simple and does not expose the examined person to unnecessary radiation, it suffers from some of the same problems as bone and dental scans. First, a wide variation may exist in the rate of development between individuals within any given group. Second, ethnicity, socio-economic, and nutritional background as well as illness may impact a child's development. Third, no neutral and culturally relevant reference sets exist, against which a child's development could be compared. Fourth, a medical examination would entail an examination of the person's genitalia, which may be uncomfortable and may raise ethical concerns. In fact, in the immigration context, United Kingdom courts have already raised concerns about using physical examinations to determine a person's age, because of the absence of rigorous protocols and because of the subjective nature of pediatric reports.[29] Australian authorities have similarly rejected the use of physical examinations in the immigration context to determine a person's age, because the procedure "involves examination of a person's genitals and is likely to cause significant distress, fear, embarrassment and discomfort."[30] In sum, it appears that physical examinations conducted toward examining a person's age are equally unreliable as bone and dental scans, but may cause greater discomfort to the person and have been rejected by government authorities of several states.

Clavicle (collar bone) X-rays or magnetic resonance imaging has also been discussed as a scientific method for determining a person's age. This procedure

27 NEW SCIENTIST, *supra* note 14.

28 Australian Human Rights Commission, *supra* note 12, at 63.

29 A v London Borough of Croydon & SSHD; WK v SSHD & Kent County Council [2009] EWHC 939, as cited in UK Border Agency, Guidelines for Assessing Age, 2011, section 6.5.

30 Australian Human Rights Commission, *supra* note 12, at 64.

may be relevant for those attempting to challenge the conclusion that they are of an adult age over eighteen, because “all other developmental systems under examination have completed their growth by this time.”[31] It appears, however, that more scientific research is needed in order to assess the reliability and accuracy of this type of medical age-determining procedure.

The use of magnetic resonance imaging to assess growth plate maturity has also been discussed in the scientific community as another method of determining age. While this method has been used in the context of age assessment for the purposes of international sporting competitions, it has not been used in other legal contexts. The George Institute for Global Health has concluded that there is no evidence to support the use of this technology for age determination of young people below fourteen years of age and above seventeen years of age, and that more research into the methodology is required.[32]

Another possible medical technique to assess age is the use of ultra sounds of the wrist and elbow. Some of the main advantages of using ultra sounds include that this is a radiation-free imaging technique, that it is relatively inexpensive and widely available, and that patient compliance is generally good. This technique does present challenges and disadvantages, which include a relatively high likelihood of error, difficulties in the technology itself, such as imaging transfer, and the lack of reliable data available regarding age determination from the ultrasound of a wrist or elbow. In sum, while this technique may have potential, it appears that at present time more research is needed into its reliability.[33]

Because none of the purely medical age-determining procedures appear to be sufficiently reliable and capable of producing accurate results, some in the scientific community have advocated for the use of multi-factorial medical tests, and for a more comprehensive approach, combining the use of non-medical tests with the above-described medical procedures. These approaches will be discussed in the sections below.

Using Multi-Factorial Medical Tests to Determine Age?

As the sections above have discussed, no single reliable age-determining method currently exists. In light of this, some experts have suggested the use of multi-factorial medical tests as the most appropriate approach toward determining age. A multifactorial approach involves combining many of the available medical processes described above on the same person, in order to predict his or her age more accurately. While it is possible that using a multifactorial approach would reduce the margin of error in a single age determination to some degree, because this approach would expose the same person to a battery of tests, it raises unique ethical issues. The Australian Human Rights Commission has noted that:

31 *Id.*
32 *Id.* at 65.
33 *Id.* at 65.

> there must be consideration of whether it is ethically justified to ask individuals to undertake more procedures when it has not been established that this will make a significant difference to obtaining an accurate assessment of chronological age.[34]

In addition, using the multifactorial approach may entail cost and practicality challenges, because multiple medical and dental practitioners would be needed in order to conduct a single age assessment procedure. It appears that if each of the medical and dental procedures described above suffers from unreliability, using a combination of such procedures would not reduce the margin of error and would instead result in equally unreliable age determinations. Thus, it is unclear that the use of a multi-factorial approach would significantly approve the accuracy of age determination procedures.

Using a Holistic or Multi-Disciplinary Approach to Assess Age?

Some experts have advocated for the use of a holistic or multi-disciplinary approach in conducting age determinations. This approach would consist of using both medical and non-medical procedures to determine a person's age. Professor Aynsley-Green has suggested the use of this approach:

> Multi-professional assessment—a 'holistic' approach—involving a team of social workers, educationists, paediatricians and psychologists working in specialised Age Assessment Referral Units or within the existing structures for child protection would seem to be a pragmatic way forward in order to obtain a consensus decision on age.[35]

The Royal Australasian College of Physicians has also recommended the use of this type of comprehensive approach, "which may include psychological, cognitive, developmental and cultural factors, as well as comprehensive efforts to source accurate documentation of age where it exists."[36] The Australian Society of Forensic Odontology has argued that within every medical age assessment, there should be a multi-disciplinary medical team present. And the Separated Children in Europe Programme's Statement of Good Practice recommends that

> [t]he [age assessment] procedure should be multi-disciplinary and undertaken by independent professionals with appropriate expertise and familiarity with the child's ethnic and cultural background. They must balance physical, developmental, psychological, environmental and cultural factors.[37]

34 *Id.* at 66.
35 *Id.* at 68.
36 *Id.*
37 *Id.*

While this approach may appear most attractive, its effectiveness may be limited by some of the same factors that exist in the context of traditional medical age-determining procedures described above. First, the rate of social and cognitive development, same as that of physical development, may be impacted by socio-economic and racial factors. Second, psychological and cognitive tests are prone to similar margins of errors as medical tests are, and may be highly subjective. Third, a court or other type of government authority may afford much greater weight to medical examinations over psychological and cognitive tests. Finally, a truly comprehensive holistic approach may be impractical because of time and cost associated with it. Thus, although using a holistic approach may appear as the best option in conducting age determinations, this method too is associated with particular challenges and complexities and it is unclear that it will become frequently used in the future.

In the context of piracy prosecutions, where age determinations are important because they determine the rights of juvenile versus adult suspects, it is important for all prosecuting nations to develop a consistent approach toward assessing a suspect's age. All of the medical, dental, and non-medical techniques described above represent viable options for piracy prosecuting nations. Piracy cases are relatively rare—the United States and European nations have prosecuted a handful of cases, and even countries that have concluded transfer agreements with capturing nations and have thus enlisted to prosecute pirates (Kenya, The Seychelles, and Mauritius) have altogether prosecuted a couple of hundred pirates. Among these cases, an even smaller subset consists of cases where suspects assert juvenile status and where this status is contested by the prosecution. In sum, the overall number of piracy prosecutions where the suspects' age is an issue is very small, and using a holistic, comprehensive approach to determine the age of piracy suspects, whenever possible, may be feasible, and may constitute the best approach. Courts of all prosecuting nations should, whenever a suspect's age is disputed, order a series of medical, dental, and non-medical tests, which could provide the court with the most accurate estimate of the suspect's age. Chapter 9 below will discuss, in more detail, specific recommendations regarding age-determination procedures.

Conclusion

Determining the age of a criminal suspect who lacks documentary evidence, such as a birth certificate or passport, is a challenging task. As this chapter has described, a multitude of medical, dental, and cognitive tests exist and can be used toward assessing a person's age. Each of these tests and techniques is prone to criticism, however, because neither of them can produce sufficiently accurate results. In other words, deciding whether someone is seventeen or nineteen may at times be medically impossible. Yet, determining a criminal suspect's age is crucial in most national criminal systems, because juveniles are typically prosecuted in different courts, using distinct procedures and approaches, which focus on the offender's rehabilitation and reintegration into society. In the piracy context, where suspects are typically prosecuted in the criminal courts of various nations, it is thus extremely important to determine such suspects' ages, in order to adequately protect the rights of those who may be juvenile. It is this chapter's conclusion that all piracy prosecuting nations should adopt comprehensive, holistic age determination procedures, which may ensure the least margin of error and may result in the most adequate treatment of juvenile suspects. The subsequent chapters (6, 7, and 8) will discuss specific piracy prosecutions in the courts of various European and non-European nations, including the United States, in order to assess how different jurisdictions have used some of these age determination procedures.

6 Recent National Prosecutions of Juvenile Suspects

European Countries

Introduction

This chapter will discuss the recent prosecution of allegedly juvenile piracy suspects in the national courts of several European nations: Germany, Spain, Italy, and France. These prosecutions are grouped together because they bear significant similarities and reflect a European/regional approach toward handling claims of juvenile status by Somali piracy suspects. In each of these national prosecutions, pirates had attacked a vessel flagged in the prosecuting state; in each of these instances, pirates were captured after an unsuccessful attack and transferred to stand trial in the courts of the victim vessel's state. Moreover, each of these prosecutions featured a group of Somali piracy suspects prosecuted together and allegations of juvenile status asserted by one or several individuals within the prosecuted group. The courts of Germany, Spain, and Italy conducted medical and forensic tests to ascertain the actual age of those individuals claiming juvenile status; it is unclear whether the French court conducted any such tests. The courts of Germany, Italy, and France accepted the juvenile status claim by some of the prosecuted piracy suspects, based on medical and forensic tests in the first two countries (it is unclear how the French authorities determined that one of the prosecuted suspects was a juvenile). The Spanish court rejected the juvenile status claim by one suspect, also based on medical and forensic tests. It appears that prosecuting authorities of each of these four European nations were willing to transfer the prosecution of juvenile suspects to their respective juvenile courts—the German and the French courts conducted the entire piracy trial under the rules of juvenile justice; the Italian authorities separated the case against juvenile suspects and prosecuted those in juvenile court; the Spanish authorities, before rejecting the juvenile status claim, appeared ready to proceed with the prosecution in juvenile court as well. Moreover, the sentences imposed on juvenile pirates by German, Italian, and French authorities were particularly lenient and reflective of international human rights law's focus on the rehabilitation of juveniles, rather than on retributivism. The lengthy sentence imposed on pirates prosecuted in Spain can most likely be explained by the Spanish authorities' determination that each of the prosecuted suspects was an adult over the age of eighteen.

This chapter will discuss the recent Somali piracy prosecutions in Germany, Spain, Italy, and France where suspects had claimed juvenile status. It wil conclude that while the prosecuting authorities of at least three of these countries (Germany, Spain, and Italy) attempted to appropriately use medical and forensic tests to determine the suspect's age, courts in each of these countries continued to face uncertainty regarding the results of these tests, which are often inconclusive, and regarding the appropriate legal regime to impose upon those claiming juvenile status. This chapter will conclude that it is crucial that all piracy prosecuting countries use medical and forensic tests to determine piracy suspects' actual ages, but that it is equally important for prosecuting nations to develop appropriate legal and policy regimes regarding the handling of such complex cases. When such regimes and policies are in place, prosecutions can proceed more efficiently and will result in less uncertainty surrounding the status of juvenile or allegedly juvenile piracy suspects.

Germany

German prosecutors faced the problem of juvenile piracy in the first German piracy trial in over 400 years. In 2010, a group of ten Somali pirate defendants was jointly prosecuted in Hamburg, on charges related to the hijacking of a German cargo ship, the *MV Taipan*, in the Gulf of Aden. The attack against the *MV Taipan* has been described as follows:

> The *MV Taipan* was headed from Haifa, Israel to Mombasa, Kenya and avoided the vicinity of Somalia in order to be relatively safe from pirate attacks. 500 nm from the Somali coast in the middle of the Indian Ocean on the April 5, 2010 they sighted the dhow Hud Hud, a kidnapped vessel, which was first deemed harmless and the threat it posed became apparent only when it sent two skiffs towards the container vessel Taipan. The crew of the Taipan, which now travelled full speed, was sent to the safe room and the master and two crew-members remained on the bridge. When the skiffs closed in and machine gun fire hit the Taipan, the master ordered everyone in the ship's citadel. The pirates on the skiffs tried to climb on board, observed by a German maritime surveillance aircraft, and eventually succeeded.[1]

The ten defendants had boarded the *MV Taipan* armed with AK-47s, but a nearby Dutch navy frigate, the *Tromp*, successfully interfered and intercepted the *MV Taipan*. The Somalis were apprehended after a brief exchange of fire; they were arrested by the Dutch frigate and eventually extradited to Germany for prosecution.[2]

1 Roger Phillips, *Long Road to Justice—The German Piracy Trial*, COMMUNIS HOSTIS OMNIUM (Oct. 21, 2012), available at http://piracy-law.com/2012/10/21/long-road-to-justice-the-german-piracy-trial/.

2 Mark A. Drumbl, *Child Pirates: Rehabilitation, Reintegration and Accountability*, 46 CASE W. J. INT'L L. 235, 254 (2013).

Five out of ten accused pirates alleged to be juveniles. Most of the accused claimed ages between sixteen and twenty-eight, but one of the defendants claimed to be only thirteen. In fact, it quickly became apparent that the suspected pirates themselves may be confused and uncertain about their own ages—one defendant stated that he had been born under a tree, and another that he had been born during the rainy season.[3] The court initially determined that one defendant, Abdiwali, was a juvenile; his detention and treatment were particularly criticized by the German press. Beate Lakotta wrote a scathing review of the German piracy trial, focusing on the detention of Abdiwali, whom she described as "an attractive boy with short-cropped hair, soft facial features and almost no facial hair" who was "scared to death" upon his transfer to Germany and his detention by German authorities; Lakotta wrote that Abdiwali was barely able to understand the nature of the German criminal system and the penalties that he may be facing.[4] Lakotta described the conditions under which Abdiwali had resorted to piracy: he had been born into poverty; his parents passed away when he was four years old; his sisters died as well; and he was raised by other siblings but forced to fend for himself at the young age of ten. In addition, Abiwali was born into a lower caste or clan within the Somali society and as such, was essentially held in slave-like servitude by members of the higher clans. According to Lakotta, the purpose of the German juvenile justice system is to rehabilitate and re-educate juvenile offenders, so that they can become, once again, productive members of German society. In the context of the Abdiwali case—a piracy prosecution of a juvenile Somali suspect—Lakotta exposed the inherent difficulty of adequately applying the goals of German juvenile justice to a foreign-born suspect, accused of serious crimes yet unfamiliar with any aspects of German life and society. "Germany's juvenile criminal law stipulates that the goal of the punishment must be to educate the offender. But Abdiwali must first be able to learn German before he can be educated."[5] Lakotta thus questioned the utility of the Hamburg piracy trial and the adequacy of detaining someone as young and destitute as Abdiwali.

In addition to the Abdiwali case, the alleged age of thirteen, by one of the other suspects, was particularly problematic for the Hamburg court, because under German law individuals younger than fourteen cannot be held criminally liable.[6] However, according to witness testimony, in this particular piracy attack the alleged thirteen-year-old had personally used a grenade launcher! Thus, in light of the gravity of the alleged criminal action, coupled with the allegation of a particularly young age, below the age of minimum criminal responsibility under German law, it became critical for the German court to use adequate procedure

3 Beate Lakotta, *Torture? Execution? German Justice Through the Eyes of a Somali Pirate*, SPIEGEL ONLINE, April 7, 2011, available at www.spiegel.de/international/world/torture-execution-german-justice-through-the-eyes-of-a-somali-pirate-a-755340–2.html.

4 *Id.*

5 *Id.*

6 Phillips, *supra* note 1.

to accurately ascertain this, and other defendants' ages. The dilemma facing the German court has been accurately summarized as follows:

> If its [the court's] purpose is to demonstrate fairness and the rule of law, its treatment of the young defendants must be exemplary. It cannot treat an adolescent pirate from Somalia worse than it would treat a young offender from Germany.[7]

The court decided to initially presume that this defendant was at least fourteen, but ordered that medical tests be conducted in order to conclusively determine this defendant's actual age. Prosecutors relied on the testimony of a Dutch and a German expert, who testified, respectively, that this defendant was either fifteen or eighteen. The defendant's defense lawyers argued, in turn, that it was wrong to compare the physical development of a Somali youth to that of a western peer, because the two groups may grow at different rates.[8] Because of the uncertainty associated with the ages of this suspect, and of the remaining defendants, the German court decided to proceed with the trial under the rules of juvenile justice, on the theory that adopting this strategy would adequately protect the interests of all, including all those who claimed juvenile status.

German authorities then conducted a series of forensic tests on all defendants claiming juvenile status, such as bone X-rays, and used expert testimony to determine the age of the remaining four defendants alleging juvenile status. The expert testimony and associated medical and forensic tests were criticized in the German press because of their uncertain and ambiguous nature:

> The court spent several days deliberating over whether so-called growth plates, which are found in the bones of children and adolescents but not of adults, could be considered reliable indicators of age. When an expert on wrist bones from the University Medical Center Hamburg-Eppendorf was called to testify, he projected X-rays onto a screen in the courtroom. He proceeded to deliver a lecture on calcification in the sesamoid bone of the thumb, bone stages and skeleton age, percentile curves, sectional imaging and summation methods, the 20-bone method, point values and diagrams — all based on data obtained from Central Europeans. But does any of this apply to people of a different ethnicity, not to mention people who were malnourished and had to work hard from an early age?[9]

As described in the quote above, the Hamburg court relied on medical tests and expert testimony to ascertain the contested age of the four defendants. However,

7 Lakotta, *supra* note 3.

8 Karin Matussek, *Somalis Face Hamburg Court in First German Piracy Trial for Four Centuries*, BLOOMBERG, Nov. 22, 2010, available at www.bloomberg.com/news/articles/2010-11-22/ten-somalis-are-tried-in-hamburg-court-over-indian-ocean-pirate-attack.

9 Lakotta, *supra* note 3.

because of different growth rates and physical development associated with Somali youth as opposed to "western" youth, it is unclear as to how exact the results of such bone X-rays and other medical tests could be.

Despite the arguably inconclusive nature of such medical tests and testimony, the Hamburg court ultimately found in early 2012 that three of the defendants were of juvenile status.[10] These defendants were prosecuted under the German juvenile justice system, each facing the maximum penalty of ten years in prison, unlike the adult suspects who faced harsher penalties. Ultimately, the trial concluded in 2012, after an usually long period of almost two years, when the Hamburg court found all ten suspects guilty.[11] The ten accused were found guilty of two crimes under the German Criminal Code: attack on maritime traffic and abduction for the purpose of blackmail.[12] However, presumably because the defendants' ages remained unverifiable, the court handed down mild sentences to all. The three youngest defendants were given two-year sentences, and because they had already served time during pre-trial detention and the trial itself, these defendants were freed immediately. The juvenile pirates had, according to German juvenile justice standards, attended school during the lengthy trial; by all accounts, they were exemplary defendants who will remain in Germany and continue to attend school and receive other rehabilitative and educational services in order to fully integrate into German society. The remaining seven adult defendants were given sentences of six to seven years. It is unclear what will happen to these pirates, but in all likelihood, they will remain in Germany as well because Germany is bound by the principle of *non-refoulement*, under international human rights law. Under this principle, Germany cannot transfer anyone to a third state if there is a danger that the transferee will be mistreated by the authorities of the place of transfer.[13]

In sum, it is unclear how successful the Germany piracy prosecution was; this uncertainty is particularly highlighted by the difficulties that the German prosecuting authorities encountered with respect to the suspects' juvenile age allegation. The age determination procedures were lengthy, expensive, and ultimately led to inconclusive results. According to Lakotta,

> Four judges, four lay judges, two prosecutors, 10 other court employees, 20 defense attorneys and three Somali language interpreters — along with numerous expert witnesses on subjects including conditions in war-torn Somalia, the estimation of age through carpal bone analysis, bullet holes and the Urdu language — have jointly managed to bring to light no more than

10 *German Prosecutor Urges Jail in Somali Piracy Trial*, REUTERS, Jan. 25, 2012, available at http://af.reuters.com/article/somaliaNews/idAFL5E8CP3HR20120125.

11 This piracy trial was the longest German criminal trial since the Second World War. Drumbl, *supra* note 2, at 16.

12 Phillips, *supra* note 1.

13 For a detailed discussion of applicable international human rights law, *see supra* Chapter 3.

> what was known from the start — after all, the 10 defendants were caught red-handed by Dutch marines who stormed the ship.[14]

The German authorities, similar to the authorities of other prosecuting nations, such as Spain, and Italy, described below, used medical procedures to determine piracy suspects' ages. Unfortunately, it appears that these procedures were less successful in Germany and led to inconclusive results, causing the Hamburg court to deliver mild sentences to all suspects involved. The section below will discuss a similar approach adopted by Spanish prosecuting authorities when faced with the issue of juvenile age claims by Somali piracy suspects.

Spain

In 2009, Spanish naval authorities captured a young suspect, named Cabdiwell Cabdullahl, and better known by his nickname, Abdu Willy. Abdu Willy and another Somali man were captured by Spanish naval forces in the Indian Ocean on October 4, 2009, two days after the hijacking of the Spanish trawler *Alarkana*.[15] Both suspects were transferred to Madrid, and Spanish authorities planned to charge both with piracy offenses.

Early in the case, Abdu Willy claimed juvenile status, which complicated prosecutorial plans because uncertainty arose as to whether this defendant should be prosecuted under special provisions of Spanish juvenile justice law, as opposed to facing charges in regular court with the other piracy defendant.[16] The judge initially ordered that Abdu Willy be placed under detention in a juvenile facility operated by the Spanish juvenile justice system—presumably in order to comply with provisions of human rights law, which obligate Spain to afford special protections to juvenile suspects, as discussed above in Chapter 3. A first battery of medical and forensic tests, including X-rays of the defendant's wrist bones, indicated that the defendant was at least seventeen; in light of these tests, Judge Pedraz, presiding over the Madrid court, ordered that the defendant be released.[17] Under Spanish law, juveniles can be prosecuted under special provisions of Spanish juvenile law, but typically only for territorial offenses involving specific crimes, such as terrorism. It remained unclear whether Abdu Willy, a potentially juvenile suspect accused of the extra-territorial offense of piracy could be lawfully prosecuted by Spanish juvenile courts. Judge Pedraz, upon releasing Abdu Willy, ordered additional tests, including a dental examination, in order to achieve a

14 Beate Lakotta, *An Expensive Farce: Germany's Somali Pirate Trial is Pointless*, SPIEGEL ONLINE, Sept. 12, 2012, available at www.spiegel.de/international/germany/german-trial-of-somali-pirates-turns-into-pointless-and-expensive-farce-a-855252.html.

15 FOX NEWS, *Somali Pirate Suspect in Legal Limbo in Spain*, October 21, 2009, available at www.foxnews.com/story/2009/10/21/somali-pirate-suspect-in-legal-limbo-in-spain.html.

16 *Id.*

17 *Id.*

more complete age assessment over the defendant. The uncertainty related to Abdu Willy's prosecution was referred to by the Spanish press as "a soap opera . . . that seems to have no end."[18] It can thus be observed that the Spanish press, like its German counterpart, was critical of a piracy trial involving a Somali suspect claiming juvenile status.

After Abdu Willy was initially released by Judge Pedraz, the juvenile section of the Madrid court ordered a series of medical and forensic tests on the defendant over a two-week period. After these tests were analyzed, the court ultimately concluded that the initial test results—indicating that the defendant was at least seventeen—had been overcome and that the defendant was in fact over the age of eighteen.[19] The court based this determination primarily on the defendant's height and weight, as well as X-rays of his clavicle bone and left hand, which all indicated that he was most likely not a juvenile.[20] The Spanish court thus used forensic procedures to ascertain a piracy suspect's age. Defendant Willy, as well as his co-defendant, was sentenced to a particularly lengthy sentence of 439 years in prison. The lengthy sentence was most likely based upon the gravity of the charges levied against the defendants, but under Spanish law, the defendants will only serve thirty years out of the entire sentence. "The hefty sentence stems from illegally detaining 36 crew members in addition to 11 years for each count of piracy. However, court officials have indicated that the maximum time each pirate will serve is likely not more than 30 years."[21] It appears that defendant Willy was sentenced to the same lengthy sentence as his co-defendant after the court rejected Willy's juvenile status claim and proceeded to treat him as an adult.

Thus, Spanish authorities, like German courts described above, resorted to medical and forensic tests to ascertain the suspect's contested age. In both Germany and Spain, the age determination tests appeared somewhat inconclusive and heavily criticized by the local press. In Spain, unlike in Germany, the court rejected the juvenile status claim and found that the defendant was an adult. The Spanish prosecution thus resulted in the imposition of a much heavier sentence, perhaps because of the adult age determination. The section below will describe a similar Somali piracy prosecution involving juvenile suspects conducted in Italy.

Italy

Italian prosecuting authorities encountered the same issue of the treatment of juvenile piracy suspects during Italy's first modern piracy trial. On October 10, 2011, the Italian-flagged cargo ship, *Montecristo*, was attacked by a group of

18 *Id.*

19 Lauren Hahn, *Juvenile Justice and Piracy: Prosecutions of Juvenile Pirates in the United States*, GEO. MASON L. REV. 241, 257–58 (2012).

20 *Id.*

21 JURIST, *Spain Court Sentences Somali Pirates to 439 Years*, May 3, 2011, available at http://jurist.org/paperchase/2011/05/spain-court-sentences-somali-pirates-to-439-years.php.

Somali pirates approximately 600 miles off the Somali coast. At the time of the attack, the *Montecristo* was en route to Yemen transporting goods from Liverpool, United Kingdom, to Vietnam. The Somali pirates approached the *Montecristo* from two skiffs and a mother ship, firing at the vessel before successfully boarding it. The *Montecristo* crew sought refuge in a fortified citadel on board the vessel, from which it could control the engine and continue steering. Approximately twenty-four hours after the attack, the *Montecristo* and its crew were rescued by United Kingdom and United States naval forces in a North Atlantic Treaty Organization (NATO) Ocean Shield operation.[22] The piracy suspects ultimately surrendered, were arrested on board another Italian vessel participating in the NATO operation, and eleven suspects were transferred to Italy for prosecution.[23]

Several of the eleven piracy suspects alleged to be juvenile; the Italian court determined that four out of eleven were juveniles. The Italian court reached this age determination based on the report of a medical forensic expert.[24] Although the public defender demanded the ordering of new forensic tests for age determination purposes over all of the defendants, the court rejected this request. It is unclear what methods the expert used in order to determine that some suspects were juvenile and others not—presumably, the expert conducted medical, dental, and other forensic tests to reach this conclusion. It is possible that the expert did not conduct any detailed tests and based his or her results on a simple physical examination of the suspects. The latter assertion may be supported by the fact that the defense counsel contested the court's conclusion regarding the age determination and asked for the ordering of additional medical and forensic tests.[25] The court rejected this demand and instead adopted the expert's conclusion that some of the suspects were juvenile and others not.

The juveniles were then separated from their adult co-defendants and prosecuted separately, in the Italian juvenile court, *Tribunale dei Minori*. The adult pirates were prosecuted in the criminal division of Rome's Third Circuit Court, the *Settore Penale della Terza Corte d'Assise*.[26] Ultimately, the adult pirates were convicted and sentenced to lengthy sixteen and nineteen-year prison terms.[27] The juveniles were sentenced to eight years in prison by the Juvenile Court in

22 Matteo Crippa, *Historic Piracy Trial Opens in Italy*, COMMUNIS HOSTIS OMNIUM, March 27, 2012, available at http://piracy-law.com/2012/03/27/historic-piracy-trial-opens-in-italy/.

23 RNW MEDIA, *High-seas Drama at Somali Piracy Trial in Italy*, available at www.rnw.org/archive/high-seas-drama-somali-piracy-trial-italy.

24 LETTERA22.IT, *A Roma il primo processo contro presunti pirati Somali* (March 23, 2012), available at www.lettera22.it/showart.php?id=12138&rubrica=122 (in Italian).

25 *Id.*

26 Brandon Gatto, *Italy Court Orders Trial for Accused Somali Pirates*, JURIST (February 21, 2012), available at http://jurist.org/paperchase/2012/02/italy-court-orders-trial-for-accused-somali-pirates.php.

27 Enzo Mangini, *Somali Pirates Sentenced*, MAR. SECURITY REV. (November 28, 2012), available at www.marsecreview.com/2012/11/somali-pirates-sentenced/.

Rome, on charges of attempted hijacking of the crew of the *Montecristo* with the purpose of taking ransom.[28]

The Italian authorities, like their German and Spanish counterparts, used forensic expertise to determine the suspects' age; it is unclear which types of tests the Italian court ordered and actually used in the age determination process. It may be that the Italian authorities did not order a full range of medical, dental, and forensic tests and instead relied simply on the expert opinion of the forensic scientists employed by the Italian court. The Italian authorities, like German courts, found that some of the suspects were juveniles and prosecuted these individuals separately, under Italian provisions of juvenile justice law. As in Germany, light sentences imposed on juvenile pirates were most likely reflective of Italian adherence to international human rights standards, requiring such lenient treatment for juveniles. The section below will discuss a piracy prosecution conducted in France, where a suspect also claimed juvenile status.

France

France encountered the issue of child piracy in 2008, when a group of six pirates hijacked a French-flagged vessel, *Carre d'As*. The yacht had been under the command of a couple traveling from Australia to France when it was attacked and successfully hijacked by a group of Somali pirates.[29] Four days later, a French frigate arrived at the scene and started trailing the hijacked yacht. The pirates were able to dock the *Carre d'As* in Puntland, along the Somali coast; they then demanded a two-million dollar ransom from the French government in exchange for the release of the two hostages. The French government refused to negotiate and instead launched a rescue operation. A team of thirty French commandos was parachuted into the Indian Ocean, to the vicinity of the hijacked yacht. The French commandos swam up to the yacht and were able to board it and overtake it by surprise. The French military team successfully captured most of the Somali pirates on board the hijacked yacht.[30]

Six of the Somali pirates involved in this incident were transferred to France for prosecution. The trial began almost three years later, and one of the six defendants claimed to have been under the age of eighteen at the time of the piracy attack. It is unclear how the French court determined this defendant's age, but it appears that the court accepted this claim and consequently transferred the

28 Enzo Mangini, *Landmark Somali Trial Climaxes*, THE ITALIAN INSIDER (July 3, 2012), available at www.italianinsider.it/?q=node/1084.

29 Bellish, Jon, *The Issue of Juvenile Piracy* 289, *in* PROSECUTING MARITIME PIRACY: DOMESTIC SOLUTIONS TO INTERNATIONAL CRIMES (Scharf *et al.* eds. 2015).

30 MARINE LOG, *Court Tells France to Pay Damages to Somali Pirates* (Dec. 5, 2014), available at www.marinelog.com/index.php?option=com_k2&view=item&id=8373:court-tells-france-to-pay-damages-to-somali-pirates&Itemid=230.

entire trial, of all six defendants, to a juvenile court.[31] As an additional measure of protection toward the juvenile defendant, the court initially planned to hold *in camera* audiences, but the juvenile suspect's attorney, at his client's request, demanded that the trial be made public.[32] The court's willingness to protect the privacy rights of the allegedly juvenile defendant may indicate that the French prosecuting authorities had firmly accepted the juvenile status claim by one of the suspects.

It appears that the lengthy pre-trial phase was problematic in this case. Although each defendant was held separately, including the juvenile defendant, it appears that French authorities had difficulty finding appropriate Somali language interpreters, and that some defendants encountered inmate violence during their pre-trial detention.[33] This type of lengthy pre-trial detention is particularly problematic in the context of the one juvenile defendant—as discussed above in Chapter 3, international human rights law attempts to minimize the amount of time juvenile suspects have to be incarcerated as a punitive measure, and only allows for pre-trial detention as a matter of last resort. In fact, Article 37 of the Convention on the Rights of the Child provides that "[t]he arrest, detention or imprisonment of a child shall be in conformity with the law and shall be used only as a measure of last resort and for the shortest appropriate period of time."[34] Jon Bellish has argued that "[l]egal norms, related to the pre-trial detention of juveniles state that such detention should be a last resort, of the shortest possible duration, and in an area separate from adults" but that "[t]he appropriate length of duration [of pre-trial detention] on shore will be driven primarily by the jurisdiction's experience in prosecuting pirates and the complexity of the legal issues at hand."[35] It is thus possible that France violated its human rights obligations when it held the juvenile piracy suspect in pre-trial detention for over two years. In fact, France was ultimately held liable, by the European Court of Human Rights, for violations of Articles 5-1 and 5-3 of the European Convention on Human Rights, which guarantee the right to liberty and security, for not having transferred the arrested piracy suspects to a French investigative judge within forty-eight hours of their arrival in France.[36] According to this holding by the European Court of Human Rights, France also violated the rights of the juvenile suspect when this suspect was not promptly transferred to the investigative judge upon his arrival in France. It can be argued that, in light of existing international human rights law on the treatment of juvenile suspects,

31 BBC NEWS, *Somali Pirates Jailed in France for Kidnapping Couple* (Nov. 30, 2011), available at www.bbc.com/news/world-africa-15976883.

32 Bellish, *supra* note 29, at 289.

33 Bellish, *supra* note 29, at 289. It is unclear whether the juvenile suspect encountered violence as well during pre-trial detention.

34 Convention on the Rights of the Child, art. 37, *opened for signature* Nov. 20, 1989, 1577 U.N.T.S. 44 (entered into force on Sept. 2, 1990).

35 Bellish, *supra* note 29, at 286.

36 *Somali pirates jailed in France*, *supra* note 31.

described in Chapter 3 above, this violation is particularly problematic in the context of the juvenile defendant.

At the trial itself, the prosecutor asked for sentences ranging between eight and sixteen years, with the lowest sentence of eight years reserved for the juvenile suspect.[37] Ultimately, the court convicted five out of the six defendants, including the juvenile, and imposed sentences ranging between four and eight years. Unsurprisingly, the juvenile defendant received the lowest four-year sentence.

The prosecuting authorities of France, like those in Germany, Spain, and Italy, were forced to conduct age determination proceedings to ascertain the age of a piracy suspect claiming juvenile status. While the French court accepted one defendant's juvenile status, it is unclear how the French court reached this conclusion and whether it ordered any medical or forensic tests. The French court, like those in Germany and Italy, imposed a light sentence on the juvenile pirate, in accordance with French obligations under international human rights law.

Conclusion

The German, Spanish, Italian, and French prosecutions of piracy suspects claiming juvenile status are somewhat similar. It appears that in Germany, Spain, and Italy, prosecuting authorities initially accepted the defendants' claim that they were under the age of eighteen, but ordered medical and forensic testing in order to more objectively ascertain their actual age. In both Germany and Spain, medical tests offered somewhat inconclusive results, causing the press in each of these countries to decry these piracy prosecutions as ineffective or speculative. The German court determined that some suspects were juvenile, while the Spanish court rejected the juvenile status claim by the only suspect raising this issue. In Italy, it is unclear what types of forensic tests the court used to ascertain the defendants' age, but as in Germany, the court determined that some suspects were indeed juvenile. In France, it is unclear whether the court ordered any medical or forensic testing, but the court ultimately found that one of the suspects was a juvenile. All prosecuting courts, where juvenile status claims by some suspects were accepted, separated those cases and tried them in juvenile court (in Germany, Italy, and France). All prosecuting courts however ultimately convicted almost all piracy suspects, including juveniles (in France, one of the non-juvenile suspects was found not guilty). In Germany, Italy, and France, those whose juvenile status was accepted by the courts were given particularly lenient sentences. In Germany, the juvenile pirates were immediately released into German society, in light of pre-trial detention time already served, with the goal of rehabilitating them within Germany. In Spain, the defendant was found to be an adult and was given the same lengthy 439-year sentence as his adult co-defendant, presumably because the court rejected the juvenile status claim and treated both defendants equally.

37 *Somali pirates jailed in France*, *supra* note 31.

The above discussion and conclusions demonstrate that European countries, such as Germany, Spain, Italy, and France, take their obligations under international human rights law seriously and are willing to at least attempt to address juvenile status claims by Somali piracy suspects, by conducting court ordered medical procedures to ascertain each defendant's contested age. However, the above discussion also demonstrates the uncertainty and complexity that the prosecuting authorities of these European nations faced in these cases—because medical age determinations often lead to inconclusive results, it appears that the German, Spanish, Italian, and French courts were initially willing to conduct all proceedings in juvenile court or under the rules of juvenile justice, to ensure that nobody's rights were offended under human rights law. This approach can be inefficient and unfair, leading to the preferential treatment of all suspects, including adults, who are not entitled to the same protection as juveniles under human rights law. It is thus important for all piracy prosecuting nations, including these European countries, to develop particular legal regimes and policies that will apply to all piracy cases involving juvenile suspects. Such a legal regime, which will be developed in more detail in Chapter 9 below, would include the imposition of mandatory medial and forensic tests for all those claiming juvenile status, age presumptions developed based on the results of such medical and forensic tests, the application of specific juvenile justice procedures to those found to be juvenile, and the development of rehabilitative and educational punishments, which would allow juvenile pirates to become productive members of either Somali or other nations' societies at the conclusion of their incarceration. If piracy prosecuting nations developed specific legal regimes and policies for the prosecution of cases involving juvenile suspects, this would lead toward more efficient prosecutions and toward a preferential treatment of all juvenile piracy suspects.

7 Recent National Prosecutions of Juvenile Suspects

Non-European Nations (India, Malaysia, and the Seychelles)

Introduction

Governments of non-European nations have encountered the issue of child piracy as well. Recently, the courts of India, Malaysia, and the Seychelles have handled cases involving juvenile piracy suspects. It appears that Indian courts have used medical and forensic testing to ascertain the suspects' ages, but it is unclear that Malaysian and Seychellois authorities have resorted to using such tests. All courts, in India, Malaysia, and the Seychelles, have accepted some juvenile status claims; in these instances, juveniles have been treated preferentially. In India, juvenile suspects are typically prosecuted under special juvenile justice laws, and such suspects are detained separately from adults. In Malaysia, it is unclear that adult and juvenile suspects face different legal regimes, but it appears that juveniles have received more lenient sentences and that Malaysian authorities have been taking into account the suspects' young age during the sentencing phase. In the Seychelles, judges have attempted to separate juvenile suspects from adults and to treat the former distinctly, by imposing more lenient sentences on juvenile pirates and by, in some instances of particularly young age, refusing to impose individual criminal responsibility against them at all. This chapter will discuss piracy prosecutions involving juvenile suspects in India, Malaysia, and the Seychelles. This chapter will conclude that, like European nations, these piracy-prosecuting countries ought to develop specific legal and policy regimes toward the treatment of juvenile piracy suspects.

India

The government of India has encountered the problem of child piracy, but its lack of specific domestic legislation on piracy has inhibited piracy cases from being resolved. According to an Indian official, "Indian legal system lacks clear and unambiguous mechanism to prosecute maritime pirates."[1] India currently lacks

1 Ranjit Sinha, *India Lacks Legal System To Prosecute Pirates*, THE ECONOMIC TIMES (Sept. 24, 2014), available at http://articles.economictimes.indiatimes.com/2014-09-24/news/54279757_1_indian-navy-indian-ocean-cbi-director-ranjit-sinha.

a criminal provision on maritime piracy; instead, India prosecutes piracy suspects for attempted murder under the Indian Penal Code or the Suppression of Unlawful Acts against Safety of Maritime Navigation and Fixed Platform on Continental Shelf Act of 2002.[2] A maritime piracy bill had been introduced to the Indian Parliament in April 2012, but as of today that bill has not become law. If passed, this law would impose a maximum penalty of fourteen years in prison plus a fine, for the crime of piracy. In addition, this bill would impose capital punishment for the crime of piracy, if a victim is killed during the commission of this crime.[3] The absence of specific piracy laws in India poses significant hurdles in the prosecution of all pirates, and in particular, when it comes to the treatment and potential prosecution of juvenile suspects.

After *Vega 5* and *Al-Murtuza*, two fishing and cargo ships, were hijacked in 2010 by the Somali pirates, the Indian Navy arrested the pirates involved. The piracy suspects were detained at a detention facility in Mumbai, India. Presumably because some of the suspects appeared very young, India's Deputy Director General of Shipping sent a letter to Indian police stating that some of the pirates were juvenile and should be prosecuted under Indian juvenile justice laws. In response, the Indian government selected nineteen suspects for age verification procedures, which included "bone, teeth and other tests."[4] According to these tests, nine out of nineteen suspects were confirmed to be adults; it is unclear what happened to the remaining ten.[5]

In addition to the above-mentioned incident, the Indian media reported on three additional captures of Somali piracy suspects, including juveniles, by the Indian naval forces. In January and February 2011, Indian forces captured a total of forty-three pirates, among whom were "a few youngsters," according to media accounts.[6] In May 2011, the Indian navy captured sixty-one suspected Somali pirates, twenty-five of whom were suspected of being fifteen years of age or younger, and four of whom were estimated as being younger than eleven.[7] In all likelihood, the presence of juvenile piracy suspects among other pirates detained by Indian forces will complicate prosecutions in Indian national courts. "With India's legal system grappling with the absence of a specific provision dealing with piracy in the Indian Penal Code (IPC), the presence of "child pirates" will further complicate matters."[8] In sum, as of June 2011, according to media

2 Bellish, Jon, *The Issue of Juvenile Piracy* 291, *in* PROSECUTING MARITIME PIRACY: DOMESTIC SOLUTIONS TO INTERNATIONAL CRIMES (Scharf *et al.* eds. 2015).

3 Sanjeet Ruhal, *The Piracy Bill 2012: A Solution or Mere Paper Tiger?*, MARITIME GATEWAY, (Apr. 23, 2014).

4 *Id.*

5 *Id.*

6 Rajat Pandit, *25 of 61 Pirates Arrested by Navy at Sea Are Children Below 15 Yrs.*, THE TIMES OF INDIA (Mar. 17, 2011), available at http://timesofindia.indiatimes.com/india/25-of-61-pirates-arrested-by-Navy-at-sea-are-children-below-15-yrs/articleshow/7723224.cms.

7 *Id.*

8 *Id.*

reports the Indian authorities had arrested a total of 106 suspected pirates in various raids; it is unclear how many in total had claimed juvenile status.[9]

Under Indian law, a juvenile's rights are protected under India's Juvenile Justice Act of 2000.[10] This act provides for the "best interest of the child" approach, and requires the creation of separate "observation homes" to be used during the pre-trial detention phase. In addition, this act stipulates that penal detention should only be used in the case of a serious offense and as a measure of last resort, and it proscribes the application of the harshest sentences, such as the death penalty or life in prison without the possibility of parole.[11] This act would apply to all juvenile piracy suspects, if their status as juvenile is accepted by the prosecuting authorities. However, Indian media has reported on persistent problems within the Indian juvenile justice system regarding age determination procedures.[12] According to the Juvenile Justice Act, courts in India are supposed to refer suspects who claim juvenile status to appropriate medical boards for medical and forensic testing, in the absence of documentary evidence, such as birth certificates.[13] Thus, under Indian law piracy suspects claiming juvenile status are entitled to appropriate medical examinations in order to determine their age. Indian judges, however, routinely forgo the ordering of such medical age determinations, and suspects are at times treated as adults, in the absence of such procedures. It is possible that Indian authorities will choose not to order necessary medical and forensic tests on piracy suspects claiming juvenile status, and it may be that juvenile piracy suspects' rights will not be adequately protected within the Indian justice system.

In sum, it appears that Indian authorities have accepted juvenile status claims by some suspects after ordering medical and forensic tests to reach specific age determinations. It is unclear, however, which tests have been used on juvenile piracy suspects, why some juvenile status claims have been rejected, and what the status of piracy prosecutions in Indian courts is as of today. According to one media account, 120 pirates have indicated their willingness to plead guilty in one court case, but it appears that these suspects were all adults.[14] It is unclear as of today what the status of juvenile suspects' cases is, and whether any juvenile suspects have already been convicted in Indian courts. Thus, it is impossible to

9 Mateen Hafeez, *Tests on Pirates to Determine Age*, TIMES OF INDIA (June 21, 2011), available at http://timesofindia.indiatimes.com/city/mumbai/Tests-on-pirates-to-determine-age/articleshow/8930959.cms.

10 The Juvenile Justice (Care and Protection of Children) Act (India, Dec. 30, 2000).

11 *Id.* Articles 8, 15.

12 Meera Vankipuram, *Juvenile Bill: Experts Claim Age Determination is Biggest Hurdle*, TIMES OF INDIA (Dec. 28, 2015), available at http://timesofindia.indiatimes.com/city/chennai/Juvenile-bill-Experts-claim-age-determination-is-biggest-hurdle/articleshow/50347863.cms.

13 *Id.*

14 Rebecca Samervel, *120 Somali Pirates Want to Plead Guilty in Court*, TIMES OF INDIA (Nov. 6, 2015), available at http://timesofindia.indiatimes.com/city/mumbai/120-Somali-pirates-want-to-plead-guilty-in-court/articleshow/49680010.cms.

ssess whether Indian authorities have complied with human rights law in their treatment of juvenile piracy suspects. The section below will discuss piracy prosecutions involving juvenile suspects in Malaysia.

Malaysia

Malaysian authorities prosecuted several juvenile piracy suspects in connection with the hijacking of a chemical tanker, *MV Bunga Laurel*, in the Gulf of Aden.[15] Although the captured piracy suspects included adults and three juveniles, Malaysian authorities decided to prosecute the entire group together, in a single criminal case.[16] Thus, unlike their German, Spanish, Italian, and French counterparts, as described above in Chapter 6, Malaysian authorities did not prosecute juvenile suspects in a distinct juvenile justice jurisdiction. It is unclear how Malaysian authorities determined the age of these piracy suspects, and whether any medical or forensic testing was used. It may be that Malaysian authorities simply accepted the three suspects' juvenile status claim, if they appeared particularly youthful. It is possible, however, that Malaysian authorities did use medical and forensic testing. As of the present, no information is available regarding this issue.

Under Malaysian law, an individual who fires a gun with the intent to injure another during the commission of a crime faces the death penalty. Thus, under Malaysian law, all piracy suspects, if they fired a gun, could potentially be eligible for capital punishment.[17] In this case, Malaysian prosecutors confirmed early on in the proceedings that the juveniles would not face the most severe penalty of execution due to their young age. Ultimately, all suspects, adult and juvenile, pleaded guilty in order to avoid the death penalty or life imprisonment.[18] A Malaysian court sentenced the three juvenile piracy defendants to a lesser sentence of eight years, while imposing a longer sentence of ten years on the adult suspects, presumably handing down the lesser sentence to juveniles on account of their age.[19] Thus, although it is unclear how Malaysian authorities determined the suspects' age, and although juvenile suspects in this case were prosecuted alongside their adult partners in crime, without having the benefit and protections of provisions of juvenile justice, Malaysian authorities did take into account the suspects' juvenile status in the sentencing phase.

The section below will discuss piracy prosecutions involving juvenile suspects in the Seychelles.

15 *See* Andrea Bottorff, *Malaysia Court Charges Suspected Somali Pirates*, JURIST (Feb. 11, 2011), http://jurist.org/paperchase/2011/02/malaysia-court-charges-suspected-somali-pirates.php.

16 J.T. Quigley, *Pirates Plead Guilty in Malaysian Navy Shooting*, THE DIPLOMAT (Sept. 3, 2013), http://thediplomat.com/asean-beat/2013/09/03/pirates-plead-guilty-in-malaysian-navy-shooting/.

17 *Id; see also* Act 37: Firearms (Increased Penalties) Act of 1971, art. 3 (Aug. 30, 1971, last amended Mar. 27, 2006).

18 *Id.*

19 Hidir Reduan, *Malaysia: Seven Somali Pirates Sentenced*, HIIRAAN ONLINE, Sept. 4, 2013.

The Seychelles

The Seychelles is an Indian Ocean island nation, which has since 2008 prosecuted over a hundred Somali piracy suspects pursuant to various transfer agreements with large maritime nations and the European Union, as discussed above in Chapter 2. The Seychelles' judges and prosecutors have encountered several cases involving juveniles.

In two earlier cases, the Seychellois court did not differentiate between juvenile and adult defendants and sentenced all convicted defendants to the same lengthy term in prison. In fact, in *Republic v. Mohamed Aweys Sayid et al.*, seven of the nine defendants found guilty of piracy claimed that they were younger than eighteen.[20] The court noted the defendants' alleged juvenile age, but determined that all the defendants had the requisite *mens rea* for the commission of the offense of piracy. The court proceeded to prosecute all defendants, children and adults alike, in a Seychellois criminal court, and then sentenced all pirates—juveniles and adults alike—to a lengthy sentence of thirty-two years in prison, with ten of those years running concurrently.[21] In *Republic v. Houssein Mohammed Osman & 10 Others*, the court noted the defendants' young age in the judgment, confirming that the investigation process and joint arraignment between adult and juvenile defendants were conducted pursuant to Seychellois law on juvenile defendants.[22] The court accepted that some of the defendants were under the age of eighteen, but concluded that in light of the gravity of the committed crime of maritime piracy, all defendants would receive the same sentence of sixteen years in prison, with six years running concurrently.[23] Thus, it appears that in these early cases, the age of the accused piracy suspect did not serve as a mitigating factor. "The lack of discussion on alternate sentencing for convicted minors further suggests that the Court did not seriously consider the young age of the accused."[24]

In subsequent cases, the Seychellois courts appeared to attempt to differentiate between juvenile and adult suspects, and to impose more lenient sentences on the former. One of seven juvenile pirates from the *Sayid* case, mentioned above, appealed his conviction to a Seychellois appellate jurisdiction (the other convicted juvenile pirates had accepted a repatriation to Somalia and were thus not parties to this appeal).[25] This juvenile pirate appealed his sentence, claiming that the trial

20 Republic v. Mohamed Aweys Sayid, Criminal Side No. 19, Sentencing Judgment, 2 (Dec. 15, 2010).

21 *Id.*

22 Republic v. Houssein Mohammed Osman, Criminal Side No. 19, para. 12 (Seychelles Oct. 12, 2011).

23 *Id.*

24 Danielle Fritz, *Child Pirates from Somalia: A Call for the International Community to Support the Further Development of Juvenile Justice Systems in Puntland and Somaliland*, 44 CASE W. RES. J. INT'L L. 891, 903 (2012).

25 Sayid v. R, Case No: SCA 2 of 2011, [2013] SCCA 24, Dec. 6, 2013, available at www.seylii.org/sc/judgment/court-appeal/2013/24.

court had erred in ordering that portions of the sentence run consecutively. The appellate court, on its own, raised the issue of juvenile status—that this defendant's rights as a juvenile suspect were not respected by the trial court because he was prosecuted as an adult, with other adults, without regard to any specific provisions of Seychellois juvenile justice law, such as the Children Act. The appellate court thus overturned this suspect's conviction.

The appellate judges held that they were "somewhat dismayed by the fact that the Court of its own volition had to raise the issue of the provisions of the Children Act."[26] In other words, it appears that the appellate court itself raised the argument that the juvenile suspect's rights, in this case, had not been respected under the Seychellois Children Act, which provides for preferential treatment of all juvenile suspects. Under section 92(1) of the Children Act, juvenile suspects are not subject to criminal prosecution unless they are charged with murder or another offense carrying the death penalty, or upon special request by the Attorney General.[27] In addition, under Section 94(2), "[n]o young person shall be sentenced to imprisonment if he can be suitably dealt with in any other way provided for under this Act."[28] Finally, section 95(1) outlines the ways in which a young offender can be punished; these include conditional discharges, probation orders, and committal orders to Juvenile Centers and imprisonment.[29] In this case, the defendant's young age and juvenile status were never disputed and appeared to have been accepted by the prosecution and noted as such. In light of the defendant's juvenile status, as well as such status by other defendants prosecuted in the same case, the appellate court concluded as follows:

> We cannot understand how charges were preferred against a number of children ranging from the ages of 13 to 16 without counsel for either party, nor for that matter the trial Judge bringing their attention to the provisions of the Children Act. These are grave criminal offences but this serious lapse cannot be condoned by the highest court and court of last resort in Seychelles whose duty it is to see that the rights of accused persons as protected by the Constitution are upheld and that justice is done, especially so when the appellant in this case is a vulnerable young person.[30]

As stated above, the appellate court overturned the juvenile defendant's conviction. This appellate ruling demonstrates that Seychellois appellate judges seemed concerned with some of the piracy suspects' young ages, and wished to ensure that

26 *Id.* at para. 5.

27 Law of Seychelles, Chapter 28, Children Act, Section 92(1), available at http://greybook.seylii.org/se/CAP28#!fragment//KGhhc2g6KGNodW5rxIVhbsSHb3JUZXh0OicnKSxsZWZ0UMSNZU5vdGVJZMSWJyxuxKNlc1F1ZXJ5xKgsc2Nyb2xsQ8SIxIo6IW7EtWVhcsSHxK/EscSzxJfFgsWExIdTxJB0QsSzUkVMRVZBTkNFLHRhYjp0b2MpKQ==.

28 *Id.* Section 94(2).

29 *Id.* Section 95(1).

30 Sayid v. R., *supra* note 25, at para. 5.

lower trial jurisdictions would protect juvenile suspects' rights under specific juvenile justice provisions of Seychelles' law.

In subsequent trial cases, Seychellois judges appeared to differentiate between juvenile and adult defendants, at least in the sentencing phase. In *Republic v. Liban Mohamed Dahir & Twelve Others*, Justice Duncan Gaswaga of the Seychelles Supreme Court sentenced three juvenile pirates aged fourteen, sixteen, and seventeen to two and a half years in prison.[31] In the same case, Justice Gaswaga determined that an eleven-year-old defendant could not face individual criminal responsibility under Seychellois law; this defendant was released. Justice Gaswaga also held that a twelve-year-old defendant could not be prosecuted in the Seychelles because of his young age; this juvenile was conditionally released back into the custody of his relatives in Somalia without facing any criminal penalty.[32] Adult defendants convicted of piracy in the same case were sentenced to thirty years—a lengthy sentence that reflected the harsh treatment imposed by Justice Gaswaga on those who employ juvenile pirates.[33] In the words of Justice Gaswaga, "[t]he seriousness of the offence of the adult accused person is aggravated by the recruitment of juveniles whom they ought to have taken care of and guide instead of encouraging them to get involved in criminal activities."[34] In another case, *Republic v. Mohamed Abdi Jama & Six Others*, Justice Gaswaga sentenced all adult piracy suspects to seven years in prison and sentenced one juvenile pirate to two years, presumably taking into consideration his young age.[35] In both the *Liban* and *Jama* cases, prosecutors chose not to challenge the defenses' assertion that various defendants were below the age of eighteen, and in both cases Justice Gaswaga accepted arguments to treat such defendants as juveniles.[36] The defendants' ages were thus not disputed in these cases, and medical or forensic testing to ascertain the defendants' ages was unnecessary. It is likely that in the *Liban* and *Jama* cases the defendants' age remained uncontested because they were particularly young, and their claims of juvenile status appeared reasonable.

In sum, it appears that in many Seychelles' piracy prosecutions some suspects have claimed juvenile status, and that Seychellois judges have, for the most part, accepted such juvenile status claims without ordering medical and forensic testing. It is unclear whether most of these juvenile suspects have appeared particularly

31 Republic v. Liban Mohamed Dahir & Twelve Others, Sentence, Crim. Side No. 7 of 2012 [16] (Supreme Ct. Sey. 2012).

32 *Id.*

33 *Id* at 18.

34 *Id.* at 19.

35 Republic v. Mohamed Abdi Jama & Six Others, Sentence, Crim. Side No. 53 of 2011 [6] (Supreme Ct. Sey. 2012).

36 Republic v. Liban Mohamed Dahir & Twelve Others, Judgment, Crim. Side No. 7 of 2012 [11], [13], [41] (Supreme Ct. Sey. 2012) (noting its decision in the Jama case and finding that in the light of no prosecutorial challenge to the age issue and the lack of other evidence proving age, the court must accept that certain defendants were juveniles and could not be legally convicted); Jama case, *supra* note 35, at [6].

youthful, or if Seychellois prosecutors and judges had other reasons to accept juvenile status claims. Moreover, it appears that in early piracy prosecutions, trial judges were unwilling to treat juvenile piracy suspects distinctly from adult suspects. This defect may have been corrected in the *Sayid* appellate judgment, discussed above, where the appellate judges reprimanded their trial court colleagues about treating children without regard to Seychellois juvenile justice law. Subsequent trial court judgments involving juvenile piracy suspects appear to reserve preferential treatment for juvenile suspects. Although juvenile suspects were prosecuted together with adults in all Seychellois piracy prosecutions, in some cases trial judges have refused to impose criminal responsibility on particularly young defendants, or have imposed more lenient sentences on convicted juveniles. The Seychellois approach toward piracy prosecutions involving juvenile suspects may be globally in line with human rights law, because juvenile suspects seem to be treated more leniently than their adult counterparts. However, it remains unclear how Seychellois courts reach specific age determinations, in the absence of medical and forensic testing, and it remains unclear whether Seychellois prosecuting authorities will agree to prosecute juvenile suspects in separate juvenile jurisdictions, under specific provisions of the Children Act, discussed above.

Conclusion

Non-European nations of India, Malaysia, and the Seychelles, have encountered the problem of child piracy. Like European nations, these countries have attempted to address the issue of child piracy through different forms of preferential treatment extended to juvenile suspects. In Malaysia and the Seychelles, this preferential treatment seems to consist of the imposition of more lenient sentences against juvenile suspects, and on the courts' willingness, in the Seychelles, to reject any imposition of individual criminal responsibility on particularly young juvenile suspects. In India, it is unclear whether any prosecutions of juvenile suspects have actually ended or resulted in criminal sentences. In addition, it appears that at least one of these nations, India, is willing to separate cases involving juvenile suspects and to prosecute those in separate juvenile justice jurisdictions. As of now, it seems that Malaysia and the Seychelles prosecute juvenile suspects in regular criminal courts, together with adult piracy suspects. Finally, it appears that one of these nations, India, has used medical and forensic testing to determine the suspects' actual age, once a juvenile status claim is raised. It remains unclear how Malaysia and the Seychelles conduct age determination procedures. In the Seychelles, the suspect's juvenile age is often uncontested, but it is uncertain as to why this is so.

These three nations, however, lack specific legal regimes and policy for the treatment of juvenile piracy suspects. It would be beneficial for these nations, as for European nations, as discussed in the previous chapter, to develop appropriate legal rules and policy guidance, which would apply to all piracy prosecutions involving juvenile suspects. The specifics of such proposed rules and policy will be discussed below, in Chapter 9.

8 Prosecuting Juvenile Piracy Suspects in the United States

Introduction

Over the past several years, the United States has prosecuted several piracy suspects in federal courts. In most instances, the prosecuted pirates attacked a United States vessel or somehow harmed American interests in another way. These prosecutions have sparked significant scholarly interest, and much of the emerging scholarship on piracy focuses on general issues pertaining to the prosecution of maritime piracy, such as universal jurisdiction, different modes of liability, such as attempts or conspiracy to commit piracy, appropriate sentencing of pirates, as well as best practices in prosecuting piracy suspects. Very little scholarly attention has been devoted thus far to the prosecution of juvenile piracy suspects in United States courts. This chapter will focus on recent American handlings of juvenile suspects, by discussing *United States v. Muse*[1] and *United States v. Hasan.*[2] In both cases, the courts essentially ignored the defendants' allegation of juvenile status and allowed the defendants to accept a plea bargain, in *Muse*, and rejected the claim of juvenile status based on testimonial evidence, in the *Hasan* case. This chapter will also briefly discuss the recent release of a juvenile suspect—most likely for lack of political and judicial will to deal with the complex issue of devising an appropriate legal and policy regime to handle the allegation of juvenile status in piracy prosecutions in federal court. This chapter will conclude that the United States should neither refuse to prosecute juvenile piracy suspects nor treat all piracy suspects as adults, without adopting appropriate age determination procedures. Instead, the United States should adopt a particular legal regime, policy, and strategy in order to adequately handle the prosecution of juvenile piracy suspects.

United States v. Muse

In 2009, the United States prosecuted Abduwali Abdiqadir Muse, a Somali pirate who had been caught during the unsuccessful piracy attack on the U.S. flagged

1 United States v. Muse, No. 1:S109-cr-00512–01-LAP (S.D.N.Y. Jan. 12, 2010).

2 United States v. Hasan, 747 F. Supp. 2d 642, 653 (E.D. Va. 2010) *aff'd sub nom.* United States v. Dire, 680 F.3d 446 (4th Cir. 2012).

vessel Maersk Alabama.[3] The ship, with a crew of twenty-three, loaded with 17,000 metric tons of cargo, was bound for Mombasa, Kenya, after a stop in Djibouti.[4] On April 8, 2009, four pirates based on another vessel, FV Win Far 161, attacked the Maersk Alabama.[5] The four pirates successfully boarded the Maersk Alabama and took its captain, Richard Phillips, as well as several crewmembers hostage.[6] During the attack on the Maersk Alabama, Muse and his fellow pirates repeatedly fired weapons, and threatened and detained crewmembers.[7] However, the pirates were unable to control the ship, and after several scuffles, Muse and his partners in crime kidnapped Captain Richard Phillips and held him hostage on a lifeboat in the Indian Ocean for five days.[8] The United States' authorities attempted to negotiate the payment of a ransom in exchange for the release of Captain Phillips, but Muse and the other pirates threatened to kill, harm, or continue to detain Phillips unless they were guaranteed a safe exit from the scene.[9] As negotiations appeared to stall, the United States Navy launched a rescue operation, during which Muse and the other pirates refused to release Captain Phillips. Members of the Navy SEALs ultimately killed all of Muse's confederates, in order to rescue Captain Phillips. The Navy captured Muse, who was transported to the United States for prosecution.[10] The Muse case represented one of the first modern-day prosecutions of a piracy suspect in the history of the United States.[11]

Muse was indicted under a host of charges, including hijacking a ship, conspiracy to hijack three ships, hostage taking, conspiracy to engage in hostage taking, kidnapping, conspiracy to engage in kidnapping, using and carrying a firearm in furtherance of a crime of violence, as well as the most serious piracy charge, under the United States federal statute on maritime piracy, 18 U.S.C. §1651.[12] Section

3 Grand Jury Indictment at 2–3, United States v. Muse, No. 1:S109-cr-00512–01-LAP (S.D.N.Y. Jan. 12, 2010), ECF No. 17.

4 *Id.* at 2–5.

5 CNN, *U.S. Warship Near Boat Carrying Pirates* (Apr. 9, 2009), available at www.cnn.com/2009/WORLD/africa/04/08/ship.hijacked/index.html.

6 Grand Jury Indictment, *supra* note 3, at 5–7; *see also* Government's Memorandum in Connection with the Sentencing of Abduwali Abdukhadir Muse at 9–10, Muse, No. 1:S109-cr-00512–01-LAP (S.D.N.Y. Feb. 09, 2011), ECF No. 29 [hereinafter Government's Sentencing Submission].

7 Grand Jury Indictment, *supra* note 3, at 5–7.

8 Lauren Hahn, *Juvenile Justice and Piracy: Prosecutions of Juvenile Pirates in the United States*, 20 Geo. Mason L. Rev. 241, 253 (2012). The piracy attack on Maersk Alabama and in particular the hijacking of Captain Phillips was the subject of the Hollywood blockbuster movie, "Captain Phillips," in 2013. Captain Phillips (Sony Pictures 2013).

9 *See* Grand Jury Indictment, *supra* note 3, at 5–7; *see also* Government's Sentencing Submission, *supra* note 6, at 11.

10 *Id.* at 253–54.

11 In fact, before the Hasan prosecution, discussed below in this chapter, and the Muse case, the last United States piracy prosecution had been the 1820 United States v. Smith Case. *See* Mike Schuler, *U.S.'s First Modern-Day Pirate Prosecutor to Step Down*, gCAPTAIN.COM (Aug. 23, 2013), available at http://gcaptain.com/united-states-modern-pirate-prosecutor-to-step-down/.

12 18 U.S.C. §1651 (West 2012).

1651 carries a mandatory life term: "Whoever, on the high seas, commits the crime of piracy as defined by the law of nations, and is afterwards brought into or found in the United States, shall be imprisoned for life."[13]

Muse subsequently accepted a plea deal whereby he pled guilty to the lesser charges, while the most serious piracy charge was dismissed; Muse thereby avoided the mandatory life sentence, which would have been imposed on him had he been convicted of piracy under Section 1651.[14] Under the terms of the plea deal, Muse was sentenced to nearly thirty-four years in prison, fined $550,000 in criminal penalties, and recommended for mental health treatment and English education in prison.[15] While Muse's participation in the piracy attack was undisputed, his young age and potential juvenile status remained unresolved. The part below will describe the ensuing legal scuffle between Muse's defense attorney and the prosecuting authority regarding Muse's claim of juvenile status.

It appears that Muse's actual age was an important factor in the United States authorities' decision, upon Muse's capture, whether to bring him to the United States to stand trial, or to consider other options, such as turning him over to Kenyan authorities for prosecution in the Kenyan courts. In the wake of Muse's capture, American authorities estimated his age to be anywhere between sixteen and twenty.[16] The United States authorities seemingly knew from the time of his capture that Muse's young age could be a challenging issue. From the outset, it was apparent that Muse's age would be impossible to verify, because of his lack of identifying documents and because of the often-inconclusive nature of medical and forensic tests carried out on individuals close to eighteen years of age.[17] In addition, United States authorities were aware that a potential prosecution in federal court could be seriously undermined if Muse was under eighteen because of difficulties linked to prosecuting juveniles in the federal system.[18] It is very rare to charge juveniles in federal court; in fact, in deciding

13 *Id.*

14 Judgment in a Criminal Case at 1, United States v. Muse, No. 1:S109-cr-00512–01-LAP (S.D.N.Y. Feb. 25, 2011), ECF No. 31; *see also* Docket Sheet, Muse, No. 1:S109-cr-00512–01-LAP (S.D.N.Y. Feb. 25, 2011).

15 *Id.*

16 Devlin Barrett, *Teen Piracy Suspect Raises Legal, Moral Issues*, SAN DIEGO UNION-TRIB. (Apr.13, 2009), available at www.sandiegouniontribune.com/news/2009/apr/13/piracy-young-suspect-041309/.

17 The various medical, dental, and cognitive tests that exist and can be used toward determining a suspect's age have been discussed above in Chapter 5. These tests include bone X-rays, dental scans, physical examinations, ultra sounds, as well as cognitive, non-medical assessments. *See supra* Chapter 5.

18 USA TODAY, *Mystery Surrounds Somali Teen Pirate* (Apr. 21, 2009, 5:50 PM), available at www.usatoday.com/news/world/2009–04–21-teen-pirate-suspect_ N.htm (reporting that New York legal experts stated that age would significantly affect how Muse would be treated in the short term and long term and that "getting [Muse] treated as an adult [would] 'avoid difficult and cumbersome proceedings"' for the federal prosecutors (quoting Professor Daniel Richman, Columbia Law School)).

when to charge a minor in federal court, the law requires officials to consider "the age and social background of the juvenile," as well as the nature of the offense.[19] It is unclear how these considerations would apply to Muse, whose age and social background could not be conclusively established. Moreover, because the United States is bound by several human rights treaties and customary laws, which dictate that juvenile suspects should be treated distinctly upon entering any criminal processes, as explored above in Chapter 3, United States authorities needed to establish how they would handle Muse—including whether to detain him separately from adult prisoners to whether to charge him in juvenile court. When asked how Muse's age might factor into the decision whether to prosecute him in the United States, then-Justice Dept. spokesman Dean Boyd stated that they were considering "the evidence and other issues" in the case.[20] This statement was overly simplistic, as it did not portray the full range of complex legal issues that the United States' authorities involved in this case had to consider before deciding to charge Muse, a defendant alleging juvenile status, in federal court in New York.

As stated, Muse was ultimately brought to the United States and indicted under a host of charges in the United States District Court for the Southern District of New York.[21] Muse's age immediately became a point of contention, with multiple national and international media outlets reporting that Muse was a juvenile.[22] Commentators predicted that if Muse were found to be a juvenile, he would be tried in juvenile court, would face lesser charges and would demand sentencing leniency.[23] In light of such predictions, prosecutors—unsurprisingly—maintained that Muse was not a juvenile.

During the proceedings, however, Muse's was an ongoing and persistent issue that was repeatedly raised by Muse's defense counsel. In order to determine Muse's age, the court first held an age hearing.[24] At the hearing, the prosecution presented

19 18 U.S.C. § 5032 (West 2012). To determine whether the transfer of a juvenile to adult status is in the "interest of justice," courts evaluate the following factors: (T)he age and social background of the juvenile; the nature of the alleged offense; the extent and nature of the juvenile's prior delinquency record; the juvenile's present intellectual development and psychological maturity; the nature of past treatment efforts and the juvenile's response to such efforts; the availability of programs designed to treat the juvenile's behavioral problems.

20 Barrett, *supra* note 16.

21 United States v. Muse, No. 1:09-cr-00512 (S.D.N.Y. Jan. 12, 2010).

22 FOX NEWS, *See Smiling Somali Pirate Weeps in Federal Court in New York City, Hearing Reopened to Public* (Apr. 21, 2009), available at www.foxnews.com/story/2009/04/21/smiling-somali-pirate-weeps-in-federal-court-in-new-york-city-hearing-reopened.html; *see also* Benjamin Weiser, *Pirate Suspect Charged as Adult in New York*, N.Y. TIMES (Apr. 21, 2009), available at www.nytimes.com/2009/04/22/nyregion/22pirate.html?pagewanted=all&_r=0; *Teenage Somali 'pirate' pleads not guilty in US court*, THE TELEGRAPH (May 21, 2009), available at www.telegraph.co.uk/news/worldnews/africaandindianocean/somalia/5364183/Teenage-Somali-pirate-pleads-not-guilty-in-US-court.html.

23 Hahn, *supra* note 8, at 254.

24 Transcript of Age Hearing, United States v. Muse, No. 1:S109-cr-00512–01-LAP (S.D.N.Y. Apr. 21, 2009).

one witness, a detective who had interviewed Muse on the flight to the United States. The detective testified that Muse told him that he was between eighteen and nineteen, but acknowledged that Muse was unable to provide him or anyone else with a birth certificate, because there had been no official birth record of when he was born.[25] The sole witness called by the defense was Muse's father. Muse's father testified that his son was born in November 1993; according to this testimony, Muse would have been sixteen at the time of the attack on the Maersk Alabama.[26] However, Muse's father's testimony was inconsistent, for example Muse's father claimed both that his fourth oldest child was born in 1990 and that Muse was his oldest child.[27] The court established, based on the persuasive nature of the detective's testimony, the conflicting nature of Muse's father's testimony, and Muse's inability to produce a birth record, which would have positively established his juvenile status, that Muse was over eighteen and subject to trial as an adult.[28] The court did not order any medical or forensic testing, unlike courts in other countries, as discussed in Chapters 6, 7, and 8 above.

Ultimately, the prosecution offered Muse a plea bargain, whereby he would plead guilty to charges other than piracy and avoid a mandatory life sentence.[29] In addition, as part of the plea bargain, the defense agreed not to pursue the age issue through an appeal.[30] This stipulation underscores further the uncertainty surrounding Muse's age. Given that Muse's age was never firmly established, the prosecution likely used the reduced sentence offered in the plea bargain to coax the defense into dropping the age issue on appeal.[31]

During sentencing, however, Muse's age remained unresolved. Because the charges Muse pled guilty to did not carry mandatory prison terms, Muse's defense chose to pursue the age argument during the sentencing phase, hoping to persuade the court to impose a more lenient sentence.[32] Muse's defense argued, in its sentencing brief, that Muse was sixteen at the time of the Maersk Alabama attack.[33] The defense introduced additional evidence to support this claim, such as affidavits from Muse's family members stating that he was under eighteen at the time of the offense.[34] Muse's mother also asserted that she had given birth to him in

25 *Id.* at 29–33.
26 *Id.* at 39–40.
27 *Id.* at 42.
28 *Id.* at 46–48.
29 Benjamin Weiser, *Leniency of Sentence for Somali Hijacker is at Issue*, N.Y. TIMES, Feb. 14, 2011, at A24.
30 Hahn, *supra* note 8, at 255.
31 *See* Hahn, *supra* note 8, at n.131 (reporting on an e-mail sent to Lauren Hahn by Philip Weinstein, Fed. Defenders of N.Y., Def. Counsel in United States v. Muse, on Sept. 7, 2011: "We resolved the issue [of age] as part of the plea negotiations so there was no litigation on that issue. In exchange for dropping the mandatory life sentence for piracy, we did not contest age").
32 Sentencing Submission of Abduwali Abdukhadir Muse, at 22–25, United States v. Muse, No. 1:S109-cr-00512-01-LAP (S.D.N.Y. Feb. 2, 2011), ECF No. 28 [hereinafter Sentencing Submission].
33 *Id.*
34 *Id.* at 22.

1993, and that he was the oldest of the four children.[35] Muse's brother claimed he was sixteen at the time he offered his affidavit, in January 2011, and that Muse was approximately one year older than him, which would mean that Muse was between fifteen and sixteen at the time of the Maersk Alabama attack.[36] In addition, the defense pointed out that Muse initially told United States authorities that he was sixteen years old; this statement was recorded in the *USS Bainbridge*'s ship log upon Muse's transfer to this ship for medical treatment.[37] The defense also explained that it chose not to submit an affidavit by Muse himself, for fear that this would violate the terms of Muse's plea bargain agreement in which he stipulated that he was eighteen and agreed to be prosecuted as an adult.[38] Finally, the defense explained that most Somalis did not know their own ages because of the lack of birth records in Somalia.[39] The defense argued instead that Muse's dental records estimated his age to be between seventeen and twenty-one, a few months after his arrest.[40] The defense cited several studies to suggest that the teeth of African youth develop more quickly than those of Western populations, often resulting in overestimates of age of such youth.[41]

The district court however chose not to acknowledge evidence related to Muse's purported juvenile age, instead deciding to treat Muse as an adult for the purposes of sentencing.[42] As stated above, Muse received a harsh sentence of nearly thirty-four years of imprisonment.[43] Arguably, had the judge found that Muse had been a juvenile, or had the judge at least taken Muse's possible young age into account at the time of sentencing, the sentence might have been lighter.

> Although the Muse Court ultimately determined Muse was an adult, the existence of an agreement not to pursue an age appeal and the evidence presented in Muse's sentencing brief present the possibility that an appellate

35 Exhibit F (Affirmation of Adar Abdirahman Hassan). 3–4, in Sentencing Submission of Abduwali Abdukhadir Muse, *supra* note 32.

36 *Id.* ¶¶. 1–3.

37 Sentencing Submission, *supra* note 32, at 22, n. 10; *see also* Exhibit L (Ship's Deck Log Sheet), in Sentencing Submission, *supra* note 32.

38 Sentencing Submission, *supra* note 32, at 22, n.10.

39 *Id.*

40 *Id.*

41 *Id.* at 23–24 (citing Lesley E. Davidson, Helen D. Rodd, Interrelationship Between Dental Age and Chronological Age in Somali Children, 18 COMMUNITY DENTAL HEALTH 27 (2001); A. Olze *et al.*, *Comparative Study on the Effect of Ethnicity on Wisdom Tooth Eruption*, 121 INT'L J. LEGAL Med. 445, 447 (2007); Andreas Olze *et al.*, Studies of the Chronological Course of Wisdom Tooth Eruption in Black African Population, 52 J. FORENSIC SCI. 1161, 1162–63 (2007).

42 MSNBC, *See Pirate Who 'Wanted to Kill Americans' Gets 33 Years for Hijacking U.S. Ship* (Feb. 16, 2011, 12:35 PM), available at www.msnbc.msn.com/id/41615693/ns/us_news-crime_and_courts/t/pirate-who-wanted-kill-americans-gets-years-hijacking-us-ship/#.Tmuf5-vgK8U.

43 The plea bargain between Muse and the government dismissed Muse's piracy charges under *§ 1651*, therefore he was not subject to the mandatory life sentence required by the statute.

> court may have found Muse to be of juvenile status. At the very least, the Muse case demonstrates that only limited avenues were taken to discover Muse's age; the government did not conduct forensic testing o Muse, but rather, avoided the issue entirely through a plea bargain.[44]

This chapter ultimately argues that the district court should have ordered appropriate medical and forensic testing in order to determine defendant Muse's age, instead of simply accepting the prosecution's account that Muse was at least eighteen. In the absence of such actions by the United States prosecuting authorities, it may be possible to argue that the United States was not fulfilling its obligations under relevant international human rights law, discussed above in Chapter 4. The section below will discuss another piracy case, *United States v. Hasan*, where the defendant alleged to be a juvenile and where the court rejected this claim without ordering medical or forensic testing. Although Hasan's age claim was not as strong as the claim asserted by Muse, the district court's actions in *Hasan*—relying solely on testimonial evidence to reject the defendant's juvenile status claim—further support the argument that the United States is not respecting its obligations under human rights law to appropriately distinguish juvenile from adult cases and to treat juvenile defendants with special dignity.

United States v. Hasan

Mohammed Modin Hasan and four other Somali pirates, Gabul Abdullahi Ali, Abdi Wali Dire, Abdi Mohammed Gurewardher, and Abdi Mohammed Umar, were involved in an attack on *U.S.S. Nicholas.* On April 1, 2010, Hasan and two of his four co-pirates launched an unsuccessful piracy attack on a ship that they thought was a merchant vessel; it turned out that the victim vessel was the *U.S.S. Nicholas*, a United States navy frigate.[45] The pirates attempted to flee, but *U.S.S. Nicholas* successfully chased and captured not only Hasan and his co-pirates involved, but also their two piracy conspirators who were waiting for them aboard a slightly larger vessel. All five defendants were transferred to the United State District Court for the Eastern District of Virginia and charged with piracy offenses under U.S.C. Section 1651, as well as with a host of other related charges.[46]

44 Hahn, *supra* note 31, at 260.

45 United States v. Hasan, 747 F.Supp.2d 642, 654–55 (2010).

46 *Id.* at 655. The defendants were originally charged with the following six offenses: (1) Piracy under the Law of Nations, in violation of 18 U.S.C. §§ 1651 and 2; (2) Attack to Plunder Vessel, in violation of 18 U.S.C. §§ 1659, 3238, and 2; (3) Assault with a Dangerous Weapon in the Special Maritime Jurisdiction of the United States, in violation of 18 U.S.C. §§ 113(a)(3), 3238, and 2; (4) Conspiracy to Use Firearms During a Crime of Violence, in violation of 18 U.S.C. §§ 924(o) and 3238; and (5) two counts of Use of a Firearm During a Crime of Violence, in violation of 18 U.S.C. §§ 924(c)(1)(A)(iii), 3238, and 2. The original indictment was amended and superseded several months later to also include the following eight charges: (1) Acts of Violence Against Persons on a Vessel, in violation of 18 U.S.C. §§ 2291(a)(6), 2290(a)(2), 3238, and 2;

Defendant Hasan asserted that he was a juvenile and that the indictment against him should be dismissed under the federal Juvenile Delinquency Act[47] because, according to Hasan, the government failed to show he was at least eighteen at the time of the alleged offenses.[48] The government based its claim that Hasan was an adult on the interviews of Hasan, and corresponding notes recorded by the United States authorities upon Hasan's arrest. In fact, after the April 1, 2010 unsuccessful attack against *U.S.S. Nicholas*, Special Agent Knox and Special Agent Mordecai interviewed Hasan and recorded Hasan's age as twenty-five and twenty-four respectively.[49] The government thus claimed that it had established that Hasan was at least eighteen at the time of the alleged piracy offense, because Hasan himself admitted that he was an adult.[50] Hasan, however, claimed that this was not accurate:

> Hasan argues that Special Agent Knox's April 4, 2010 notes from his interview with Hasan do not indicate Hasan's actual age. Instead, according to Hasan, the notes indicate that Hasan said he did not know his age, and that Special Agent Knox simply assumed Hasan was 24 or 25 years old.[51]

Because it remained unclear how Special Agents Knox and Mordecai reached the above-mentioned age determinations, the district court held a special evidentiary hearing, in September 2010, at which both agents, as well as Hasan and a Somali interpreter, testified.[52] Hasan claimed, at the evidentiary hearing, that he never told special agents Knox and Mordecai that he was twenty-four or twenty-five years of age; he instead told the court that he was eighteen (at the time of the

(2) Conspiracy to Perform an Act of Violence Against Persons on a Vessel, in violation of 18 U.S.C. §§ 2291(a)(9), 2290(a)(2), and 3238; (3) Assault with a Dangerous Weapon in a Special Maritime Jurisdiction of the United States, in violation of 18 U.S.C. §§ 113(a)(3), 3238, and 2; (4) two counts of Assault with a Dangerous Weapon on Federal Officers and Employees, in violation of 18 U.S.C. §§ 111(a)(1), 111(b), 3238, and 2; (5) Using, Carrying, and Possessing a Destructive Device in Relation to a Crime of Violence, in violation of 18 U.S.C. §§ 924(c)(1)(A), 924(c)(1)(B)(ii), 3238, and 2; (6) Carrying an Explosive Device During the Commission of a Felony, in violation of 18 U.S.C. §§ 844(g)(2), 3238, and 2; and (7) Conspiracy to Carry an Explosive During the Commission of a Felony, in violation of 18 U.S.C. §§ 844(m) and 3238. *Id.* at 655–56.

47 18 U.S.C.A. § 5031 (West 2012).

48 The Hasan court approvingly discussed the Ninth Circuit Court of Appeals precedent, according to which "the government bears the initial burden of proving defendant's age and `must offer prima facie evidence of defendant's adult status." *Id.* at 673 (citing United States v. Juvenile Male, 595 F.3d 885, 896–97 (9th Cir.2010), quoting United States v. Salgado-Ocampo, 50 F.Supp.2d 908, 909 (D.Minn.1999)). The Hasan court thus accepted that the government, not Hasan, had the initial burden to establish that the defendant was not a juvenile.

49 United States v. Hasan, 747 F. Supp.2d 642, 673 (E.D. Va. 2010) *aff'd sub nom.* United States v. Dire, 680 F.3d 446 (4th Cir. 2012).

50 *Id.* at 672–74.

51 *Id.* at 674.

52 *Id.* at 674.

evidentiary hearing itself, in September 2010) but that, like most Somalis, he did not know his actual date of birth.[53] Special Agent Mordecai testified that his notes from Hasan's interview accurately represented Mordecai's recollection that Hasan stated that he was twenty-four years of age.[54] Special Agent Knox's testimony was less precise—Knox's handwritten notes from the April 2010 interview of defendant Hasan contained the phrase "unknown age—maybe 25," but Knox was unclear about why Mordecai would have recorded Hasan's age as twenty-four, and why Knox himself wrote in a subsequent email that Hasan was twenty-six.[55] Finally, Mr. Ismail, the Somali interpreter who interpreted at both of Hasan's interviews with the United States authorities as well as at many other interviews of alleged Somali pirates, also testified at the evidentiary hearing. Ismail confirmed that it would be common for Somalis not to know their exact age, and also testified that in his experience most captured Somali pirates claim to be under the age of eighteen.[56]

Following the somewhat conflicting testimony the court had to determine whether the government had in fact established that Hasan was over the age of eighteen. The court found that Special Agents Knox and Mordecai were credible witnesses, and that, although their notes and testimony were somewhat uncertain, the age range, between twenty-four and twenty-six, was likely accurate and corroborated by other material evidence.[57] The court thus held that the government met its burden and established that Hasan was over the age of eighteen, based on Hasan's statements to Knox and Mordecai, which the court found were accurately reflected in the agents' notes and further supported by the agents' testimony at the evidentiary hearing.[58] The court then explained that the burden shifted to defendant Hasan to disprove the government's age-related determination and evidence.[59] It held that Hasan's evidence, consisting of his own testimony at the evidentiary hearing, was not sufficient to overcome the government's age determination.[60] According to the court, Hasan was not a

53 *Id.* at 674–75.

54 *Id.* at 675.

55 *Id.*

56 *Id.* at 676.

57 *Id.*

58 "Although the agents' notes and testimony varied slightly from each other, the variance was effectively explained by Special Agent Knox's testimony, which suggested that Hasan gave them an age range of 24 to 26 years old. The totality of the evidence compels the conclusion that Special Agent Knox's notes simply reflected the middle number in that range, and his subsequent email reflected the higher number, whereas Special Agent Mordecai's notes reflected the lower number. More importantly, nowhere in their notes or testimony is there any suggestion whatsoever that Hasan told them he was under the age of 18. Based on the Court's observation of Special Agents Knox and Mordecai during their testimony, and based on the content of that testimony, the Court finds them both to be credible witnesses, and their testimony to be credible and substantially consistent in all material respects." *Id.* at 676.

59 *Id.*

60 *Id.*

credible witness, because his testimony was inconsistent, and he failed to produce any other age-corroborating evidence or to call any other witnesses who could support his juvenile-age claim.

> Hasan's testimony thus stands uncorroborated, and flatly contradicted by all of the other testimony and documentary evidence presented to the Court at the evidentiary hearing. Based on the Court's observation of Hasan during his testimony, as well as on the content of that testimony, the Court finds Hasan not to be a credible witness, and accords minimal weight to his self-serving testimony that he is currently only 18 years old. The Court is also mindful that, even if Hasan is correct in asserting that he is 18 years old, since he testified that he does not know his birth date, one must wonder how, a mere five months after his arrest, he knows that he was less than 18 years old at the time of his arrest. Furthermore, Hasan's testimony that he was told he was 18 years old by people in his Mogadishu neighborhood suggests that such statements were made to him prior to the April 1, 2010 incident at issue, meaning he would have been 18 years old at that time.[61]

The court thus established that Hasan was not a juvenile and rejected Hasan's motion to dismiss the indictment against him under the Juvenile Delinquency Act.[62] The court reached this conclusion based solely on testimonial evidence. It did not order any medical or forensic testing. The *Hasan* age determination is thus consistent with *Muse*, described above, where the court similarly rejected the defendant's juvenile status claim based solely on testimonial evidence.[63] While Muse accepted a plea bargain whereby he agreed not to pursue his juvenile status claim on appeal, Hasan challenged the district court's age determination on appeal with the Fourth Circuit.[64] The Fourth Circuit affirmed the district court's decision, holding that in light of its deferential standard of review of the lower court's evidentiary findings, it would not disturb the latter's determination that Hasan was between twenty-four and twenty-six at the time of the alleged piracy offenses.[65] The Fourth Circuit did not appear troubled by the district court's procedure in reaching the adult-age determination, or by the district court's failure to conduct proper medical or forensic tests to reach such age determinations. One could argue that even in light of appellate court's deferential review standard of any lower court's factual determinations, such as the age determination in Hasan, the failure to conduct medical and/or forensic tests to accurately ascertain the defendant's age amounts to a serious error and a potential violation

61 *Id.* at 677.

62 *Id.*

63 *See Transcript of Age Hearing* at 36–37, United States v. Muse, No. 1:09-cr-00512 (S.D.N.Y. June 16, 2009), ECF No. 10.

64 United States v. Dire *et al.*, 680 F.3d 446 (4th Cir. 2012).

65 *Id.* at 55.

of international human rights law, which should be corrected on appeal. It is this chapter's overall conclusion that United States authorities should not determine any suspect's age based only on testimonial evidence, in cases where the defendant's juvenile status claim appears reasonable.

In sum, like Muse's age, Hasan's *actual* age remained unclear. Although it may appear that Muse's age-related claim was stronger than Hasan's, the fact remains nonetheless that United States courts have been unwilling to devote time and resources toward conducting appropriate medical and forensic testing to determine piracy suspects' actual age. United States courts and other legal authorities have thus far chosen not to develop specific age-determination regimes for piracy suspects, and have not developed specific policies for the treatment of alleged juvenile suspects. Because human rights treaties, which bind the United States, demand that juvenile suspects be treated in a distinct manner, and because the United States seems unwilling to devote significant time and resources toward developing a legal regime to adequately handle the prosecution of juvenile piracy suspects, it appears that the United States has chosen not to prosecute at least some juvenile suspects, even when they are caught attacking an American vessel. This attitude is equally unfortunate, because juvenile piracy suspects should not be caught-and-released, especially if the release to Somalia will likely result in recidivism. The following section will discuss the recent release of a juvenile pirate by United States authorities.

Recent Release of a Juvenile Pirate

Following a February 2011 piracy attack on a United States civilian vessel, *S/V Quest*, American authorities briefly dealt with another juvenile pirate. After a group of Somali pirates attacked the *S/V Quest* and killed four civilians traveling on this vessel, United States authorities boarded this vessel and arrested fifteen pirates responsible for the attack and the murders.[66] However, one of the fifteen pirates was juvenile and Neil MacBride, the U.S. Attorney for the Eastern District of Virginia, released him, according to a statement. The juvenile pirate was released, according to MacBride, because of his juvenile status and because he apparently played a limited role in this attack.[67] It is unclear, however, how this suspect's age was determined. It is unlikely that a series of medical and forensic tests were performed on board any United States vessels. This suspect was never brought to the United States and was thus never subject to any official age determinations by American authorities on American soil. It may be that this suspect looked very young and that United States authorities took his claim of juvenile status at face value, without conducting any additional investigations.

66 NBC NEWS, *14 Indicted for Piracy Over US Yacht Killing* (Mar. 10, 2011), available at www.nbcnews.com/id/42007399/ns/us_news-crime_and_courts/t/indicted-piracy-over-us-yacht-killings/#.VtdB4o-cGUk.

67 *Id.*

It is also very likely that the United States authorities simply did not want to face the legal and procedural complexities involved in the handling of a juvenile suspect in federal court and that they simply declined to prosecute on American soil.

It is this chapter's, and this book's, overall argument that the catch-and-release attitude often adopted by piracy-fighting states when captured suspects allege juvenile status and appear to be juvenile is undesirable. Juvenile suspects returned to Somalia most often return to the same coastal villages where they came from and most often fall prey again to the enticing recruitment efforts by piracy attack organizers. Many juvenile suspects re-enlist to become pirates again, often for lack of other educational or work opportunities. Because juvenile piracy suspects are most vulnerable and because they have the highest potential for rehabilitation, it would be preferable for piracy-fighting states to either prosecute juvenile suspects in their own courts, with adequate juvenile justice processes and opportunities for rehabilitation, or to attempt to build appropriate rehabilitation and re-education opportunities in Somalia. These issues will be further discussed in the Conclusion below. The section below will discuss particular legal challenges pertaining to the prosecution of juvenile piracy suspects in the United States. This discussion may help to illustrate why prosecuting juvenile suspects is as complex in the United States, and why American authorities may be unwilling to grapple with these legal issues.

Legal Issues Pertaining to the Prosecution of Juvenile Piracy Suspects in United States Courts

Particular constitutional issues impact the potential prosecution of juvenile piracy suspects in the United States. In fact, the Eighth Amendment to the United States Constitution prohibits the imposition of cruel and unusual punishment against any individuals.[68] The Supreme Court has interpreted this prohibition in the context of juvenile defendants and convicts, by holding in *Graham v. Florida*[69] that the imposition of life imprisonment without parole for a juvenile who commits a non-homicide offense violates the Eighth Amendment.[70] The Supreme Court held that a non-homicide juvenile offender should always have a "chance to demonstrate growth and maturity," and that overwhelming global opinion regarding the treatment of juvenile offenders supported the Court's view that the imposition of live without parole on non-homicide juveniles constituted a cruel and unusual punishment.[71] The Supreme Court thus directed states to ensure that every convicted juvenile should have a "realistic opportunity to obtain release before the end of [the prison] term."[72]

68 U.S. Const. amend. VIII.

69 Graham v. Florida, 560 U.S. 48 (2010).

70 *Id.* at 70–80.

71 *Id.* at 73.

72 *Id.* at 83.

The *Graham* case is relevant in the context of maritime piracy, because the applicable American law on piracy, as described above, carries with it a mandatory life sentence.[73] In other words, anyone convicted of piracy by a United States court, like defendant Muse, will receive the mandatory life imprisonment sentence. Thus, even juvenile piracy suspects, if charged with a piracy offense and convicted as adults, will be sentenced to life imprisonment. If such juvenile pirates have not committed a homicide during the piratical act for which they are prosecuted, their sentence would become unconstitutional under *Graham*. In other words, charging a non-homicide juvenile offender under the United States' piracy statute would result in a violation of the Eighth Amendment.

In order to avoid this conflict, the United States could argue that the Eighth Amendment does not apply to non-citizens—most piracy suspects are Somali nationals, and under this rationale, convicting juvenile Somali pirates of piracy and sentencing them to life imprisonment would not result in a constitutional violation. It is questionable, however, whether this rationale would withstand scrutiny. The Supreme Court has repeatedly held that the due process and equal protection clauses apply to non-citizens. The Court has held that the protections guaranteed by the Fifth, Sixth, and Fourteenth Amendments were "not confined to the protection of citizens" and that all persons found within the United States must be entitled to due process and other procedural protections guaranteed by these amendments.[74] In recent piracy cases, courts have reaffirmed this understanding of legal protections extended to non-citizens. In other cases, our courts have implicitly held that the Eighth Amendment protections apply to all those sentenced in the United States, whether they are citizens or non-citizens. "Cases involving Eighth Amendment claims by non-citizens, when taken in combination with the aforementioned precedent regarding the applicability of constitutional trial protections to non-citizens, support the conclusion that all those tried within the U.S. justice system receive basic constitutional trial protections, including the protection against cruel and unusual punishment in the sentencing context."[75] Thus, in light of the above, it is reasonable to argue that the imposition of a mandatory life sentence on non-homicide juvenile pirates would constitute a violation of the Eighth Amendment, even though such juvenile pirates are non-citizens.

Additionally, the United States could attempt to avoid the Eighth Amendment conflict by arguing that the mandatory sentencing portion of the piracy statute is severable from the rest of the statute, as applied to juveniles. The United States Supreme Court has held that severability is dependent on legislative intent and that, when interpreting a statute, the Court could either declare the entire statute void because of its unconstitutionality, or sever the unconstitutional provision

73 18 U.S.C. § 1651 (West 2012).
74 Yick Woo v. Hopkins, 118 U.S. 356, 369 (1886).
75 Hahn, *supra* note 31, at 263.

from the rest of the statute.[76] Although a presumption in favor of severability applies, the Court has warned that it should not use its interpretative powers to circumvent legislative intent.[77] In order to determine whether a portion of any statute is severable, the Court must decide whether "the balance of the legislation is incapable of functioning independently" from the severed provision.[78] If this analysis is applied to the sentencing portion of the United States piracy statute, its outcome would strongly tip in favor of finding the sentencing portion non-severable, because of "the framework of the piracy statute, the effect of severance on sentencing discretion, and the purpose of the piracy statute."[79]

The mandatory sentencing portion of the United States piracy statute is not severable from the remainder of this statute for several reasons. First, Section 1651, is short, direct, and it clearly mandates a sentence of life imprisonment for anyone convicted of piracy.[80] On its face, it appears that the sentencing portion of Section 1651 is not severable, because of the statute's brevity and conciseness. The Court has found that a provision of a statute cannot be severable if the Court would have to re-write the statute in order to ensure that it remained operable.[81] In the context of Section 1651, the Court would have to write additional words into Section 1651 in order to sever the sentencing portion from the remainder of this statute, because the severed sentencing provision would read ". . . shall be imprisoned for life." This short phrase is inoperative, because it is grammatically incomplete and the Court would have to essentially re-write it. This would likely be contrary to Congressional intent, when Congressional members wrote Section 1651 and envisioned that its provisions would operate together.[82]

Second, if the sentencing provision of Section 1651 were severed, this would allow for complete judicial discretion in sentencing pirates, because the severed statute would not provide any guidance to our judiciary on appropriate sentences for convicted pirates. This is also contrary to Congressional intent, because the legislative history behind Section 1651 seems to suggest that the legislature did not wish to allow for judicial discretion in sentencing pirates. Piratical activity posed incredible danger in the seventeenth and eighteenth centuries; in light of such danger, the Constitution specifically grants Congress the power to define piracy

76 United States v. Booker, 543 U.S. 220, 247 (2005) (citing Welsh v. United States, 398 U.S. 333, 361 (1970) (Harlan, J., concurring in result).

77 *Id.* at 257–58.

78 United States v. Mathurin, No. 09–21075–Cr, 2011 WL 2580775, at 4 (quoting United States v. Romero-Fernandez, F.2d 195, 196 (11th Cir. 1993) (per curiam)).

79 Hahn, *supra* note 31, at 265.

80 U.S.C. § 1861 (West 2012).

81 The Supreme Court has held that it should not "use its remedial powers to circumvent the intent of the legislature." *See Booker*, 543 U.S. at 247 (citing Heckler v. Mathews, 465 U.S. 728, 739 n.5 (1984)).

82 *See*, e.g., Gubiensio-Ortiz v. Kanahele, 857 F. 2d 1245, 1267 (9th Cir. 1988), *vacated sub nom.* United States v. Chavez Sanchez, 488 U.S. 1036 (1989).

and punish pirates.[83] The original piracy statute was enacted during the First Congress, and it contained the word "Punishment."[84] When the fifteenth Congress revised the piracy statute in 1819, it also included the word "punish" in the statute's title.[85] When the piracy statute was revised again in 1948, the only change was to change a mandatory death sentence to a mandatory life imprisonment sentence.[86] The legislative history behind section 1651 seems to highlight Congress's willingness to specifically prescribe punishment for those who engage in piracy. This type of congressional purpose and intent is contrary to the idea that judges should have discretion in sentencing convicted pirates, a conclusion that militates against the severability of Section 1651's sentencing portion.

> For over 200 years, the piracy statute has carried a penalty of no less than life imprisonment upon conviction; it does not rationally follow that the legislature would have enacted the piracy statute 'had it known [that] the constitutional invalidity of [the sentencing portion] of the statute' would result in complete judicial discretion in the sentencing of juvenile pirates. Thus, in repeatedly providing a clear-cut, direct sentencing mandate for a piracy conviction for over two centuries, Congress has demonstrated intent to retain discretion over the sentencing of pirates.[87]

In light of the above, it can be concluded that the sentencing provision in Section 1651 is not severable from the remainder of the piracy statute. If the sentencing provision is not severable, it applies to juveniles and as such constitutes a cruel and unusual punishment and a violation of the Eighth Amendment of the United States Constitution. Thus, because of a likely conflict with the Eighth Amendment, juvenile piracy suspects should not be charged as adults under Section 1651. The section below will outline recommendations for United States authorities involved in the prosecution of juvenile piracy suspects; these recommendations will be addressed further and in more detail in Chapter 10 below.

Recommendations and Conclusion

The United States has avoided addressing legal issues raised by the prosecution of juvenile piracy suspects by either rejecting the suspect's juvenile status, as in *Muse* and *Hasan*, or by declining to prosecute suspects for whom juvenile status

83 U.S. CONST., art. I, section 8, cl. 10.

84 *An Act for the Punishment of Certain Crimes Against the United States*, ch. 9, § 8, 1 Stat. 112, 113–14 (1790).

85 *An Act to Protect the Commerce of the United States, and Punish the Crime of Piracy*, ch. 77, 3 Stat. 510, 510 (1819).

86 *See* Samuel Pyeatt Menefee, *"Yo Heave Ho!": Updating America's Piracy Laws*, 21 CAL. W. INT'L L.J. 151, 161 (1990).

87 Hahn, *supra* note 31, at 267.

would have definitely attached. However, the United States may not be able to avoid this issue in the future and should instead develop a legal regime and policy recommendations to adequately address this complex legal quandary.

First, the United States should attempt to determine the suspect's age by using appropriate medical, dental, forensic, and other technology. Although these tests are not perfect, they nonetheless provide more accurate and comprehensive strategies in assessing the defendant's real age. These types of tests were not used in *Muse* or *Hasan*, where the courts instead relied on purely testimonial evidence to ultimately determine that each defendant was an adult.[88] Because of the severity of the crime of piracy and the corresponding mandatory life sentence under United States law found in Section 1651, it is crucial that American courts conduct appropriate age determinations, to both avoid sentencing non-homicide juvenile suspects to life imprisonment without parole—a likely constitutional violation—as well as to ensure that adult defendants are not claiming juvenile status in order to avoid the applicability of Section 1651. In fact, as mentioned above in the section discussing the *Hasan* case, most Somali piracy suspects claim to be under the age of eighteen. It is likely that piracy suspects do so because of at least some awareness of the harsh sentencing laws applicable to adult pirates in the United States, and because of some superficial understanding that a claim of juvenile status will benefit the suspect's treatment, detention conditions, and overall judicial and prosecutorial strategy. "The United States needs an age determination strategy that is accurate and dependable enough to deter piracy suspects from false claims of juvenile statute; the use of medical and forensic testing, when added to testimonial evidence, is more likely to deter pirates than the use of testimonial evidence alone."[89]

Second, if a United States court determines that a piracy suspect is a juvenile, it should avoid charging the suspect with piracy under Section 1651, because of this section's non-severable sentencing provision, which would impose a mandatory life sentence on non-homicide juvenile offenders, in violation of the Eighth Amendment.[90] Instead, American prosecutors could bring cases under Section 2280, the federal law implementing the Violence Against Maritime Navigation Convention.[91] Section 2280 offers a comprehensive list of prohibited acts of maritime violence, and its contemporary sentencing framework would provide judges with necessary sentencing discretion in imposing appropriate punishment on juvenile offenders, in line with *Graham*. Prosecutors could also bring additional charges against juvenile defendants, under an additional section of federal law, which outlines offenses applicable to non-citizen pirates and mandates sentences

88 *See Transcript of Age Hearing* at 36–37, United States v. Muse, No. 1:09-cr-00512 (S.D.N.Y. June 16, 2009), ECF No. 10; United States v. Hasan, 747 F. Supp. 2d 642, 673 (E.D. Va. 2010) *aff'd sub nom.* United States v. Dire, 680 F.3d 446 (4th Cir. 2012).

89 Hahn, *supra* note 31, at 271.

90 See *supra* pp. 11–14 for a more general discussion.

91 Violence Against Maritime Navigation Convention, 18 U.S.C. § 2280.

less than life imprisonment. However, if United States authorities pursue claims against juvenile piracy suspects in federal court, such suspects should be treated with special dignity, in accordance with international human rights law on the treatment of juveniles discussed above in Chapter 4. In addition, any punishments that such suspects face should always take into account the suspect's young age and promote the desirability of his or her re-education and rehabilitation.

Third, the United States should not simply catch-and release juvenile piracy suspects. If released, child pirates typically return to their communities and resort again to the same type of criminal endeavors. Often they are caught-and-released multiple times. This policy is harmful to child pirates, as it does nothing to promote their rehabilitation and reintegration into society.

In sum, the United States should develop appropriate policy and a specific legal regime, which would apply to all juvenile piracy suspects. In this manner, the United States would be able to contribute to the global fight against piracy by prosecuting all offenders, including juveniles, while respecting international human rights law and other legal regimes mandating a disparate treatment of all juvenile suspects.

Part IV

Recommendations and Best Practices

Part IV develops a set of recommendations and best practices for all piracy-prosecuting nations regarding the treatment of juvenile piracy suspects. Chapter 9 discusses these recommendations in detail; these include ensuring that age assessments are conducted through the use of appropriate medical and forensic procedures, that if results of such procedures are inconclusive, states should adopt a presumption of juvenile status, that juvenile suspects should be treated in accordance with international human rights law, and that those who employ juvenile pirates should be treated more harshly. The conclusion then sums up the entire book, by going over the problem of child piracy and by summarizing some of the solutions proposed in this book.

9 Recommendations for Best Practices Regarding the Prosecution of Juvenile Piracy Suspects

Introduction

This chapter develops a set of recommendations for states involved in the prosecution of juvenile piracy suspects. These recommendations are based on the examination of the existing Somali piracy model, as detailed in Chapters 1 and 2 above, on a review of existing human rights law, in Chapter 3 above, on a comparison between issues raised by child soldiering and child piracy, in Chapter 4 above, on a review of existing age determination procedures, in Chapter 5 above, and on a survey of national piracy prosecutions involving juvenile piracy suspects, in Chapters 6, 7, and 8. These recommendations, if adopted, would enable all piracy prosecuting countries to develop legal regimes and policies that would apply to juvenile piracy suspects and that would ultimately lead toward more efficient prosecutions, where defendants' rights would be protected in light of existing international human rights law.

First, states should use medical and forensic tests to determine the suspected pirates' age, whenever such testing is necessary (if a suspect's age is disputed and cannot be determined through documentary or testimonial evidence). Second, if forensic and medical tests are inconclusive as to a suspected pirate's age, that defendant should be treated as a juvenile. Third, if the apprehending or prosecuting state determines that a suspected pirate is a juvenile, that state should ensure that the suspect is treated in accordance with international human rights law standards on the treatment of juveniles. Fourth, an adult suspect apprehended onboard a pirate vessel with juvenile pirates should be sentenced more harshly.

These recommendations apply to all pirate apprehending and prosecuting states, in light of the above-discussed international human rights law provisions on the treatment of juvenile suspects. It is this book's conclusion that if states follow these recommendations, they will be in compliance with their international legal duties, and they will be able to conduct efficient and lawful piracy prosecutions against juvenile suspects.

Recommendation #1: States Should Use Medical and Forensic Tests to Determine the Suspected Pirates' Age

It is this book's recommendation that piracy prosecuting states should conduct medical and forensic tests to determine the suspected pirate's age, if his or her age is contested and if other reliable documentary or testimonial evidence is not available.

Once any state authorities apprehend and detain suspected pirates, they should first conduct interviews with the detained suspects. As part of the initial interview, state authorities should inquire into the suspects' ages. If a suspect claims that he is under the age of eighteen, state authorities should separate him from the rest of the suspects and detain him separately for the remainder of the suspect's stay onboard the detaining country's vessel. Once the suspect is transferred to the authorities of the apprehending state or a third state for prosecution purposes, the prosecuting state should order that the suspect remain separated from the other adult suspects, and should initially detain the suspect in its juvenile detention facilities. The separation of alleged juveniles from adult piracy suspects is particularly important, because human rights treaties, such as the Convention on the Rights of the Child, require this type of segregation between juvenile and adult suspects.[1] By initially accepting all claims of juvenile status, for the purposes of early detention, authorities of the capturing state and the prosecuting state will ensure that nobody's rights are violated and that all relevant international human rights law provisions are respected.

As early as possible in the criminal proceeding against allegedly juvenile suspects, the prosecuting nation should conduct a hearing to determine the suspect's age, if the age is contested. For the purposes of the hearing, the competent judge should first examine documentary evidence, if available. In the case of most Somali piracy suspects, documentary evidence in the form of birth certificates or passports is unavailable. In these instances, the competent judge should solicit testimony by a suspect's family members or friends who may know the suspect's actual age. If the suspect's age remains contested, the judge should order that medical and forensic examinations be performed on the defendant. These examinations may include height and weight determinations, bone X-rays, dental examinations, as well as any other medical and non-medical procedures that may be relevant for the purposes of determining a person's age. These age determination procedures have been discussed above in Chapter 5.

Age determination procedures should be conducted in a manner that respects the dignity of the young suspect. According to a 2013 UNICEF technical note, which reviewed relevant legal norms and state practice regarding age determination, these determinations should only be initiated in the best interests of the child and as a measure of last resort, while maintaining a friendly perspective; they should be undertaken without discrimination; the child should have a special guardian appointed to support the child throughout the age assessment procedure; children should be informed about age assessment procedures and must give informed consent; an age assessment must uphold the dignity of the child and remain sensitive to gender and culture; every age assessment should

1 For a full discussion of the Convention on the Rights of the Child and other human rights law, such as the International Covenant on Civil and Political Rights, *see supra* Chapter 3.

take on a holistic approach. It is this book's recommendation that age determination procedures should be conducted in a manner consistent with and similar to the UNICEF guidelines described directly above.[2]

While age determination procedures do not always lead toward perfectly accurate results, if coupled with evidentiary and testimonial evidence, they may lead the court to an age determination less susceptible to significant errors. The competent judge should make an appropriate age determination, in light of the results of all the above-mentioned medical and forensic examinations, as well as all available evidentiary and testimonial evidence.

Once a suspect is transferred to the prosecuting state, in some cases prosecution may choose not to contest the defendant's juvenile status claim. It may be appropriate for the competent judge to accept the defendant's claimed age if the judge determines that the defendant reasonably appears to be a juvenile.[3] In all cases where the judge cannot make such a determination based purely on the defendant's physical appearance, the judge should order the above-described forensic testing and examination procedures.

Recommendation #2: If Forensic and Medical Tests Are Inconclusive as to a Suspected Pirate's Age, That Defendant Should be Treated as a Juvenile

If no documentary or testimonial evidence regarding the piracy suspect's age is available, and if the competent judge orders forensic and medical testing that yields inconclusive results, the defendant should generally be treated as a juvenile. In other words, any time the defendant's age is contested, the presumption should be in favor of juvenile status, unless the state's authorities can offer a significant amount of additional evidence proving that the defendant is over the age of eighteen. Any time that medical and forensic evidence yields inconclusive results, the burden should be on the state authorities to disprove a defendant's juvenile status.[4] As a matter of policy, a presumption in favor of juvenile status

2 Terry Smith and Laura Brownlees, *Age Assessment: A Technical Note* 11–12 (UNICEF Working Paper January 2013).

3 Arguably, this is what happened in the Seychelles' prosecutions described above. *See supra* Chapter 7. This is also what may have happened in the Italian and Malaysian prosecutions, where those countries' authorities decided to treat several piracy suspects as juveniles, but where very little public information is available as to how those age-related determinations were reached. *See supra* Chapters 6 and 7.

4 German authorities adopted this approach when faced with a juvenile status claim: the Hamburg court proceeded to treat several defendants as juveniles, despite the inconclusiveness of forensic evidence, and once it became apparent that all defendants' ages were contested, the court handed down mild sentences to everybody, presumably because of the potential that all defendants were juveniles. *See supra* Chapter 6. American authorities adopted the opposite approach in the Muse case: although the defendant's age was contested throughout the proceedings, the court rejected the defendant's juvenile status claim and sentenced him as an adult. The court thus adopted a presumption against juvenile status. *See supra* Chapter 7.

mitigates the risk that the prosecuting state will violate its international obligations to treat suspect juveniles with dignity and distinction by treating them as adults. This recommendation is in line with the 2013 UNICEF technical note mentioned above—this note stipulates that where there is margin of error, this should be applied in favor of the child and in favor of accepting juvenile status.[5]

As discussed above in Chapter 5, most age-determining procedures, such as bone and dental X-rays, physical examinations, ultra sounds, and cognitive tests produce results, which are subject to a significant variance of plus or minus at least one year. Thus, if a forensic expert concludes, based on an age determination test, that a suspect is eighteen, this suspect could in reality be seventeen or nineteen. If age determinations are blindly accepted by courts, there is a significant probability that many juveniles aged sixteen or seventeen will be treated as adults, because their bones or teeth may have matured somewhat early.[6] Adopting a presumption in favor of juvenile status any time that age determination tests produce somewhat inconclusive results would ensure that all juvenile defendants are treated in accordance with international human rights law.

Critics may point to the fact that this recommendation would lead toward an over-inclusive approach, where some young adults may be treated as children. In other words, a presumption in favor of juvenile status may allow some nineteen and twenty-year-old piracy suspects to enjoy the unwarranted privileges of juvenile status and to escape the harsher treatment reserved for other adult suspects. This may be true, but this book's conclusion is that this error is harmless. First, the number of prosecuted piracy suspects across the globe is low, and the number of prosecuted suspects whose age is contested is even lower. The number of those suspects aged nineteen or twenty, who end up being treated as children because age determination results are inconclusive, is minute. If a handful of young piracy suspects enjoy the privileges of juvenile status, this will in no manner undermine the overall effectiveness of piracy prosecution. Second, the treatment of young adults as juveniles does not put piracy prosecuting nations in violation of international human rights law. However, treating juveniles as adults, because their age has been wrongly determined, does expose prosecuting nations to significant violations of international human rights law. The latter error is not harmless. Third, the treatment of very young adults as children may in reality be in line with international standards of juvenile justice. In some legal systems, the defendant's young age (over eighteen) may be taken into account during the criminal proceedings, and in particular during the

5 Smith and Brownlees, *supra* note 2.

6 This is what may have happened in the Spanish prosecution of defendant Abdu Willy. In that case, the Spanish authorities conducted a bone X-ray, which determined that the defendant was not a juvenile. The Spanish court accepted this determination and treated the defendant as an adult, sentencing him to 439 years in prison. In reality, this defendant's age remained uncertain and it is entirely possible that he was under the age of eighteen at the time of the piracy offense. *See supra* Chapter 6.

sentencing phase. Thus, treating very young adults as juveniles and imposing lighter sentences because of their young age may be a preferential policy under human rights law and standards of juvenile justice. In sum, the risks of treating juvenile suspects as adults because of unreliable age determinations far outweighs any inconvenience posed by the treatment of a handful of young adults as children.

Recommendation #3: If the Apprehending or Prosecuting State Determines that a Suspected Pirate is a Juvenile, that State Should Ensure That the Suspect is Treated in Accordance with International Human Rights Law Standards on the Treatment of Juveniles

Should the judge find that the suspect is a juvenile, the case against that person should proceed in accordance with the prosecuting nation's juvenile justice provisions. Most states that are signatories to the International Covenant on Civil and Political Rights and the Convention on the Rights of the Child will have domestic laws implementing these treaties. Most of these domestic laws will adopt a best-interest-of-the-child approach and will have provisions stipulating that pre-trial detention should only be used as a measure of last resort in cases involving juveniles, requiring separate detention facilities for juveniles as well as rehabilitation and re-education opportunities post-conviction, and demanding leniency in the sentencing phase.[7]

Piracy prosecuting nations may be justified in detaining a juvenile suspect on board the capturing ship, but should be careful not to impose an overly long pre-trial detention period on juvenile suspects. "The question of last resort [regarding pre-trial detention] will depend primarily on the availability of less institutionalized options for pre-trial detention, which will vary based on the jurisdiction in which the suspected child pirate is to be tried. Cultural considerations will also come into play here."[8] Thus, piracy-prosecuting nations should ensure that juvenile piracy suspects are not detained for overly long pre-trial periods. In addition, as discussed in Chapter 3 above, juveniles are, pursuant to most states' juvenile justice penal systems, typically given more lenient sentences, which take into consideration the person's young age at the time that the relevant crime was committed. In fact, pursuant to human rights law, as contained in the above-mentioned treaties, juveniles may not face the death penalty or imprisonment without the possibility of parole. Thus, it is this book's recommendation that piracy prosecuting nations impose adequate penalties on juvenile pirates,

7 For a discussion of relevant human rights law, such as the Convention on the Rights of the Child and the International Covenant on Civil and Political Rights, *see supra* Chapter 3. For an overview of different national laws on juvenile justice, *see supra* Chapter 5.

8 Jon Bellish, *The Issue of Juvenile Piracy* 286, *in* PROSECUTING MARITIME PIRACY: DOMESTIC SOLUTIONS TO INTERNATIONAL CRIMES (Scharf *et al.* eds. 2015).

which take into account their young age. After a juvenile is sentenced, he should serve his sentence at an appropriate detention facility, where only juveniles are housed, and where he will be afforded adequate rehabilitation opportunities, including schooling, vocational training, and job preparedness, as required by international human rights law. A state that willingly chooses to prosecute a suspected juvenile pirate has a duty, under international human rights law, to provide a convicted juvenile pirate with these opportunities.[9]

Last but not least, juvenile suspects may have additional rights during the criminal proceeding, which are dictated by human rights law. Juveniles have the right to have their parents or legal guardians contacted and apprised of the situation.[10] While it may not be possible to contact each juvenile Somali piracy suspect's family members, because many Somalis may be unreachable by telephone or electronic mail, it is this book's recommendation that prosecuting nations should expend reasonable efforts to contact each juvenile suspect's family members. Second, juvenile suspects may have a right to special representation during trial.[11] It is this book's recommendation that juvenile suspects should be given separate counsel at trial, who could argue specifically toward the best interest of the juvenile, in line with international human rights law protections available for juvenile suspects.

In sum, all piracy prosecuting nations have a duty to ensure that juvenile piracy suspects' rights are adequately protected, by guaranteeing that cases against juveniles are separated from cases pending against adults, that criminal proceeding against juvenile piracy suspects are conducted with a best-interest-of-the-child approach, with representation by special counsel and information to the juvenile's family, and that penalties imposed are more lenient and allow for rehabilitative and re-educational opportunities.

Recommendation #4: Juvenile Pirates Should Not be Caught-and-Released

Juvenile pirates should not be simply released, however. The catch-and-release policy, which has resulted in the unjustified liberation of many suspected pirates, should not apply to juvenile suspects either.[12] A released juvenile will return to Somalia, after which he will most likely re-engage in piracy. Many juveniles

9 According to media accounts, this is what happened in the Hamburg (Germany) piracy prosecution, where juvenile suspects were detained at appropriate juvenile detention facilities, where they were given access to education, including German language classes, and where they were able to integrate into German society upon their release from detention. *See supra* Chapter 6.

10 Bellish, *supra* note 8, at 287.

11 *Id.* at 287–88.

12 Estimated rates of "catch-and-release" range from 57 to 80 percent of all pirates caught at sea. *See* John H. Pendleton, *Maritime Security: Actions Needed To Assess and Update Plan and Enhance Collaboration Among Partners Involved in Countering Piracy off the Horn of Africa*, GAO REPORT TO CONGRESSIONAL REQUESTERS 64 (Sept. 2010); Bernd Debusmann, *Why High-Seas Piracy Is Here to Stay*, REUTERS, Mar. 4, 2011.

do not have extended families in Somalia or have been separated or displaced from their families; thus, they will easily fall prey to another piracy scheme organized by a Dubai or London-based financier. Jon Bellish has argued that states have a legal obligation, under the International Labor Organization Child Labor Convention, "to prevent children from returning to situations that require them to perform illicit activities in exchange for money."[13] It is thus critical that apprehended juvenile piracy suspects be transferred to an appropriate prosecution venue, where each criminal case can be handled by well-trained juvenile justice authorities, and where each suspect will be provided with meaningful rehabilitative and educational services. A juvenile pirate should face responsibility and should have to face his accusers, but his age should serve as a guiding factor in his treatment, incarceration, and punishment.

Recommendation #5: A Suspect Apprehended Onboard a Pirate Vessel with Juvenile Pirates Should be Sentenced More Harshly

A corollary to any state's obligation to treat juveniles with a particular type of dignity is the necessity for states to treat those who employ juvenile criminals more harshly. Pirates who work onboard vessels with other juvenile pirates should be dealt harsher sentences because any sentencing judge should take into consideration the fact that a suspect was engaged in a criminal enterprise with a minor. International criminal law, as discussed above, stipulates that enlisting children in an armed conflict is a war crime.[14] The International Criminal Court and the Special Court for Sierra Leone have already convicted individual suspects of war crimes for having enlisted children.[15] Because piracy typically occurs outside the armed conflict paradigm, enlisting pirates cannot be viewed as a war crime. However, the parallel between child soldiers and juvenile pirates is sufficiently strong to warrant harsher treatment and sentencing of those who employ juvenile pirates within any nation's domestic penal system. In one of the Seychelles' cases mentioned in Chapter 7 above, Justice Gaswaga engaged in this type of reasoning when he chose to sentence adult pirates, caught alongside juvenile pirates, to lengthy thirty-year sentences, and when he chose to impose lenient punishments on the juveniles.[16] Other domestic tribunals should follow Justice Gaswaga's example and treat the employment of juvenile pirates as a sentencing factor when imposing sentences on adult pirates. The deterrent effect of any future harsh sentences pronounced against those who choose to engage in piratical acts with minors onboard may play a significant role in the future organization of piracy schemes in Somalia and elsewhere.

13 Bellish, *supra* note 8, at 285.
14 *See supra* Chapter 4.
15 *Id.*
16 *See supra* Chapter 7.

Conclusion

If piracy prosecuting nations adopt the recommendation discussed above, they will be able to conduct more efficient prosecutions that will respect international human rights law obligations and ensure that all juvenile suspects' rights are adequately protected. Ideally, piracy prosecuting nations would embrace these recommendations as part of their national legal regimes and policy applicable to the treatment of juvenile piracy suspects. Prosecuting states would thus be able to process piracy cases involving juvenile suspects more efficiently, because the treatment of such suspects would be dictated by relevant law and policy and judges would not face uncertainty and unnecessary delays. The adoption of these recommendations would ensure that all prosecuting states comply with relevant international human rights law on the treatment of juvenile suspects. Moreover, each juvenile suspect's rights would be adequately protected, and children would not be placed in dangerous detention situations nor would they face disproportionately harsh penalties. Juveniles would be offered meaningful rehabilitative and educational opportunities, which in turn would increase the likelihood that juvenile pirates would someday become productive members of the Somali, or another nation's society.

Conclusion

> Modern maritime piracy is a complex, multi-faceted problem and [it] will only be overcome by complex, multi-faceted solutions. There is no doubt, for example, that an important part of the solution lies in giving young men in the regions experiencing a high incidence of piracy genuine alternatives to piracy as a means of livelihood.[1]

Somali piracy is a serious economic and humanitarian problem, that arose a decade ago off the coast of Somalia, and that has proliferated to the West African Coast, to the Gulf of Guinea, as well as to parts of Asia. Piracy attacks are typically organized by businessmen in London or Dubai, and executed by Somali youth, desperate to make a living and often unaware of the dangers associated with piracy. Recruitment into piracy often takes place in coastal Somali villages, and those who "sign up" are at times as young as twelve.[2]

The international community has invested significant efforts in the global fight against Somali piracy; these efforts include both law enforcement operations as well as prosecutorial efforts. On the prosecution side, many in the international community have expressed outrage over the "catch-and-release" phenomenon, whereby pirates were caught in the middle of the Indian Ocean but then released back to Somalia, for lack of available prosecutorial options. In fact, although piracy is the original universal jurisdiction crime and although most nations have the option of prosecuting Somali pirates under this type of expansive jurisdiction, the political will to exercise this prosecutorial option is currently lacking in most countries. Universal jurisdiction prosecutions are costly and legally complex, and bring very little advantage to the prosecution nation, in an instance where pirates have not harmed the prosecution nation in any concrete manner. To circumvent

1 Kenneth Scott, *Prosecuting Pirates: Lessons Learned and Continuing Challenges*, OCEANS BEYOND PIRACY, available at http://oceansbeyondpiracy.org/sites/default/files/attachments/ProsecutingPiratesReportDigital_2.pdf.

2 For a general discussion of the Somali piracy model, *see supra* Chapter 1. For a discussion about the use of child pirates, *see supra* Chapter 2.

this issue, most major maritime nations have concluded transfer agreements with countries willing to prosecute Somali pirates under the universal jurisdiction model—Kenya, the Seychelles, and Mauritius.[3] Other countries have at times prosecuted groups of piracy suspects, when such suspects have attacked the prosecuting country's vessels or harmed their nationals.

While prosecutions of adult piracy suspects have been relatively successful, a vexing and complex legal issue that prosecuting nations have faced is how to treat juvenile piracy suspects. Under international human rights law, juvenile suspects in criminal proceedings are entitled to special protections.[4] They are entitled to be held at separate detention facilities, and within most national systems, they are prosecuted in juvenile courts under special provisions of juvenile justice. In most national systems, juveniles do not face the harshest criminal penalties, and their punishment must take into account their young age and provide opportunities for their rehabilitation and eventual re-integration into society. Thus, according to human rights law, juvenile piracy suspects, if prosecuted within a domestic criminal system, are entitled to protections otherwise unavailable to their adult peers. This type of preferential treatment of juvenile piracy suspects is parallel to the treatment of child soldiers.[5] The most prominent academics agree that child soldiers are both victims and perpetrators, and that they need to face justice but under conditions conducive to their eventual rehabilitation. Although child pirates are not child soldiers, because piracy does not exist within an armed conflict paradigm, the parallel between the two groups is sufficiently strong to warrant the same treatment and to insist on the same types of protections and precautions in their treatment.

In several national prosecutions of Somali piracy suspects, at least some of the suspects have claimed juvenile status. Some prosecuting nations, for lack of concrete legal solutions to this issue, have treated all suspects within the same group as juveniles and have transferred such cases to juvenile courts. Others have rejected juvenile status claims and have instead tried all suspects as adults. And most have engaged in arduous age determination procedures, in order to assess the suspect's age and reach the legal conclusion as to whether the suspect should be prosecuted as an adult or as a child.[6]

Age determination procedures are often costly and time-consuming, and they often produce inconclusive results. Existing procedures involve the use of bone

3 *See supra* Chapter 2 for a more detailed discussion of transfer agreements involving Kenya, the Seychelles, and Mauritius.

4 For a discussion of international human rights law on the treatment of juvenile suspects, *see supra* Chapter 3.

5 For a detailed discussion on child soldiers, *see supra* Chapter 4.

6 For a discussion of national prosecutions of piracy suspects involving juveniles, *see supra* Chapters 6 (a discussion of European countries' prosecutions: Germany, France, Italy, and Spain), 7 (a discussion of non-European countries' prosecutions: India, Malaysia, and the Seychelles), and 8 (a discussion of the United States' prosecutions).

and dental X-rays, ultra sounds, magnetic resonance imaging, physical examinations, and mental and cognitive assessments.[7] Each of these procedures carries a significant margin of error, and it is often impossible to conclusively determine that a Somali piracy suspect is nineteen and not seventeen. In the absence of other documentary and testimonial evidence, as is often the case, courts are left to their own devices to determine how to treat a suspect. In Germany, where a lengthy piracy prosecution involved a group of suspects, some of whom claimed juvenile status, and where age determinations produced uncertain results, the court dealt with this challenge by transferring the entire case to a juvenile jurisdiction and by imposing light sentences on everyone. The German case is emblematic of the challenges that all piracy-prosecuting nations face when grappling with claims of juvenile status by one or more suspects.

In light of the significant challenges associated with the prosecution of juvenile piracy suspects, it was this book's aim to develop a set of recommendations and best practices for the treatment of juvenile suspects. These recommendations include the following:

1 all piracy prosecuting nations should use medical and forensic procedures to determine a suspect's age, if his age is contested and if other documentary or testimonial evidence is not conclusive;
2 if the results of medical and forensic age determining tests are inconclusive and if the margin of error is too significant, the prosecuting state should adopt a presumption of juvenile status;
3 if the prosecuting nation determines that a suspect is a juvenile, the state should treat the juvenile suspect in accordance with relevant provisions of international human rights law, which dictate that juvenile cases be prosecuted within separate jurisdictions and juvenile suspects treated with special dignity;
4 if adult piracy suspects are caught alongside children, adult suspects should be treated more harshly in the sentencing phase, because employing children as pirates is a serious crime, contrary to human rights law and international labor laws.[8]

It is this book's overall conclusion that the above guidelines would lead toward more efficient piracy prosecutions, because prosecuting authorities would no longer face legal uncertainty as to how to treat juvenile suspects. Prosecuting authorities could also employ appropriate medical and forensic experts who could conduct age determinations expeditiously, ensuring that suspects, including juveniles, do not face lengthy pre-trial detention. In addition, the above guidelines would ensure that all juvenile suspects were treated in accordance with

7 For a discussion of age determination procedures, *see supra* Chapter 5.
8 For a detailed discussion of these recommendations, *see supra* Chapter 9.

international human rights laws. While the adoption of these guidelines may benefit some young adult suspects, because under the presumption of juvenile status approach some nineteen and twenty-year-olds may become entitled to the protections of juvenile status, this problem is minute compared to the alternative. In other words, if many juvenile suspects are denied the protections of human rights law on children's rights, the prosecuting states will be in violation of international law and the harm committed to those suspects will be irreparable. Child pirates are neither "Lost Boys" nor hardened criminals. Like child soldiers, they need to face justice and respond to the harm that they have committed, but the penalties imposed thereon need to be proportionate to their young age and need to provide for their rehabilitation and eventual reintegration into society.

Bibliography

Ahmed, Mohamed, *Pirate Stock Exchange Helps Fund Hijackings*, FIN. POST (Canada), (Dec. 1, 2009), available at *www.financialpost.com/newssectors/story.html?id=2289558*

Amann, Diane Marie, *Calling Children to Account: The Proposal for a Juvenile Chamber in the Special Court for Sierra Leone*, 29 PEPP. L. REV. 167 (2002).

Australian Human Rights Commission, Age assessment in people smuggling cases—Inquiry into the treatment of individuals suspected of people smuggling offences who say that they are children, available at www.humanrights.gov.au/our-work/asylum-seekers-and-refugees/projects/age-assessment-people-smuggling-cases-inquiry

Azubuike, Lawrence, *International Law Regime Against Piracy*, 15 ANN. SURV. INT'L & COMP. L. 43 (2009).

Bahar, Michael, *Attaining Optimal Deterrence at Sea: A Legal and Strategic Theory for Naval Anti-Piracy Operations*, 40 VAND. J. TRANSNAT'L L. 1 (2007).

Baird Mar., *InterManager: Criminalisation and Piracy Damage Seafarer Recruitment*, (Mar. 22, 2010), www.bairdmaritime.com/index.php?option=com_content&view=article&id=6004:intermanager-criminalisation-and-piracy-damage-seafarerrecruitment&catid=113:ports-and-shipping&Itemid=208

Barrett, Devlin, *Teen Piracy Suspect Raises Legal, Moral Issues*, SAN DIEGO UNION-TRIB. (Apr.13, 2009), available at www.sandiegouniontribune.com/news/2009/apr/13/piracy-young-suspect-041309/

Barrios, Erik, *Casting A Wider Net: Addressing the Maritime Piracy Problem in Southeast Asia*, 28 B.C. INT'L & COMPO L. REV. 149 (2005).

BBC News, *Charles Taylor War Crimes Conviction Upheld* (Sept. 26, 2013), available at www.bbc.com/news/world-africa-24279323

BBC News, *Deaths of hostages held by Somali pirates 'increasing'* (June 22, 2012), available at www.bbc.com/news/world-africa-18548810

BBC News, *Freed Somali pirates 'probably died'—Russian source* (May 11, 2010) available at http://news.bbc.co.uk/2/hi/8675978.stm

BBC NEWS, *Somali Pirates Jailed in France for Kidnapping Couple* (Nov. 30, 2011), available at www.bbc.com/news/world-africa-15976883

Beekarry, Sulakshna, *Legal, Political and Strategic Initiatives of Mauritius, with Special Focus on Collaboration Between Developed and Developing Countries*, *in* MARITIME SECURITY AND PIRACY: GLOBAL ISSUES, CHALLENGES AND SOLUTIONS 1, 1–6 (Bimal N. Patel & Hitesh Thakkar eds., 2012).

Bellish, Jon, *The Issue of Juvenile Piracy*, *in* PROSECUTING MARITIME PIRACY: DOMESTIC SOLUTIONS TO INTERNATIONAL CRIMES (Scharf *et al.* eds., 2015).

Bottorff, Andrea, *Malaysia Court Charges Suspected Somali Pirates*, JURIST (Feb. 11, 2011), available at http://jurist.org/paperchase/2011/02/malaysia-court-charges-suspected-somali-pirates.php

Captain Phillips (Sony Pictures 2013).

Charles Taylor's Conviction Upheld: A Message That Recruiters of Child Soldiers Will Be Held Accountable, U.N. Special Representative Child. & Armed Conflict (Sept. 26, 2013), available at https://childrenandarmedconflict.un.org/press-release/charles-taylors-conviction-upheld/

Child Recruitment and Use, Off. Special Representative of Secretary-Gen. Child. & Armed Forces, available at https://childrenandarmedconflict.un.org/effects-of-conflict/six-grave-violations/child-soldiers/

Child Soldiers Int'l, *About the Issues*, available at www.child-soldiers.org/faq.php

Child Soldiers Int'l, *Special Court for Sierra Leone—Appeals Chamber Confirms Conviction of Charles Taylor* (Sept. 26, 2013), available at www.child-soldiers.org/news_reader.php?id=704

Chinoy, Kaivan H., *Anarchy on the High Seas—Is Arming Merchant Vessels the Way Forward?*, Ava Marine Surveyors & Consultants, available at http://psm.du.edu/media/documents/industry_initiatives/industry_reports/ava_marine-high-seas-piracy-and-arming-vessels.pdf

Cipriani, Don, Children's Rights and the Minimum Age of Criminal Responsibility: A Global Perspective 98–108 (2009).

CNN.com, *U.S. warship near boat carrying pirates* (Apr. 9, 2009), available at www.cnn.com/2009/WORLD/africa/04/08/ship.hijacked/index.html

Coalition to Stop the Use of Child Soldiers, Child Soldiers Global Report 2012 (2012).

Coalition to Stop the Use of Child Soldiers, Child Soldiers Global Report 2008 (2008), available at file:///Users/elisabethleonard/Downloads/2008globalreport1245411.pdf

Conradi, Carl, *Mitigating Children Involvement in Maritime Piracy*, 10 Canadian Nav. Rev. 16 (2014), available at www.navalreview.ca/wp-content/uploads/public/vol10num2/vol10num2art3.pdf

Conradi, Carl, *The Invisible Phenomenon of Child Piracy*, Canadian Naval Rev. (Feb. 6, 2013), available at www.navalreview.ca/2013/02/the-invisible-phenomenon-of-child-piracy/

Counter-Piracy Programme: Support to the Trial and Related Treatment of Piracy Suspects, 7 UNODC, Sept.–Oct. 2011, www.unodc.org/documents/Piracy/UNODC_Brochure_Issue_7_WV.pdf

Crippa, Matteo, *Historic Piracy Trial Opens in Italy*, COMMUNIS HOSTIS OMNIUM, March 27, 2012, available at http://piracy-law.com/2012/03/27/historic-piracy-trial-opens-in-italy/

Custer, Michael, *Punishing Child Soldiers: The Special Court for Sierra Leone and the Lessons to be Learned from the United States' Juvenile System*, 19 Temp. Int'l Law & Comp. L.J. 449 (2005).

Customary IHL, Rule 120. Accommodation for Children Deprived of Their Liberty, Int'l Comm. of the Red Cross, www.icrc.org/customary-ihl/eng/docs/v1_rul_rule120.

Dallaire, Romeo, Williamson, Hugh, and Whitman, Shelly, *Child Pirates Are Everybody's Problem*, THE GLOBE AND MAIL (Feb. 10, 2012).

Dalton, Jane G. *et al.*, *Introductory Note to United Nations Security Council: Piracy and Armed Robbery at Sea—Resolutions 1816, 1846 & 1851*, 48 INT'L LEGAL MATERIALS 129 (2009).

Debusmann, Bernd, *Why High-Seas Piracy is Here to Stay*, REUTERS (Mar. 4, 2011).

Defimedia, Bernd, *Pirates to be Prosecuted in Mauritius* (Jan. 13, 2012), available at www.defimedia.info/newssunday/nos-news/item/4435-pirates-to-be-prosecuted-in-mauritius.html?tmpl=component&print=1

Department of Homeland Security Office of Inspector General, Age Determination Practices for Unaccompanied Alien Children in ICE Custody, November 2009, available at www.oig.dhs.gov/assets/Mgmt/OIG_10–12_Nov09.pdf

DISCOVER MAURITIUS, available at www.mauritius.net

Drumbl, Mark A., *Child Pirates: Rehabilitation, Reintegration and Accountability*, 46 CASE W. J. INT'L L. 235 (2013).

Drumbl, Mark A., *Reimagining child soldiers in international law and policy* (2012).

Facebook, Today in Seychelles, *Detaining and Protecting Child Pirates* (Mar. 18, 2014), www.facebook.com/todayinsey/posts/635900863114394

Fact Sheet No. 2 (Rev. 1), the International Bill of Human Rights, U.N. OFF. OF THE HIGH COMMISSIONER OF HUM. RTS. www.ohchr.org/Documents/Publications/FactSheet2Rev.1en.pdf

Fox News, *Smiling Somali Pirate Weeps in Federal Court in New York City, Hearing Reopened to Public* (Apr. 21, 2009), available at www.foxnews.com/story/2009/04/21/smiling-somali-pirate-weeps-in-federal-court-in-new-york-city-hearing-reopened.html

Fox News, *Somali Pirate Suspect in Legal Limbo in Spain* (October 21, 2009), available at www.foxnews.com/story/2009/10/21/somali-pirate-suspect-in-legal-limbo-in-spain.html

Fritz, Danielle, *Child Pirates From Somalia: A Call for the International Community To Support The Further Development of Juvenile Justice Systems in Puntland and Somaliland*, 44 CASE WES. RES. J. INT'L L. 891 (2012).

Gathii, J.T., *Jurisdiction to Prosecute Non-National Pirates Captured by Third States Under Kenyan and International Law*, 31 LOY. L.A. INT'L & COMP. L. REV. 363 (2009).

Gatto, Brandon, *Italy Court Orders Trial for Accused Somali Pirates*, JURIST (February 21, 2012), available at http://jurist.org/paperchase/2012/02/italy-court-orders-trial-for-accused-somali-pirates.php

Grossman, Nienke, *Rehabilitation or Revenge*, 38 GEO. J. INT'L L. 323 (2007).

Guled, Abdi, *Somali Pirates Kill Hostage Over Delayed Ransom*, THE WORLD POST (Sept. 1, 2012), available at www.huffingtonpost.com/2012/09/01/somali-pirates-hostage-killed_n_1848937.html

Haaba, *Seychelles MPs Adopt Anti-Piracy Law* (Mar. 16, 2010), available at www.haaba.com/node/395898/topic/it

Haddon, Harry, *Recession Hits Somalian Pirates: Kingpin Quits As Hijackings Dry Up*, 2OCEANSVIBE.COM (Jan. 11, 2013), available at www.2oceansvibe.com/2013/01/11/recession-hits-somalian-pirates-kingpin-quits-as-hijackings-dry-up/

Hafeez, Mateen, *Tests on Pirates to Determine Age*, TIMES OF INDIA (June 21, 2011), available at http://timesofindia.indiatimes.com/city/mumbai/Tests-on-pirates-to-determine-age/articleshow/8930959.cms

Hahn, Lauren, *Juvenile Justice and Piracy: Prosecutions of Juvenile Pirates in the United States*, GEO. MASON L. REV. 241 (2012).

Halberstam, Malvina, Benjamin N. Cardozo School of Law, Comments at the American Society of International Law Annual Meeting (Mar. 26, 2009).

Happold, Matthew, *Child Soldiers: Victims or Perpatrators?*, 29 U. LA VERNE L. REV. 56 (2008).

Happold, Matthew, *The Age of Criminal Responsibility in International Criminal Law*, *in* INTERNATIONAL CRIMINAL ACCOUNTABILITY AND THE RIGHTS OF CHILDREN 6 (Karin Arts & Vesselin Popovski eds. 2006).

Hoge, Robert D., *Introduction to the Canadian Juvenile Justice System*, RESOURCE MATERIAL SERIES No.78, at 59, available at www.unafei.or.jp/english/pdf/RS_No78/No78_11VE_Hoge3.pdf

Holland, Emily, *Hijacked Childhoods, Under the Radar: How the International Community Can Help the Youth Associated with Somali Piracy-and Why It Must*, 17 UCLA J. INT'L L. & FOREIGN AFF. 175 (2013).

Houreld, C., *Warships Fill Up with Pirates after Kenya Bails*, ASSOCIATED PRESS (April 15, 2010), available at http://abcnews.go.com/International/wirestory?id=10384342 &page;eqI

Human Rights Watch, *Sierra Leone: Landmark Convictions for Use of Child Soldiers* (June 20, 2007), available at www.hrw.org/news/2007/06/20/sierra-leone-landmark-convictions-use-child-soldiers

ICC Com. Crime Servs., *IMB Advises Continued Vigilance as Maritime Piracy Attacks Decline*, (Apr. 15, 2013), available at www.icc-ccs.org/news/841-imb-advises-continued-vigilance-as-maritime-piracy-attacks-decline

ICC Com. Crime Servs., *Piracy Attacks in East and West Africa Dominate World Report*, (Jan. 19, 2012), available at www.icc-ccs.org/news/711-piracy-attacks-in-east-and-west-africa-dominate-world-report

International Committee of the Red Cross, *How is the Term "Armed Conflict" Defined in International Humanitarian Law?*, Opinion Paper, March 2008, available at www.icrc.org/eng/assets/files/other/opinion-paper-armed-conflict.pdf

International Committee on the Red Cross, Treaties and State Parties to Such Treaties, Protocol Additional to the Geneva Conventions of 12 August 1949, and relating to the Protection of Victims of International Armed Conflicts (Protocol I), June 8, 1977.

JURIST, *Spain Court Sentences Somali Pirates to 439 Years* (May 3, 2011), available at http://jurist.org/paperchase/2011/05/spain-court-sentences-somali-pirates-to-439-years.php

Juvenile Law Center, Juvenile and Criminal Justice, Miller v. Alabama; Jackson v. Hobbs, available at www.jlc.org/legal-docket/miller-v-alabama-jackson-v-hobbs

Kaplan, Eben, *Child Soldiers Around the World*, COUNCIL ON FOREIGN REL. (Dec. 2, 2015), available at www.cfr.org/human-rights/child-soldiers-around-world/p9331#p6

Konge, Paola, *International Crimes & Child Soldiers*, 16 SW. J. INT'L L. 41 (2010).

Kontorovich, Eugene, *International Legal Responses to Piracy off the Coast of Somalia*, ASIL INSIGHTS (Feb. 6, 2009), www.asil.org/insights/volume/13/issue/2/international-legal-responses-piracy-coast-somalia

Kontorovich, Eugene and Art, Steven, *An Empirical Examination of Universal Jurisdiction for Piracy*, 104 AM. J. INT'L L. 436 (2010).

KOUROUMA, AHMADOU, ALLAH N'EST PAS OBLIGE 100 (2000).

Kraska, James and Wilson, Brian, *Combatting Piracy in International Waters*, WORLD POL'Y BLOG (Feb. 23, 2012), available at www.worldpolicy.org/blog/2011/02/23/combatting-piracy-international-waters

Kraska, James and Wilson, Brian, *Fighting Pirates: The Pen and the Sword*, 25 WORLD POL'Y J. 41(2009).

Kraska, James and Wilson, Brian, *Piracy Repression, Partnering and the Law*, 40 J. MAR. L. & COM. 43, 43 (2009).

Lakotta, Beate, *An Expensive Farce: Germany's Somali Pirate Trial Is Pointless*, SPIEGEL ONLINE (Sept. 12, 2012), available at www.spiegel.de/international/germany/german-trial-of-somali-pirates-turns-into-pointless-and-expensive-farce-a-855252.html

Lakotta, Beate, *Torture? Execution? German Justice Through the Eyes of a Somali Pirate*, SPIEGEL ONLINE (Apr. 7, 2011), available at www.spiegel.de/international/world/torture-execution-german-justice-through-the-eyes-of-a-somali-pirate-a-755340.html

LETTERA22.IT, A Roma il primo processo contro presunti pirati Somali (March 23, 2012), available at www.lettera22.it/showart.php?id=12138&rubrica=122 (in Italian)

Levin, John Clark, *Arming Captain Phillips*, WALL ST. J. (Oct. 16, 2013) www.wsj.com/articles/SB10001424052702304106704579137903414164412

Mangini, Enzo, *Somali Pirates Sentenced*, MAR. SECURITY REV. (November 28, 2012), available at www.marsecreview.com/2012/11/somali-pirates-sentenced/

Mangini, Enzo, *Landmark Somali Trial Climaxes*, THE ITALIAN INSIDER (July 3, 2012), available at www.italianinsider.it/?q=node/1084

MARINE LOG, *Court Tells France to Pay Damages to Somali Pirates* (Dec. 5, 2014), available at www.marinelog.com/index.php?option=com_k2&view=item&id=8373:court-tells-france-to-pay-damages-to-somali-pirates&Itemid=230

Matussek, Karin, *Somalis Face Hamburg Court in First German Piracy Trial for Four Centuries*, BLOOMBERG, Nov. 22, 2010, available at www.bloomberg.com/news/articles/2010–11–22/ten-somalis-are-tried-in-hamburg-court-over-indian-ocean-pirate-attack

Menefee, Samuel Peatt, "*Yo Heave Ho!*": *Updating America's Piracy Laws*, 21 CAL. W. INT'L L.J. 151, 161 (1990).

Messaoudi, Sonia, *Child Pirates: A Key Issue For Respecting Child's Rights And Halting Piracy*, COMMUNIS HOSTIS OMNIUM (Oct. 23, 2012), available at http://piracy-law.com

MSNBC, *Pirate Who 'Wanted to Kill Americans' Gets 33 Years for Hijacking U.S. Ship* (Feb. 16, 2011, 12:35 PM), available at www.msnbc.msn.com/id/41615693/ns/us_news-crime_and_courts/t/pirate-who-wanted-kill-americans-gets-years-hijacking-us-ship/#.Tmuf5-vgK8U

Mudi, Maureen, *Kenya: Special Court to Hear Mombasa Piracy Case*, NAIROBI STAR (Sept. 30, 2011), http://allafrica.com/stories/201109301201.html

Mukinda, Fred and Shiundu, Alphonce, *Kenya Laments Pirates' Burden*, DAILY NATION (Mar. 20, 2012) www.nation.co.ke/News/-/1056/889976/-/vrw9dl/-/index.html

Murdoch, Lindsay, *Australia Imprisons Indonesian Boys*, THE NATIONAL AGE (June 14, 2011), available at www.theage.com.au/national/australia-imprisons-indonesian-boys-20110613–1g0il.html

Murdoch, Lindsay, *Indonesian Children Released From Adult Prison*, THE SYDNEY MORNING HERALD (June 18, 2011), available at www.smh.com.au/national/indonesian-children-released-from-adult-prison-20110617–1g7yq.html

NBC News, *14 Indicted For Piracy Over US Yacht Killing* (Mar. 10, 2011), available at www.nbcnews.com/id/42007399/ns/us_news-crime_and_courts/t/indicted-piracy-over-us-yacht-killings/#.VtdB4o-cGUk

NEW SCIENTIST, *With No Paper Trail, Can Science Determine Age?* (May 9, 2012), available at www.newscientist.com/article/mg21428644–300-with-no-paper-trail-can-science-determine-age/

Obert, Steven R., *Using Force on Land to Suppress Piracy at Sea: The Legal Landscape of a Largely Untapped Strategy*, 25 DUKE J. COMP. & INT'L L. 197 (2014).

Osinowo, Adeniyi Adejimi, *Combating Piracy in the Gulf of Guinea*, AFRICA SECURITY BRIEF, No. 30 (February 2015), available at http://africacenter.org/wp-content/uploads/2015/02/ASB-30-Feb-2015-Combating-Piracy-in-GoG.pdf

Pandit, Rajat, *25 of 61 Pirates Arrested by Navy at Sea are Children Below 15 Yrs.*, THE TIMES OF INDIA (Mar. 17, 2011), available at http://timesofindia.indiatimes.com/india/25-of-61-pirates-arrested-by-Navy-at-sea-are-children-below-15-yrs/articleshow/7723224.cms

Pendleton, John H., *Maritime Security: Actions Needed to Assess and Update Plan and Enhance Collaboration Among Partners Involved in Countering Piracy off the Horn of Africa*, GAO Report to Congressional Requesters (Sept. 2010).

Peppetti, Jon D., *Building the Global Maritime Security Network: A Multinational Legal Structure to Combat Transnational Threats*, 55 NAVAL L. REV. 73 (2008).

Phillips, Roger, L., *Long road to justice—The German piracy trial*, COMMUNIS HOSTIS OMNIUM (Oct. 21, 2012), available at http://piracy-law.com/2012/10/21/long-road-to-justice-the-german-piracy-trial/

Philips, Roger L., *Kenya: No Jurisdiction to Try Piracy?*, COMMUNIS HOSTIS OMNIUM (Jan. 27, 2011), http://piracylaw.com/2011/01/27/kenya-no-jurisdiction-to-try-piracy/

Quigley, J.T., *Pirates Plead Guilty in Malaysian Navy Shooting*, THE DIPLOMAT (Sept. 3, 2013), available at http://thediplomat.com/asean-beat/2013/09/03/pirates-plead-guilty-in-malaysian-navy-shooting/

RADIO CANADA INTERNATIONAL, *Child Pirates: Raising Awareness About a Serious Issue* (Mar. 20, 2013), available at www.rcinet.ca/english/daily/interviews-2012/14–23_2013–03–20-child-pirates-raising-awareness-about-a-serious-issue/

Rass-Masson, Nathy, *Study on Children's Involvement In Judicial Proceedings, Contextual Overview For The Criminal Justice Phase: France*, available at http://bookshop.europa.eu/en/study-on-children-s-involvement-in-judicial-proceedings-pbDS0313668/?CatalogCategoryID=WTQKABsteF0AAAEjKpEY4e5L

Rass-Masson, Nathy, *Study on Children's Involvement in Judicial Proceedings, Contextual Overview for the Criminal Justice Phase: England, Wales and Northern Ireland*, available at http://bookshop.europa.eu/en/study-on-children-s-involvement-in-judicial-proceedings-pbDS0313686/?CatalogCategoryID=WTQKABsteF0AAAEjKpEY4e5L

Reduan, Hidir, *Malaysia: Seven Somali Pirates Sentenced*, HIIRAAN ONLINE (Sept. 4, 2013).

REUTERS, *German Prosecutor Urges Jail in Somali Piracy Trial* (Jan. 25, 2012), available at http://af.reuters.com/article/somaliaNews/idAFL5E8CP3HR20120125

RNW MEDIA, *High-seas Drama at Somali Piracy Trial in Italy*, available at www.rnw.org/archive/high-seas-drama-somali-piracy-trial-italy

Roach, J. Ashley, *Countering Piracy Off Somalia: International Law and International Institutions*, 104 AM. J. INT'L L. 397 (2010).

Role of the International Criminal Court, OFF. SPECIAL REPRESENTATIVE SECRETARY-GEN. CHILD. & ARMED CONFLICT, available at https://childrenandarmedconflict.un.org/our-work/role-of-the-icc/

Ruhal, Sanjeet, *The Piracy Bill 2012: A Solution or Mere Paper Tiger?*, MARITIME GATEWAY (Apr. 23, 2014).

Rule of Law in Armed Conflicts Project, Somalia, available at www.geneva-academy.ch/RULAC/applicable_international_law.php?id_state=204

Ryan, Jennie, *Seychelles President Urges Greater Anti-Piracy Measures*, JURIST (Dec. 5, 2011), http://jurist.org/paperchase/2011/12/seychelles-president-urges-greater-anti-piracy-measures.php

Samervel, Rebecca, *120 Somali Pirates Want to Plead Guilty in Court*, TIMES OF INDIA (Nov. 6, 2015), available at http://timesofindia.indiatimes.com/city/mumbai/120-Somali-pirates-want-to-plead-guilty-in-court/articleshow/49680010.cms

Scharf, Michael P., *Introduction*, *in* PROSECUTING MARITIME PIRACY: DOMESTIC SOLUTIONS TO INTERNATIONAL CRIMES (Scharf *et al.* eds. 2015).

Schuler, Mike, *Suspected Pirates Found Not Guilty in Mauritius*, GCAPTAIN.COM (Nov. 6, 2014), http://gcaptain.com/2014/11/06/suspected-pirates-found-not-guilty-in-mauritius/#.VqfXX4-cGUk

Schuler, Mike, *U.S.'s First Modern-Day Pirate Prosecutor to Step Down*, GCAPTAIN.COM (Aug. 23, 2013), available at http://gcaptain.com/united-states-modern-pirate-prosecutor-to-step-down/

Scott, Kenneth, *Prosecuting Pirates: Lessons Learned and Continuing Challenges*, OCEANS BEYOND PIRACY, available at http://oceansbeyondpiracy.org/sites/default/files/attachments/ProsecutingPiratesReportDigital_2.pdf

Seth, Joshua, *Age of Criminal Responsibility*, THE EXAMINER (Nov. 22, 2012), available at www.examiner.com/article/age-of-criminal-responsibility

Sinha, Ranjit, *India Lacks Legal System to Prosecute Pirates*, THE ECONOMIC TIMES (Sept. 24, 2014), available at http://articles.economictimes.indiatimes.com/2014–09–24/news/54279757_1_indian-navy-indian-ocean-cbi-director-ranjit-sinha

Smith, Terry and Brownlees, Laura, *Age Assessment: A Technical Note* 11–12 (UNICEF Working Paper January 2013).

Snow, Anita, *UN Envoy: Rehabilitate Child Pirates*, ARAB NEWS.COM (Nov. 9, 2010), available at http://arabnews.com/world/article184520.ece

SPIEGEL ONLINE, *A Precedent or a Farce? Court Faces Daunting Hurdles in Hamburg Pirate Trial* (Jan. 18, 2011), available at www.spiegel.de/international/world/a-precedent-or-a-farce-court-faces-daunting-hurdles-in-hamburg-pirate-trial-a-740122.hml

Sterio, Milena, *Piracy off the Coast of Somalia: The Argument for Pirate Prosecutions in the National Courts of Kenya, the Seychelles, and Mauritius*, 4 AMSTERDAM L.F. 104 (2012).

Taussig-Rubbo, Mateo, *Pirate Trials, the International Criminal Court, and Mob Justice: Reflections on Postcolonial Sovereignty in Kenya*, Humanity: An International Journal of Human Rights, Humanitarianism and Development, 2010–1.

The International Criminal Courts Kenya Monitor, *How the ICC Became Involved in Kenya*, available at www.icckenya.org/background/ (last visited Feb. 7, 2016).

THE TELEGRAPH, *Repelling Pirate Attacks: The Measures to Protect a Ship* (Feb. 10, 2014), available at www.telegraph.co.uk/sponsored/culture/captain-phillips-film/10367534/security-against-pirate-attacks.html

THE TELEGRAPH, *Teenage Somali 'Pirate' Pleads Not Guilty in US Court* (May 21, 2009), available at www.telegraph.co.uk/news/worldnews/africaandindianocean/somalia/5364183/Teenage-Somali-pirate-pleads-not-guilty-in-US-court.html

Treves, Tullio, *Piracy, Law of the Sea, and Use of Force: Developments off the Coast of Somalia*, 20 EUR. J. INT'L L. 399 (2009).

USA Today, *Mystery Surrounds Somali Teen Pirate* (Apr. 21, 2009, 5:50 PM), available at www.usatoday.com/news/world/2009–04–21-teen-pirate-suspect_ N.htm

Vankipuram, Meera, *Juvenile Bill: Experts Claim Age Determination is Biggest Hurdle*, TIMES OF INDIA (Dec. 28, 2015), available at http://timesofindia.indiatimes.com/city/chennai/Juvenile-bill-Experts-claim-age-determination-is-biggest-hurdle/articleshow/50347863.cms

VICTIMS OF INTERNATIONAL CRIMES: AN INTERDISCIPLINARY DISCOURSE 141 (Thorston Bonacker and Christoph Safferling, eds. 2013).

Walt, Vivienne, *Why the Somali Pirates Keep Getting Their Ransoms*, TIME (Apr. 20, 2009), www.time.com/time/world/article/0,8599,1892366,00.html

Weiser, Benjamin, *Leniency of Sentence for Somali Hijacker is at Issue*, N.Y. TIMES (Feb. 14, 2011), at A24

Weiser, Benjamin, *Pirate Suspect Charged as Adult in New York*, N.Y. TIMES (Apr. 21, 2009), available at www.nytimes.com/2009/04/22/nyregion/22pirate.html?pagewanted=all &_r=0

Whitman, S. *et al.*, *Children and Youth in Marine Piracy—Causes, Consequences and the Way Forward*, DALHOUSIE MARINE PIRACY PROJECT (Dec. 2012), available at www.childsoldiers.org/wp-content/uploads/2014/02/Children-and-Youth-in-Marine-Piracy-RDCSI.pdf

Whitman, Shelly, L., *Children and Marine Piracy*, 46 CASE W. RES. J. INT'L L. 213 (2013).

Yacht Pals, *Pirate Attacks on Sailing Yachts-Piracy Warnings* (Oct. 2, 2009), available at, http://yachtpals.com/pirates-yachts4092 (reporting on several pirate attacks off the Seychelles' coast in 2009).

Legal Documents and Cases

18 U.S.C. §1651 (West 2012)

U.S.C. § 1861 (West 2012)

18 U.S.C.A. § 5031 (West 2012)

18 U.S.C. § 5032 (West 2012)

A v London Borough of Croydon & SSHD; WK v SSHD & Kent County Council [2009] EWHC 939

African Charter on the Rights and Welfare of the Child, art. 2 OAU Doc. CAB/LEG/ 24.9/49 (entered into force Nov. 29, 1999)

Amicus Curiae United Nations Special Representative of the Secretary-General on Children and Armed Conflict Submitted in application of Rule 103 of the Rules of Procedure and Evidence at Apex. A pg. 5, Prosecutor v. Thomas Lubanga Dyilo, Case No. ICC-01/04–01/06, Judgment (Mar. 14, 2012)

An Act for the Punishment of Certain Crimes Against the United States, ch. 9, § 8, 1 Stat. 112, 113–14 (1790)

An Act to Protect the Commerce of the United States, and Punish the Crime of Piracy, ch. 77, 3 Stat. 510, 510 (1819)

Attorney Gen. v. M. M. Dashi *et al.*, (2010) K.L.R. (Ct. App. Nairobi) (Kenya) http://kenyalaw.org/CaseSearch/view_preview1.php?link=38656751089581753125617

C182—Worst Forms of Child Labour Convention, INT'L LAB. ORG. (Nov. 19, 2000), available at www.ilo.org/dyn/mormlex/en/f?p=1000;11300:0::NO:11300:P11300_INSTRUMENT_ID:312327

Cape Town Principles and Best Practices (Apr. 27–30, 1997) (definitions), available at www.unicef.org/emerg/files/Cape_Town_Principles(1).pdf

Convention Concerning the Prohibition and Elimination of the Worst Forms of Child Labor (No. 182) arts. 3(b), 3(d)

Convention on the Rights of the Child, art. 1, *opened for signature* Nov. 20, 1989, 1577 U.N.T.S. 44 (entered into force on Sept. 2, 1990)

Convention for the Suppression of Unlawful Acts Against the Safety of Maritime Navigation art. 3, Mar. 10, 1988, 1678 U.N.T.S. 221

Draft Statute of the International Criminal Court, Report of the Preparatory Committee on the Establishment of an International Criminal Court, Addendum, Part One, UN Doc. A/CONF.183/2/Add.1, 14 April 1998, p. 21

G.A. Res. 40/33, United Nations Standard Minimum Rules for the Administration of Juvenile Justice (the "Beijing Rules"), annex ¶ 4.1, (Nov. 29, 1985)

G.A. Res. 44/25, Status of the Convention on the Rights of the Child, Nov. 20, 1989, https://treaties.un.org/Pages/ViewDetails.aspx?src=IND&mtdsg_no=IV-11&chapter=4&lang=en

G.A. Res. 45/112, United Nations Guidelines for the Protection of Juvenile Delinquency (the "Riyadh Guidelines")

G.A. Res. 45/113, United Nations Rules for the Protection of Juveniles Deprived of Their Liberty (Dec. 14, 1990)

G.A. CODE ANN. § 15–11–560 (West 2012)

Geneva Declaration on the Rights of the Child, League of Nations (1924)

Graham v. Florida, 560 U.S. 48 (2010)

Gubiensio-Ortiz v. Kanahele, 857 F. 2d 1245, 1267 (9th Cir. 1988), *vacated sub nom.* United States v. Chavez Sanchez, 488 U.S. 1036 (1989)

Hassan M. Ahmed v. Republic, (2009) K.L.R. (H.C.K.) (Kenya) (Azangalala, J.)

ICTY, The Prosecutor v. Dusko Tadic, Decision on the Defence Motion for Interlocutory Appeal on Jurisdiction, IT-94–1-A, 2 October 1995, para.70

705 ILL. COMP. STAT. ANN. 405/1–8

25th International Conference of the Red Cross, Res. IX; 26th International Conference of the Red Cross and Red Crescent, Res. II

27th International Conference of the Red Cross and Red Crescent, Res. I (adopted by consensus)

International Covenant on Civil and Political Rights, art. 10, *opened for signature* Dec. 19, 1966, 999 U.N.T.S. 171 (entered into force on Mar. 23, 1976)

International Legal Standards for the Protection of Children, UNICEF (Sept. 2002), www.unicef.org/emerg/files/ICJC.pdf

Jackson v. Hobbs, No. 10–9647 (2012)

Law of Seychelles, Chapter 28, Children Act, Section 92(1), available at http://greybook.seylii.org/se/CAP28#!fragment//KGhhc2g6KGNodW5rxIVhbsSHb3JUZXh0OicnKSxsZWZ0UMSNZU5vdGVJZMSWJyxuxKNlc1F1ZXJ5xKgsc2Nyb2xsQ8SIxIo6IW7EtWVhcsSHxK/EscSzxJfFgsWExIdTxJB0QsSzUkVMRVZBTkNFLHRhYjp0b2MpKQ==

Law on the Establishment of the Extraordinary Chambers in the Courts of Cambodia for the Prosecution of Crimes Committed During the Republic of Kampuchea, art. 33, NS/RKM/1004/006 (Oct. 27, 2004)

Letter dated 24 January 2011 from the Secretary-General to the President of the Security Council, Annex (Report of the Special Adviser to the Secretary-General on Legal Issues Related to Piracy off the Coast of Somalia)

M.M. Hashi *et al.*, (2009) K.L.R. (H.C.K.) (Kenya) http://piracylaw.files.wordpress.com/2011/01/in-re-mohamud-mohamed-hashi-et-al1.pdf

Miller v. Alabama, 567 U.S. _ (2012)

Miranda v. Arizona, 384 v.s. 436 (1966)

N.C. GEN. STAT. ANN. § 7B-1501

N.H. REV. STAT. ANN. § 628:1

Optional Protocol to the Convention on the Rights of the Child on the Involvement of Children in Armed Conflict art. 1, May 25, 2000, 2173 U.N.T.S. 222 (entered into force Feb. 12, 2002).

Or. Rev. Stat. Ann. § 419A.004 (West 2012)

Org. of African Unity [OAU], Council of Ministers, Res. 1659 (LXIV) (1993).

Penal Code (Amendment) Bill, 2010, § 65 (Sey.) (amending Penal Code 1955, CAP. 73 (Sey.))

Piracy and Maritime Violence Act 2011, (No. XXVIII), art. 3 (Dec. 13, 2011) (on file with author)

Prosecutor v. Furundzija, Case No. IT-95–17/1-T, Trial Chamber, Judgment, 284,291 (ICTY 1998)

Prosecutor v. Lubanga Dyilo, Case No. ICC-01/04–01/06, Judgment, ¶ 1 (Mar. 14, 2012)

Prosecutor v. Lubanga Dyilo, Case No. ICC-01/04–01/06, Confirmation, (Dec. 1, 2014)

Prosecutor v. Norman, Case No. SCSL-2004–15-AR72(E), Decision on Preliminary Motion Based on Lack of Jurisdiction (Child Recruitment), (May 31, 2004), available at www.rscsl.org/Documents/Decisions/CDF/Appeal/131/SCSL-04–14-AR72(E)-131.pdf

Prosecutor v. Taylor, Case No. SCSL-03–01-T, Judgment, ¶ 12 (May 18, 2012), available at www.scsldocs.org/documents/view/6662–19559

Protocol Additional to the Geneva Conventions of 12 August 1949, and Relating to the Protection of Victims of International Armed Conflicts (Protocol I), art. 77(4), June 8, 1977, 1125 U.N.T.S. 3

Protocol Additional to the Geneva Conventions of 12 August 1949, and Relating to the Protection of Victims of Non-International Armed Conflicts (Protocol II), art 1, para. 1, June 8, 1977, 1125 U.N.T.S. 3

Report of the Secretary-General on the Establishment of a Special Court for Sierra Leone, U.N. SCOR, 52d Sess., U.N. Doc. S/2000/915 (2000)

Republic v. Houssein Mohammed Osman, Criminal Side No. 19, para. 12 (Seychelles Oct. 12, 2011)

Republic v. Liban Mohamed Dahir & Twelve Others, Sentence, Crim. Side No. 7 of 2012 [16] (Supreme Ct. Sey. 2012)

Republic v. Mohamed Abdi Jama & Six Others, Sentence, Crim. Side No. 53 of 2011 [6] (Supreme Ct. Sey. 2012)

Republic v. Mohamed Aweys Sayid, Criminal Side No. 19, Sentencing Judgment, 2 (Dec. 15, 2010)

Rome Statute of the International Criminal Court art 8(2)(b)(xxvi), (e)(vii), U.N. Doc. A/ CONF.183/9* (1998), available at www.un.org/law/icc/statute/contents.htm

Roper v. Simmons, 543 U.S. 551 (2005)

Ruling on Defense Motion for Dismissal Due to Lack of Jurisdiction Under the MCS in Regard to Juvenile Crimes of a Child Soldier para. 18, Khadr, No. D-022 (Military Comm'n, Apr. 30, 2008)

Sayid v. R, Case No: SCA 2 of 2011, [2013] SCCA 24, Dec. 6, 2013, available at www.seylii.org/sc/judgment/court-appeal/2013/24

S.C. Res. 827, Statute of the International Criminal Tribunal for the Former Yugoslavia (May 25, 1993), available at www.icty.org/x/file/Legal%20Library/Statute/statute_sept09_en.pdf

S.C. Res. 955, Statute of the International Tribunal for Rwanda (Nov. 8. 1994), available at www.ohchr.org/EN/ProfessionalInterest/Pages/StatuteInternationalCriminalTribunalForRwanda.aspx

S.C. Res. 1261, ¶2 (Aug. 25, 1999)

S.C. Res. 1816, (June 2, 2008)

S.C. Res. 1851, (Dec. 16, 2008)

S.C. Res. 1846, (Dec. 2, 2008)

S.C. Res. 1844, (Nov. 20, 2008)
S.C. Res. 1838, (Oct. 7, 2008)
S.C. Res. 1816, (June 2, 2008)
S.C. Res. 1897 (Nov. 30, 2009)
S.C. Res. 1918 (Apr. 27, 2010)
S.C. Res. 1950, ¶13 (Nov. 23, 2010)
S.C. Res. 1976, ¶17, ¶26 (Apr. 11, 2011)
S.C. Res. 2015, ¶4 (Oct. 24, 2011)
Statute of the Special Court for Sierra Leone, art. 7, ¶1 (Aug. 14, 2000)
The Director of Public Prosecutions v. Abdoulkader Mohamed Ali *et al.*, 2015, No. 8702, 452 SCJ (Mauritius)
The Juvenile Justice (Care and Protection of Children) Act (India, Dec. 30, 2000)
The Paris Principles: Principles and Guidelines on Children Associated with Armed Forces or Armed Groups (February 2007), Prin. 2.1, available at www.child-soldiers.org/childsoldiers/Paris_Principles_March_2007.pdf
The Republic v. Abdi Ali, Sentencing, Crim. Side No. 14, ¶ 2 (Nov. 3, 2010) (Sey.) (citing Penal Code 2010, § 65 (Sey.)) (on file with author)
The Republic v. Mohamed Aweys Sayid, Crim. Side No. 19, ¶¶ 11–12, (Dec. 15, 2010) (Sey.) (citing Penal Code, 2010 § 65(4) (Sey.)) (on file with author)
United Nations Convention on the High Seas, Apr. 29, 1958, 450 U.N.T.S. 11, 90
United Nations Convention on the Law of the Sea, Oct. 7, 1982, 1833 U.N.T.S. 41–42
United Nations Convention on the Rights of the Child, G.A. Res. 44/25, Art. 1, Annex, U.N. Doc. A/RES/44/25 (Nov. 20, 1989) (entered into force Sept. 2, 1990)
United Nations Security Council, Report of the Secretary-General, S/2010/394 (July 26, 2010), pp. 21–22, para. 46
United Nations Transnational Administration for East Timor, on Transitional Rules of Criminal Procedure, Rule 45.1, UN Doc. UNTAET/REG/2000/30 (Sept. 13, 2000)
United Nations Treaty Collection, Status of the International Covenant on Civil and Political Rights, https://treaties.un.org/pages/ViewDetails.aspx?src=IND&mtdsg_no=IV-4&chapter=4&lang=en
U.S. Const. amend. VIII
U.S. Const., art. I, section 8, cl. 10
United States v. Booker, 543 U.S. 220, 247 (2005)
United States v. Hasan, 747 F.Supp.2d 642, 654–55 (2010)
United States v. Hasan, 747 F.Supp. 2d 642, 653 (E.D. Va. 2010) *aff'd sub nom.* United States v. Dire, 680 F.3d 446 (4th Cir. 2012)
United States v. Mathurin, No. 09–21075–Cr, 2011 WL 2580775
United States v. Muse, No. 1:S109-cr-00512–01-LAP (S.D.N.Y. Jan. 12, 2010)
United States v. Dire *et al.*, 680 F.3d 446 (4th Cir. 2012)
Violence Against Maritime Navigation Convention, 18 U.S.C. § 2280 (2012)
Yick Woo v. Hopkins, 118 U.S. 356, 369 (1886)

Index

For Product Safety Concerns and Information please contact our EU representative GPSR@taylorandfrancis.com
Taylor & Francis Verlag GmbH, Kaufingerstraße 24, 80331 München, Germany

www.ingramcontent.com/pod-product-compliance
Ingram Content Group UK Ltd.
Pitfield, Milton Keynes, MK11 3LW, UK
UKHW011018180926
475701UK00004B/805
* 9 7 8 1 0 3 2 2 4 2 1 2 5 *